Susan Mitchell broke new ground when she wrote her first book, *Tall Poppies*, intimate portraits of successful Australian women. In her following twelve books she has continued to document and celebrate the lives of Australian women in sport, politics, the arts, business and many other aspects of Australian life, together with the lives of ten American writers whose books have changed the world. Her books have been published in the USA, the UK, Germany, Holland and New Zealand.

Born in Adelaide, she has degrees from the University of Adelaide and Flinders University and is a former senior lecturer in Literature and Creative Writing at the University of South Australia. She has lived and worked in London, New York, Melbourne, Brisbane and Sydney.

Her passion for communicating with the widest possible audience has included broadcasting her own programs on both the ABC and commercial radio, and presenting her own television programs, *Tall Poppies* and *Susan Mitchell in Conversation*.

She has been a director on the Literature Board of the Australia Council, Film Australia and the South Australian Tourism Commission. She is a book reviewer, a columnist and a public speaker.

Her heroines are Simone de Beauvoir and Mae West.

Also by Susan Mitchell

All Things Bright and Beautiful: Murder in the City of Light
Splitting the World Open
Be Bold!
Icons, Saints and Divas
The Scent of Power
Public Lives Private Passions
Tall Poppies Too
Hot Shots
The Matriarchs
Winning Women
Tall Poppies

Margaret Whitlam

a biography

Susan Mitchell

RANDOM HOUSE AUSTRALIA

Random House Australia Pty Ltd
Level 3, 100 Pacific Highway, North Sydney, NSW 2060
www.randomhouse.com.au

Sydney New York Toronto
London Auckland Johannesburg

First published by Random House Australia 2006
Paperback edition first published 2007

National Library of Australia
Cataloguing-in-Publication Entry

Mitchell, Susan.
Margaret Whitlam.

ISBN 978 1 74166 487 4(pbk.).

1. Whitlam, Margaret, 1919– . 2. Prime ministers' spouses – Australia – Biography. I. Title.

994.0092

Internal design by Greendot Design
Typeset in Goudy by Midland Typesetters, Australia
Printed and bound by Griffin Press, South Australia

10 9 8 7 6 5 4 3 2 1

CONTENTS

To Mary, whose story is yet to be told

There is no experience from which you can't learn something. The purpose of life, after all, is to live it, to taste experience to the utmost, to reach out eagerly and without fear for newer and richer experience.

You can only do that if you have curiosity and an unquenchable spirit of adventure.

Eleanor Roosevelt, 1960

PROLOGUE

The first time I visited the Whitlam residence was early in 1986, after a great deal of angst. I had been trying, unsuccessfully, to make contact with Margaret for weeks as I wanted to include her in my book *The Matriarchs*. After many attempts and no response I had retreated to the Blue Mountains to stay with a friend, who suggested that as a last resort I send Mrs Whitlam a telegram, her theory being that women of her generation seemed to respond to them – it was something to do with the war, she advised.

My telegram read, 'Desperately seeking Margaret Whitlam. Sincerely, Susan.'

It worked, and a few days later I pressed the security buzzer to Margaret's apartment at Darling Point and first met her face to face. I found her then, as I have found her many times since, warm, unaffected and viewing life from a somewhat bemused perspective.

Twenty years later I was pressing the buzzer again, actually feeling rather nervous because it was the beginning of my interviews for my biography of her. Now I was truly desperately in search of her. I had been undecided about what to bring for this momentous occasion. Was it to be chocolates, or flowers? Knowing that she was on a fairly strict regime for her health I decided on flowers.

When I thrust them towards her at the door, she asked cheekily, 'What's this, a bribe?'

'Certainly not,' I replied, 'I don't need to bribe you to tell the truth.' She immediately placed the flowers in a vase, assuring me they were gorgeous. They were wrapped with a red satin ribbon and she confessed, popping it into a drawer, that I'd probably get it back one day, recycled.

Even though the sun was shining through the window it was chilly inside the small apartment. She turned on the heater, made me a cup of coffee and placed a plate of biscuits and nuts next to me. Her leg was troubling her so she lay on the couch.

'So go ahead. Analyse me,' she chortled. We warmed up.

When I was leaving she showed me the third bedroom, known as the archives or, in her childrens' words, 'Mum's Nostalgia Nest'. It was crammed floor to ceiling with old boxes, files, folders and a strange assortment of plastic bags. Thank God, I thought, that she is a dedicated hoarder. Manna from heaven for the biographer. As we walked past their bedroom I asked, 'Do you both still sleep in that bed?'

'Yes, we do. It's queen size, perfectly fine. Besides, we couldn't fit anything larger in this small bedroom.'

On the bed between the pillows I noticed she had placed a small cushion on which was embroidered the words, 'Old friends are the best friends.' She watched me taking note of it.

'I thought that would amuse you,' she teased.

MOTHER AND FATHER

Margaret Whitlam's earliest memory is of herself aged four dressed as a fairy, complete with wand, having her photo taken by her mother on the front lawn of their semi-detached house in Bondi. She can't remember why she was dressed as a fairy, but she suspects that it was simply because, like many little girls, she had desperately wanted to be one. Her mother had made her the dress and taken the photo because she had thought Margaret had better have a fairy dress before she got too large.

In this photo her legs are already very long and skinny and she is acting up for the camera, smiling cheekily, her arms outstretched to show off the tiered layers of white organdie skirt threaded with ribbons and the matching organdie wings. A sparkling star sits in the middle of her headband.

This first memory tells us a great deal not just about Margaret as a child, but also about the woman who emerged. It also tells us about her mother.

It's a confident child who expresses an early wish to dress up in an imaginary costume, a child with an inclination towards performance. It's a loved child who has her wish granted, has a special fairy dress made for the occasion and then has it captured in a photo.

It's a thoughtful and far-sighted mother who indulges her daughter's wish because she doesn't want her to miss out on anything simply because she is already so tall.

It's a mother who makes things happen. It's a mother who is determined that her daughter is going to have every opportunity that she didn't have in her life.

Above all, it's a mother who wants her daughter to have fun.

Margaret Whitlam was destined by birth to stand out. She is tall. Very tall. In her prime she was 6 foot 2 inches, without shoes. Now, in her eighty-seventh year, she measures less than 6 foot due to osteoporosis and spinal deterioration. Nevertheless her head is visible above any crowd and her long legs still take up more room than the average Australian's.

Being very tall if you are a man may be an advantage, but as a young girl born in 1919, her height was something that set Margaret apart, something that people endlessly felt the need to comment upon – 'My, what a tall girl you are' – as if your height was something of which you needed to be made constantly aware. Thoughtless remarks like, 'How's the air up there?' are hard to answer with civility, especially when you have been asked that question a thousand times. Clearly, at a very early age, when it is obvious that you are always going to be much taller than the average girl, you have to develop a means of dealing with your difference in a way that doesn't demonstrate a general outlook of either bitterness or superiority. How you learn to deal with your departure from the so-called 'norm' is usually determined by your parents. Margaret's tallness was going to set her apart from other girls of her own age and the task ahead for her parents was to help her feel confident as she strode into the world, and not let her difference blight her happiness.

Margaret Elaine Dovey was the first-born of Wilfred Robert Dovey and Mary Dorothy Duncan. Margaret's maternal grandfather was William Duncan. Born in 1864, William's family was from Portlethen outside Aberdeen in Scotland, and they were farmers and fishermen. William himself was a carpenter before arriving in Australia in 1884 when he was twenty. Margaret still has what her mother always called 'Dadda's little blue book', in which he has written in pencil the account of his journey out to Australia. There were eight sons in the family and William came out on his own, but soon afterwards his brother Alex joined him and the two of them became master builders of pubs and terrace houses in Paddington, then a working-class inner-city suburb of Sydney.

William married Margaret Charlton, who was one of numerous daughters of Julia Austen, a widow who owned a boarding house where he lived in Phillip Street, in the city of Sydney. In 1893 they had a daughter, Mary – Margaret's mother.

But thirteen years later Margaret Charlton died tragically, due to the contraction of an ear infection which led to meningitis. She was pregnant at the time she died and left behind Mary and two siblings who were nine, seven and two at the time. Her headstone in Waverley cemetery in Sydney is inscribed 'Maggie Duncan', although Margaret's mother always said that she liked to call herself Marguerite.

In 1907, after his wife's death, William's work took him to the town of Casino, which is situated on one of the northern rivers in New South Wales. Normally he would return home to Paddington for the weekend to be with the children, but one weekend it was hot and there was still work to be finished, so he decided to stay up there with the other men. They jumped into the river for a long cooling swim and almost as soon as he hit the water William had a heart attack and drowned. Margaret still has the letters of condolence.

Margaret's paternal grandfather, Thomas Robert Dovey, was a corn, hay and chaff merchant and the sign on the side of his shop is still visible in Kelso, which is now a suburb of Bathurst in New South Wales. He married Winifred Isabel (always called Mardi) and they had a son – Margaret's father, Wilfred Robert Dovey, who was born in Bathurst in 1894. Mardi later gave birth to twins. Mardi and Robert eventually separated, and Mardi became a trained midwife, greatly in demand in country areas. She would live in with a family for a month before their baby was due and stay on for a couple of months afterwards. In between work, not having a settled abode, she would stay with Wilfred. Margaret remembers her as a grand-looking woman – never, it seemed, without a hat. She always wore her full uniform when she was working as a nurse. Dressing in proper uniforms befitting the task was very important in that era: every service job, no matter how menial, had one.

When she retired from midwifery Mardi made a life for herself in organisations such as the Historical Society, which she attended frequently. Her parents had what was then termed a 'mixed' marriage, so having converted of her own choice aged fourteen from Catholicism to Anglican, she was a regular church-goer. Cricket was her greatest passion and during the Test season she would go to matches every day with her little bag full of her lunch and knitting.

Wilfred grew up to be a bright student at the regional Bathurst schools in Kelso and White Rock, and he won a secondary scholarship to Sydney Grammar, the prestigious private boys' school in College Street in the centre of Sydney. He boarded with a family in Stanmore for seven years and went on to win a bursary to Sydney University, where he first completed an arts degree and then began law, until World War I interrupted his studies.

Remembering him now, Margaret describes him as 'six foot three, with thick dark hair, brown eyes, rather aquiline features, handsome, with olive skin'. He had a wonderful singing voice and a warm, rich, deep speaking voice. A man well known and well liked about Sydney, he smoked a pipe and in his later life often wore a monocle.

She remembers how as a child she'd hear the latch go on the back gate at Bondi and she would watch him walk into the living room, where Margaret or her mother would have his black leather slippers at the ready. He'd kiss his wife and daughter, take off his jacket and his shoes and slide his feet into his slippers. His next move would be to the sideboard, where he'd pour himself a scotch with a spray of soda from the siphon. He would ask his wife, whom he always called 'girl', if she'd like a drink and she would usually decline. It was only when they were out that she would have a cocktail because it was fashionable.

The main room of the Bondi house was very long, with the living room at one end and the dining room at the other. They had a big, solid oak table that extended into an oval shape and could seat a large number of people. Dinner was two courses, one always a pudding of some description. A roast of beef, lamb or pork was served on Sundays and Wednesdays. Chicken was special in those days, reserved for birthdays or parties. On the in-between days they had steak and kidney pie, or casseroles, or tripe.

The family never drank wine with meals and only her father would have a beer with dinner. Later on, when they had moved to Vaucluse, Margaret's mother might join him. He'd say, 'Will you have some, girl?' And girl would reply, 'Oh, I'll just have a little one.' So he'd say, 'A peanut-butter glass?' And girl would say, 'Yes.' Her mother was never bossy with her father – he was a very strong-willed man. She was always playful with him, almost kittenish.

Whenever Margaret's friends came to visit he was very warm and friendly and always interested in them. She says he was 'a lovely man, a mix of hale fellow well met and dignified and stately'.

Margaret's mother, Mary Dorothy Duncan, was tall for those days – around 5 foot 10 – and very slim. A framed photo of her in Margaret's apartment reveals a peach-skinned, clear-eyed, dark-haired, good-looking young woman with a Greer Garson-style face. Margaret believes, 'She was one of the unsung beauties of her period.' Photographs of her in her youth show her dressed in white linen, white cotton, or voile with inset lace. Black shoes, usually patent, were always worn with white dresses.

When Mary's mother died, although her aunts, grandmother and her Uncle Alec came to the rescue, she was still given a great deal of responsibility at a young age, and was expected to take charge. And so she did. It was a stance she was to assume for the rest of her life.

She won a scholarship to the coveted Sydney Girls' High (a selective school for intelligent girls) and achieved academic prizes while studying there. She then won a bursary to study arts at Sydney University (Margaret has, of course, still got it), which included tuition and £20 for the first year, with the possibility of an extension.

Unfortunately for the young Mary Duncan, her father's sudden death forced her to leave Sydney University in her second year: the bursary money had run out and her Uncle Alec, who had taken over the running of the household, wouldn't pay for the continuation of her studies – attitudes at that time deemed the advanced education of women a waste of money. It was a huge disappointment to her and, having made many friends, she deeply resented being forced to leave. She'd loved university and had been determined to make the most not only of the academic study but the many social events. She had joined every club that captured her interest. The Glee Club was the university musical society and it was there that Mary met Wilfred Dovey, who loved to sing and perform on stage. They were married in August 1914, and four days later Wilfred was sent off to war, at only twenty years of age. Mary was almost a year older than her husband, a fact that she disguised for most of her life.

After leaving university Mary became a teacher at several small private primary schools, in both academic subjects and sports. When Wilfred returned from the war after fifteen months with dengue fever, he was judged no longer fit for active service. After his discharge he took a job teaching at Brisbane Grammar School and completed his law degree by correspondence. Mary spent many hours summarising law books from the library in order to lessen her husband's workload, while continuing her own war work with the Red Cross, making quilts and sewing on the red cross for the army hospitals. She was to continue her charity work for the Red Cross for the rest of her life, assuming various positions of leadership.

By the time they returned to Sydney Wilfred had graduated in law and before being admitted to the bar in 1922 he became the associate to the Chief Justice of Australia, Sir Samuel Walker Griffith. This meant he had to travel around the country and he often took his wife and baby on his visits to Melbourne. Mary later told Margaret that she had hired a baby-sitter to look after her when she was only one year old and she later discovered that the young girl had taken Margaret down to the beach-front at St Kilda, so she could meet her boyfriend there. She had kept Margaret quiet by constantly feeding her chocolates. When she recounts the story she chuckles at her ability to go with the flow and scoff the chocolates. 'For a one-year-old baby it wasn't too bad, was it?'

Margaret remembers her mother with tremendous love and fondness. Mary was very proud of her Scottish heritage and according to Margaret 'played it up for all it was worth'. They often went to watch highland dancing but Margaret regrets that she never had the opportunity to learn it. Instead, in later years she would take her own daughter, Catherine, and live vicariously through her dancing. Accompanying parents were allowed to sit on the sidelines but Margaret admits that she could barely stop herself from leaping up and joining in.

She says she never stopped hearing about the grandfather she hadn't known because her mother was constantly talking about her Dadda: 'Dadda this and Dadda that and Dadda said and Dadda looked.' She even tormented her own husband, who was a freemason, with her knowledge of masonry gained from inspecting her Dadda's masonic accoutrements. She teased him that she knew all their rituals – a sacrilege to an all-male secret society.

Having been forced to take on the role of manager of the housekeeping money at such a young age, by the time Mary was married she was well equipped for budgeting. Margaret still has her housekeeping book in which every penny is accounted for. It has a regular entry of threepence for Margaret, which was her week's pocket money. Because of Mary's Scottish frugality and her 'keeping of the coin' Margaret has always been a careful manager of her own housekeeping money. She also remains a great user of leftovers, and a keeper of old string, paper bags and wrapping paper. Even today her children open a kitchen drawer and will ask, 'Mum, what are you keeping all this stuff for?' She still has a bag of ribbons that are constantly recycled. Her mother had one drawer in which was stored every paper bag that had ever entered the house. When the sugar was emptied the bag would be kept. Thrift was for her a habit of a lifetime, even when it was no longer necessary.

Mary loved grand occasions and her greatest thrill was attending the Queen's Coronation to which she and her husband were invited. She went alone because Wilf had just been appointed to the bench and felt he couldn't take the time off. She stayed on after the event, visiting Scotland, and was very excited about meeting the cousins with whom she had been corresponding all her life.

Mary sewed beautifully. This was wonderful for Margaret who, from an early age, could never fit into clothes off the rack. It meant that her mother always decided what she would wear, but as Margaret considered her to have good taste it didn't worry her unduly. She describes Mary as obsessed with dressing well. 'She always looked very snappy.'

Only once in her life did she criticise her mother's dress sense, and Margaret still remembers it with embarrassment. 'She came to secondary school wearing a linen dress with embroidery on it and I said, "Please don't come to school again in a doily." She must have looked gorgeous and it was ridiculous of me to say such a thing.'

The genteel and feminine skills of sewing, knitting, crocheting and tatting were shared among the women in her family, Margaret's Aunty Bessie being the expert on tatting and crocheting. Margaret still insists on using hankies and has several with Aunty Bessie's tatting on them. Her paternal grandmother, Mardi, taught her how to knit when she was five and from then on she has continued to do so constantly. She has never liked to be idle. She once even knitted herself a dressing gown, under Mardi's instruction. It wasn't really wide enough but she was so thin she could make it stretch around her.

When Margaret thinks of the word that most characterises her mother, it is 'gay'. Almost as an antidote to the disasters that had struck in her early life, she was determined to seize the day, or even the moment. The old-fashioned definition of gay is 'light-hearted, carefree, sportive' and her mother always insisted on making the most of every occasion, her early life having been blighted by sadness. Margaret's university friend Georgie Swift described Mary as 'a giggler'. Her favourite saying was, 'We have to celebrate.' And, indeed, everything possible was celebrated. Margaret recalls:

> We celebrated birthdays and Christmas and cracker nights and especially Empire Day, which was her big thing and the day before Mother's birthday. She was a bit of a hoot. I can see her now riding my little brother's hobby-horse around the garden. Dad always set up the crackers and she prepared the supper for afterwards. All the relatives and the neighbours were always invited. She was forever going off to bridge parties that included lunch afterwards. She didn't take her bridge-playing too seriously, but it came easily to her and she had a good circle of friends in the Bondi–Waverley area where they all played, taking it in turns at each other's houses. She was an excellent cook and didn't drink at all when she was young, though it gradually increased as she got older.

Mary's party favourite was a manhattan cocktail, which was whiskey and sweet vermouth. This was the era of cocktails and when it became fashionable she moved on to a martini. Margaret later shared her taste and, even now, she loves to enjoy a martini before dinner.

Hats were a necessity for the well-dressed woman and her mother would go to the top milliners of the day where a hat would cost £5. If you couldn't afford it, the milliners would let you secure it with a deposit. It was very important for her to always have a new hat for the races. She didn't so much love the actual racing, but she always placed the odd little bet on a horse and she adored the social scene.

Although her mother was quite girlish, with her own sense of fun, she was also a very proper person, in the sense of being critical if things were not done in the correct way. She was determined to be 'genteel', which Margaret does not think is always an enviable quality. Most importantly, she passed on to her daughter the confidence and the belief that she was as good as anybody else and that she would do well at whatever she tried. She was never pushy with her, or overly gushing with applause at her successes, but she conveyed her firm belief that Margaret would always be, as she says, 'top of the pops'.

In the public eye she was a dignified and stately woman and if Margaret did anything or said anything of which she disapproved she would give her 'the look'. Her blue eyes would become focused on her daughter, and very steely. If Margaret was rude as a child she was given a good slap on the arm and sent to her room which, by the time her brother had arrived and they had moved to their second house in Bondi, she shared with her grandmother when she was in town. Margaret actually slept out on the verandah, which was protected by big blinds and positioned so that it didn't suffer the brunt of the weather.

Margaret admits that her mother was a major influence in her life and that she was very dependent on her without really being conscious of it.

I only really noticed my dependency when she died. As a child I was very unsophisticated and I always let her decide what I was going to wear because she was going to make it. So I had to mind my ps and qs, otherwise she'd say, 'I'm not going to finish that.' Whenever I had differences of opinion with her, I'd always have to apologise. Sometimes I was a bit wistful about everyone else getting wonderful dresses from shops while I was forced to always wear home-made clothes. Then they would say they were jealous of me because I had so many more dresses. For practically every party I went to Mother would make me a new dress and often they would have the same one. She took part in every aspect of my life and tried to make it fun. As an adult I'd talk to her on the phone most days, just about things I was doing. After she died, around the cocktail hour I'd often go to ring her and then realise she wasn't there. That was distressing. A lot of my widowed friends often ring me in the late afternoon when there's no one to have a cocktail with. I've realised that's their lonely time.

It was her mother who taught Margaret how to overcome her shyness.

She always had great confidence going into a room and bounding up to people and chatting away to them. I used to think, 'I don't know any of these people.' It was awful. I was very shy with people I didn't know. She jollied me out of it by saying, 'Just stand there by the door, Margaret, look around, and if you know anybody, go up to them. If you don't know anybody, then find out who they are. You know full well that you look just as good as anybody in that room, so off you go.'

Georgie Swift says she liked to go over to Margaret's house and spend time with her family because 'having fun' was one of their major goals in life. There was also a constant pattern in Mary's attitude to parenting: you encourage your child to join as many organisations and to participate in as many different activities as possible, to facilitate and support anything in which your child shows an interest. Unlike her own childhood, which had been overshadowed by the death of both her parents, she was determined that her daughter would miss out on nothing. This became the template for how Margaret brought up her own children.

Margaret Elaine Dovey was a long-awaited and much wanted baby. Grandmother Mardi delivered her granddaughter at home in the parental bedroom in Bondi on 19 November 1919. Margaret still thinks 19/11/1919 is the best birth date anyone can have.

She was a 9½ pound, long-legged, healthy, happy baby – a bonny child, in the words of her Scottish forebears. Her parents were both delighted with their first-born, especially as they had waited five years for Mary to become pregnant. In fact, her mother was seven months pregnant before the doctor finally admitted that she didn't have 'the growth' that he had previously diagnosed, but was about to have a baby. Her father was so furious with the doctor's misdiagnosis that he threatened to refuse to pay him the full fee.

The family Christmas card of 1920 has on its cover a photo of a large, chubby-cheeked baby in a beautiful crocheted lace dress with a bonnet to match. She has pretty, sensual lips and the steady gaze of a child who has clearly just been propped against the wall on a small table in order to have her photo taken. She stares directly at the camera as if interested in what is happening – neither smiling nor fearful, nor on the edge of tears, merely bemused. It is an expression that many photographers will capture throughout her life. Inside the card is the message 'Margaret wishes you a Merry Christmas'.

When Margaret looks at the photo now she says, 'I looked like a proper baby, didn't I? Well cared for. Loved and wanted.' Delivered by her own grandmother in her mother's matrimonial bed, she made her entrance already safe, secure and protected. To be assisted lovingly out of the womb by your grandmother's hands into the waiting arms of your mother is a most desirable way to enter a strange world. Perhaps this is why as a baby, a child, a schoolgirl and a woman of varying ages Margaret has never looked at the world with fearful eyes, but rather with curiosity and a sense of adventure. 'What's next?' her eyes always appear to be saying, almost anticipating something interesting: something different and exciting.

Her first home was a rented semi-detached house in Bondi with an upstairs and downstairs and a neat little garden. Her parents had a special nameplate made for it which read 'Kabakaul', the town her father had been sent to in 1914 with the first Australian expeditionary force to New Guinea.

When Margaret was five Mary enrolled her into ballet classes, which were held in the basement of the old Maccabean Hall in Darlinghurst. They would go to the lessons hand in hand and, together with a long line of little people, Margaret would curtsy to Madame. At the end of the lesson she would line up, curtsy good night, put on her togs and her mother would take her home. So confident was she regarding her ballet skills that when she was seven and her mother took her to see the great ballerina Anna Pavlova, she stood up during the 'dying swan' scene and announced loudly, '*I* can do that.' Her mother told her, 'Margaret, sit back on your seat,' but she refused and kept insisting loudly, 'I can do that.' It was all her mother could do to stop her demonstrating her skills in the theatre.

Her mother also organised piano lessons with a Miss McGarrity, who would walk up the hill from her home nearby at 7.30 in the morning, climb the steep steps to the Doveys' front door and teach Margaret twice a week. Margaret practised hard and liked the playing but, even though she passed all her exams, she describes her skill as a pianist as merely adequate.

Just as her mother had enabled Margaret to enjoy the fairy dress, she taught her daughter to swim and then encouraged her to join the Bondi Swimming Club, of which Mary had become president. Not only was it an activity that she and her husband loved but it was a sport in which being tall could be an advantage. 'I can still remember the thrill of ducking under the beam that separated the shallow end from the deep section of the pool, venturing out for the first time on my own,' recalls Margaret.

She showed an early talent for the sport: by the time she was seven she was already swimming competitively and aged nine she was in the club finals. The district swimming carnivals on Saturday night were mostly held at the Coogee Aquarium which, during the summer, was used as a swimming pool. (A shark once actually disgorged a human arm there.) Margaret and her mother would catch a tram from Bondi Beach to Bondi Junction, then change for Coogee. Her father would attend the major heats but, unlike her mother, he wasn't prepared to sit out the twenty-five heats that led up to the final. Sometimes Margaret would travel with the team, but her mother would always turn up a little later. She never missed a competition. Margaret would look up into the spectators' gallery and see her mother's smart little red or green hat among the crowd and know she was sitting there, cheering her on.

In 1924 Margaret's brother, Will, or William Griffith Dovey, was born. Margaret was four and wasn't particularly pleased that Will had interrupted her lovely life with her parents. She was no longer the centre of their attention, but now her relationship with her father became especially close.

Once Will arrived Margaret remembers feeling that both her grandmother Mardi and her mother favoured him above Margaret, in the manner of mothers and their sons. Her mother would give Willie big helpings of Margaret's favourite coffee ice-cream and when she'd question why he was given more than her, her mother would simply say, 'Because he's little and he likes it.' Margaret would become very cross and reply, 'Well, when I'm grown up I'm going to buy a whole block and I'm going to eat it all by myself.'

Willie was an outgoing, funny boy, and physically tall like Margaret, whom he nicknamed 'Big Snozzle'. She called him 'Little Rat'. Within the family and by close friends he was called 'Impy', which he had named himself when he heard his parents saying, 'Where's that little imp?'

As a means of making up for her mother's apparent preference for her little brother, Margaret's father made a point of taking her to Bondi Beach every Sunday morning. She loved striding along the beach with him and together they would jump into the surf. He was a competent swimmer but not as good as her mother, who had swum competitively at school. She adored their special

Sunday visits to the beach, where they would sit on the sand, Margaret wearing an eye shade, both of them slathered in coconut oil, getting brown. (Unfortunately, she didn't have his olive skin and to this day is regularly having small skin cancers removed from various parts of her body.)

When Willie was one, grandmother Mardi brought Alice, who was a country girl, to live in with the family as a maid. Margaret and her brother nicknamed her 'Bottle' because they thought she was shaped like a beer bottle.

Both children liked Alice, and Margaret still has a picture of her holding little Willie by the hand; she was very much a part of their family. It was quite common at that time for middle-class families to have live-in maids. She was given her 'keep', her uniforms and 25 shillings a week. Alice was very fond of her uniforms, which were either blue or pale yellow with white pinnies and caps. She, too, had her set routines. On Mondays she'd do the washing, on Tuesdays the ironing, and she did all the cooking except on Thursdays, which was her day off. On Thursdays Margaret's mother would say, 'I'm going to town today, I'll bring home pies,' and her father would reply, 'If we're having pies I'm not coming home. I'll stay at the club.'

Alice always baby-sat the children and when Margaret's parents were out she'd sit at the dining room table and read them stories from Arthur Mee's *Children's Encyclopaedia*. She was a very keen movie-goer and loved to tell young Margaret stories from films, leaving out any sexy bits. She was very jolly and cheerful and stayed with the family for about twenty years.

Margaret started school when she was five at Bondi Infant School, which was part of the local Bondi public school in Wellington Street. It is a lovely old red-brick building that is still standing. (In August 2005 Margaret returned to the old classrooms to open an artist-in-residence studio named after her.)

She remembers taking to school her slate, her slate pencil and a damp cloth (to wipe the slate) in a little tin. In school photos everyone is wearing a pale-coloured dress but Margaret is wearing a dark one. Her mother had made it, thinking it was smarter and a more appropriate colour.

She enjoyed primary school, although she can't remember too much about it now, except that her headmistress was Mrs Gardiner and her special friend was Peggy Charleton, who went to the Catholic school on the corner. They would always walk the three blocks there together before going their separate ways.

Being taller than the other children was only a problem when she and her mother went into town to buy clothes. They could never buy according to age, only according to size, and the shop assistant's would inevitably remark, 'Oh, what a big girl you are.' Her mother would ignore that and simply say to Margaret, 'Come on, darling, try this on – it suits you.' Mostly, however, she made Margaret's clothes. She also made special little play clothes in heavy brown cotton for Willie that were like carpenters' aprons. Margaret admits, 'He was really rather cute – Willie in his pinny.' But by the time he was walking Margaret was into her ballet lessons, her books and her swimming and she tried very hard to ignore him.

Her mother continued to encourage Margaret to participate in whatever interested her. Her father would refer to her myriad activities as 'her uniforms'. He'd say, 'Good God, what uniform will we see the girl in next?' Girl Guides was one thing, but when she turned up to show him her Greek dancing costume, he said he couldn't quite come at it.

And then there was sport. Apart from the swimming there was basketball, hockey and tennis, and even though she wasn't a great runner she would often do the hurdles at school just for fun. In the summer she was always at the Bondi pool in the early morning and after school; in the winter she would play in the back lane with all the neighbouring kids. The girls spent a lot of time on rope-skipping games and when the boys were present they would all play cricket – serious test matches with proper scores. Margaret found it very exciting, particularly when she won. She was also keen to demonstrate her gymnastic skills on the lawn to anyone who would watch, particularly her handstands and Catherine wheels.

Drama was another of her great joys and, even if it meant playing the male leads because of her height, she couldn't wait to get onto the stage. She also loved to sing, especially at Sunday School, which was at 3 pm every Sunday at St Matthew's Anglican church in Bondi, after the roast lunch. She would wear her best dress – white silk, long-sleeved – matched with black patent-leather shoes with little straps. When she returned home she had to take the shoes off immediately, cover them with Vaseline and put them away.

From the age of eight her mother took her regularly to symphony concerts at the town hall, where they'd sit up in the gallery behind the orchestra because that's all Mary could afford at the time. Margaret loved it there because you could see the faces and hands of the musicians, and the face of the conductor. Her father would occasionally join them, but he preferred the opera and adored all the latest musicals. Margaret was automatically included in the music and theatrical tickets purchased by her parents. She particularly remembers *The Desert Song*, and all the Madge Elliott and Cyril Ritchard shows. Her parents also loved to go to the Tivoli, but they didn't take her when she was younger because her mother thought it was a little vulgar. Margaret still loves to tell the story of Mo (of comic act Stiffy and Mo) who used to say, 'There are two sorts of Sheilas – those that are good, and those that are good-oh!'

When she was ten she was invited to go in her mother's place with her father to see a show at the Theatre Royal. She was so excited. All dressed up in the silk party dress that her mother had made especially, she was even wearing a pair of her mother's silk stockings. As her father was escorting her back from drinks in the manager's office at the interval (there were no bars in theatres in those days), she snagged a stocking on the side of the seat. When she sat down she said quite loudly, 'Pa, I tore my stocking.' He said quietly, 'Don't worry about it, girl.' She said more loudly, 'But they're Mum's, they're Mum's.' He had to calm her down, and was rather embarrassed by his daughter making such a stir. Her mother described this as her 'extrovert stage', but her father always assured her that she was unconditionally loved, however she behaved.

Encouraged by her mother and adored by her father, young Margaret existed in a protective bubble, while the world outside her family was focused on the deprivations and desolation of the Depression. Margaret, however, was oblivious to anything outside her immediate world. All her needs were attended to and fulfilled. Her parents did their best to protect her from the harsher realities. Life was a series of everyday rituals.

Despite the Depression, Wilfred Dovey was doing well enough as a barrister to send Margaret to a private secondary school. There was a great deal of discussion about whether to send her as a boarder to NEGS (New England Girls' School) in Armidale, but in the end her mother refused to send her away. Then, there was a toss-up between St Gabriel's or St Catherine's in nearby Waverley. Eventually, somehow SCEGGS (Sydney Church of England Girls' Grammar School) in inner-city Darlinghurst won.

In the middle of 1930 her father took Margaret, aged ten, on the tram and walked with her to the school for her first day. When they were going down the hill of Forbes Street in Darlinghurst, famous for its prostitutes, he said to her, 'Now, Margaret, when you're coming to school there's no need to look to the left or the right, just look straight ahead because you're going to walk past dens of iniquity.' She used to wonder what on earth 'a den of iniquity' was, until it dawned on her that this was where the street girls operated. She didn't think too much about it because she was always in such a hurry to get to school. She liked to get there early so she could 'hit up', which meant she'd get a couple of tennis balls from the staff-room, go behind the gym where the height of a tennis net was marked on the back wall and hit the balls. She used to do the same against their garage door at home.

Getting to school early also meant being first to get the swing under the big tree in the schoolyard, and she often stayed late after lessons just to muck around in the gym. When she was older she joined in sessions in the prefects' study and spent time discussing their forthcoming dramatic performances at the school. She would often play the clown, dressing up in anything that was to hand, such as curtains. She has a photo of herself outside the prefects' study with her tunic tucked into her pants doing a minuet with her best friend, Sonya.

In September 2005 Margaret took me to visit SCEGGS as I was not educated in Sydney and therefore was unfamiliar with the school. As we parked the car and walked past the award-winning Harry Seidler apartment building 'The Horizon' I noticed a couple of prostitutes standing around on the street corner. 'Look neither to right nor left, Margaret,' I said. 'There's still dens of iniquity here.' She laughed and said, 'Have you seen the one that's all purple inside on Ocean Street in Woollahra?'

'No,' I replied. 'How do you know it's purple?'

'I couldn't resist it and peeked inside one day.'

'You see, this school has been a bad influence on you.'

As she slipped her hand through my arm for support, her stick in the other hand – all the better to get her balance over the uneven surface of the footpath – I wondered how many times as a cheeky, bright-eyed, gangly school-girl she had loped through these iron gates.

Margaret didn't know whether she believed in God, but she was confirmed an Anglican when she was fourteen. Her mother was a Presbyterian and her father, although baptised an Anglican, seldom went to church. But Margaret liked the colour and ritual of the church services and attended chapel every day at SCEGGS. She continued to love singing hymns and was always in the choir at secondary school.

Though at that stage she was never really sure what she believed in, she now thinks that there has to be somebody up there responsible for the universe. What she certainly believes in is not exactly turning the other cheek, but turning a blind eye. Her mother used to say 'anything for a quiet life' and Margaret will always settle for a consensus rather than engage in conflict or acts of revenge, unless she is openly provoked.

Margaret was most self-conscious about her height during her teenage years. By the time she was fourteen she had reached her full height of 6 foot 2 inches, and her most embarrassing times were the agony of school dances. It was traditional to have dance cards and her school friend Jeanette Leahy remembers Margaret filling in her empty card with imaginary names to make light of it all. She said hardly anyone ever asked her to dance and if one of the boys did screw up his courage, when they were dancing he would usually be staring at her navel. Even though, like most adolescent girls, she fought a great deal with her mother during her teenage years, her mother was determined to never let her dwell on her self-consciousness. She constantly encouraged her to fill her life with other activities that gave her pleasure, telling her that everything would improve once she reached university.

With her father's encouragement, she loved showing off her speaking talents and still does. Those were the days of elocution and eisteddfods, and in the last three years of school Margaret competed in what was called 'reading at sight'. She came third when she was fifteen, second when she was sixteen and in her last year she won the top prize. She was thrilled to finally be a winner and to receive her award standing on the stage of the Sydney Conservatorium.

At this point she had decided she would like to be a famous stage actor, but unfortunately the school didn't have drama teachers, so she had to content herself with participating in the annual school plays put on by the English teachers. While she admits to always feeling a little bit nervous beforehand, it was never enough to let it spoil her performance.

In August 2004 Margaret and Gough talked about what Shakespeare meant to them at a fund-raising event for the Bell Shakespeare Company at the Art Gallery of New South Wales. There they were, Margaret aged eighty-five and Gough aged eighty-eight, billed as the first two performers. Margaret told me she was asked whether she wanted to go first and she said, 'I don't care, which would you prefer?' The woman who was organising it replied, 'I think you should go first because we can't always be certain that Gough's not going to take a long time and then you wouldn't have much time left yourself.' 'So,' Margaret said, 'I went ahead and talked about my own experience in reading Shakespeare at school and performing. I made it clear that while I read all the leading parts, I played the extras and the walk-on male roles like Stephano in *The Merchant of Venice*, who was a servant to Portia. I had six lines. But I was in a doublet and hose and I had good legs. It was such fun.'

Margaret won a collected *Works of Shakespeare* (which she has still) as a school prize for what was called 'home reading'. Every year when you returned to school after the holidays you had to write a little resumé of the books you had read. This was no hardship for Margaret who, as a passionate reader, was always curled up with a book. 'I can see the chair now, it was wide with big armrests covered with chintz, and I'd sit sideways in it with my legs hanging over the edge.'

Her mother would tell her to go outside and play in the sun and get some fresh air. She'd simply take her book, sit on the swing outside the back door and continue to read. Her father always gave her books for birthdays and Christmas. '*David Copperfield* I remember most clearly – it's such a great story. And then I went on to read most of Dickens. Before that he gave me Kipling – his *Just-So Stories* and the two *Jungle Books*. But I'd read anything I could get my hands on – comics like *Schoolgirls' Own*, and even boys' comics that were about impossible things like planes taking off from ships in the middle of the ocean. I'd think, What a load of rubbish, and of course it's all come true.'

SCEGGS would take its pupils to school concerts in the town hall, where Sir Bernard Heinze would talk them through the orchestra, describing the various instruments and demonstrating their sounds. Margaret continued to learn music as an extra subject at secondary school and was soon addicted to the romantic composers, particularly the Russians. She admits that her addiction to the romantics remains and it was only thirty years ago that she extended it to include Mozart and Wagner.

When Margaret was thirteen Sonya Johnston arrived at SCEGGS. Margaret was assigned to show her around, and they became close friends for life. She was devastated when Sonya died in 1994 from lung cancer, even though she had never smoked.

> I always think of Sonya as being a pink and white person because I was so jealous of her bedroom, which was all pink and white and pretty. It was lovely. My bedroom was mainly walnut furniture, brown furniture. When we moved to Vaucluse in my last year of school, I was given all new furniture for my bedroom and I chose white painted furniture, which I thought was rather dishy. I came home to find that Mother had changed her mind and ordered this walnut. She said, 'I decided, darling, that you'd like that better.' So I had to like it better. I was very disappointed.
>
> Sonya was very musical. She played the piano beautifully. She, too, was in the choir, of course. She was always the woman and I was the man in the minuet in our dressing-up. She was gentle – that goes with pink and white, doesn't it? But she was equally good at making decisions. I do miss her, even now, so many years after her death. My dear pink and white friend.

Holidays were great fun because Margaret went on organised school trips with Sonya. Once, they were taken on an expedition to Heron Island before it was, as Margaret says now, 'all glossified'.

The sports mistress, Beatrice Ogilvy, would also take them skiing at Mount Kosciusko every September. It was while in Kosciusko that a boy called Margaret 'a big Jew with a big nose'. Even though she wasn't Jewish she was very tall and had a prominent nose. It was her first taste of overt discrimination and she was stunned and shocked that anyone would attack her for no reason.

Margaret had no sense that the life she led was privileged and, like most children who attend private schools, simply took such trips and treats for granted.

> I was a foxy kid. Sometimes on Friday after school I'd go into town – either legitimately to the dentist, or I would just want to go in and shop. In those days you'd have to get permission to go into town in your school uniform. I'd always pop into my father's chambers because I knew he'd say, 'Here, girl, here's two bob.' Two bob was fabulous. He'd say, 'Go and buy a milkshake,' and then he'd tap me on the back and say, 'Stand up, Sam,' when I'd be getting all round-shouldered, as I am now. Sam was his pet name for me and he always encouraged me to stand up tall and straight.

To hear Margaret tell it, her time at SCEGGS was all good fun and a smooth ride, though she was cross that she was never made a prefect. Neither was Sonya or her other close friend Philippa (Pip) Street, daughter of the famous Jessie and sister of Sir Laurence. Sonya didn't care two hoots about the prefectship but Margaret and Pip were furious with the staff who made the decision. Margaret admits that it was mostly because they were never able to wear the coloured badge that would have been emblazoned on their blazer pockets.

There were other injustices that stung Margaret. Her father was particularly keen on horse racing and Margaret had always run a sweep in her class for the Melbourne Cup. There was nothing unusual in that – all the other classes had done the same and so did the staff – but Margaret was caught passing a result to a student. She was given a Saturday-morning detention, which was 'the worst sort'. Her mother was furious because she considered it to be so hypocritical, and she went to the school on Margaret's behalf to confront the headmistress. The word 'ridiculous' was used a lot. Her mother won. Margaret was given a regular Wednesday detention instead, but her mother didn't tell her what she had done until the detention had been changed. Margaret was very pleased that her mother had taken up her cause because she had felt it was so unfair. Fairness was to become one of her touchstones in life.

At heart Margaret was an unsophisticated girl and she says it really didn't take much to make her happy. She was happy at SCEGGS, but not so happy that she was devastated when it was time to leave. She was amazed at the girls who spent their last few days there with their arms around each other, weeping. She said she thought to herself, 'What is this all about?' Years later she realised they were probably sobbing because they were leaving the mistresses. Or each other. She certainly had adolescent crushes on some of the older, good-looking girls, and would hang around them, but she never thought of any of them as particularly special. She says she was far too concerned with her own life and what was going to happen tomorrow. Her life always seemed so full of possibilities and she couldn't wait for it all to happen.

Margaret was never by nature or inclination introspective, nor was anyone in her family: life was about doing things, not lying around thinking about them. She admits that she hadn't really studied very hard at school and had spent time in Latin class reading novels under the desk instead of Cicero, but her final academic results were worse than she had anticipated. Even though she had matriculated, she had not passed well enough in Latin or maths to qualify to do an arts degree at Sydney University, which is all she had ever wanted to do.

She was absolutely shattered when she found out she couldn't study arts. For the first time in her life she was barred from doing something she wished to do. She simply couldn't believe it could happen to her. What's more, neither of her parents could fix it. Her parents didn't ever tell her whether they were disappointed in her academic results, and they certainly didn't admonish her. Her father continued to encourage her to aim high. When she expressed some interest in doing nursing like her grandmother, her father said, 'Why not do medicine?' As a means of giving her confidence he took her up to the old medical school, but seeing all the dead babies in bottles and specimens of body parts put an end to that idea.

When she decided that she was interested in journalism her father took her to meet Frank Packer, for whom he did legal work. At a meeting in his office Packer, who was the largest owner of newspapers and magazines in Australia at the time, said, 'So, girlie, what do you want to do – the social notes?' Margaret replied that while she liked socialising, she didn't want to write about it. 'Well, what *do* you fancy doing?' he queried again.

'Court reporting, or something like that,' she announced rather boldly.

'Oh no, girlie,' he said, 'our girls only do social rounds.'

That ruled out journalism.

Despite her failure to be admitted to do an arts degree, at the end of 1937 Margaret was looking forwards not backwards: 'I always feel when something ends, something new is going to begin and it's going to be just as exciting.'

Margaret had a good relationship with both her parents and for the most part refrained from indulging in bouts of adolescent angst and teenage rebellion. Her mother was the disciplinarian and was very firm about what Margaret was allowed and not allowed to do. She would not stand rudeness or Margaret fighting with Will.

Margaret and her father never argued and she can remember only one incident when, thinking she was 'smart', she called him a moron. He was so shocked and hurt at his beloved daughter that he didn't speak to her for three days. He adored her and couldn't believe she would call him such a name. Neither, now, can she. She still snorts with derision at herself for her burst of teenage arrogance.

Her parents tried to be present at all her activities, and her father especially was puffed-up proud of her swimming achievements. She trained with determination: summers meant swimming every day after school. (People rarely swam in the winter as there were no heated pools in Sydney.) Not that training for competitions was so onerous in those days. For a 100- or 200-yard race she would do 600 yards at a steady pace. Breaststroke became her favourite stroke and her strength. Mostly she did twelve laps of the pool for either a two-lap or four-lap race. Then she'd practise starts and finishes, followed by a couple of 100 yards focused on improving her style, when she would do a slow but beautiful breaststroke.

Kathleen Buckle, who ran the Bondi Ladies' Amateur Swimming Club, was her coach. Mrs Buckle had been an English showgirl who had married an Australian. She was known to be a gifted coach and ran the club entirely with help of two other women: Mrs Cox and Beryl Etheridge, who lived next door to Margaret.

'With the help of her little black book Mrs Buckle had everyone listed in order – fastest to slowest – adding a handicap by way of a number. "M. Dovey," she'd call out crisply. "Here," I'd reply. "Go!" she'd shout.'

Mrs Cox was married to one of the local Bondi dentists and she did the books and helped with the judging, as did Beryl. When you were really swimming well you would be selected to be part of a small team who was often asked to compete in Wollongong or Ramsgate, or to open a new pool.

Selected members would be asked to do an exhibition of their particular stroke. Exhibitions were common in those days – every swimming carnival held one.

> The first one I went to was by Fanny Durack and Mina Wylie. Fanny was the Olympic gold medallist at the 1912 games in the 100 metre freestyle, and Mina the silver medallist in the same event. They had special styles. Fanny used a six-beat crawl, which was considered very adventurous, while Mina used the old trudgeon, which was freestyle with your arms and a sort of sidestroke with the legs. If you gave an exhibition you were a star.

All Margaret's years of training and swimming in carnivals at the Bondi Club finally paid off. She competed successfully in all the inter-club meetings and inter-club championships and in 1937 she was chosen to be part of the state team, with all her expenses paid, including money for a milkshake and travel fares. A white-haired chap called Pop Hooton was her coach for the state championships and she would travel from Bondi to the Coogee Aquarium to be coached by him. 'Back then you could use butterfly in the last ten yards of a breaststroke race, but I found I was too pooped at the end of the race. I regarded butterfly as a rather exhausting stroke, whereas doing breaststroke I felt like a swan.'

Her team-mates in the state team included Joan Thomas, Pat Norton and Clare Dennis. Pat had made it to the final in the 1936 Olympics in backstroke. Clare had won the 200 metre breaststroke at the 1932 Los Angeles Olympics with a time that was unbeaten for some years. Today the times for breaststroke are at least a minute faster than Margaret's times.

In 1937 she had the strong feeling that she was hitting top form in the breaststroke and her father was terribly excited at the prospect of her competing in the Australian championships. She overheard him telling a neighbour, 'If Margaret wins the national championships I won't call Bob my uncle.' She was privately delighted that he was so proud of her.

And so it was that in the new North Sydney pool Margaret Dovey became the 1937 Australian breaststroke champion. This meant that she also qualified to be part of the team to compete in the British Empire Games the following year. She was thrilled at this prospect, and her coach thought she had a definite chance of winning at least a place. Her father was bursting with pride for his daughter and told everyone he knew about his Margaret being chosen to swim for Australia in thc Empire Games.

A photo taken during the Australian championships shows her talking to one of her competitors. Her body, although long and thin, looks strong and her thighs are very lean and powerful. She is standing with her left foot slightly raised, a stance that she often has today whenever she is talking earnestly to someone. In the photo she looks like a fresh-faced schoolgirl who would be eager to have a chat. She has an open, innocent face framed by a warm smile. Her long brown hair, which she had been growing since she was a child, hangs in perfectly braided plaits down her back.

Both her mother and her father had given her all the gifts of good parents. They both loved her unconditionally and they both encouraged her in every activity in which she was interested. They gave her a loving, warm, safe home and family life which enabled her to approach the world without fear. They both made it absolutely clear to her that her height would be no impediment to her fulfilment in life.

UNIVERSITY

In 1938 Hitler moved his army into Austria and Czechoslovakia, but Australia, like Britain, was desperate to avoid another war and advocated the policy of appeasement.

Margaret Whitlam was starting an economics degree at the University of Sydney and like many Australians was blissfully unaware of any clouds on her horizon. Her main concern was working out how to squeeze into the day and the night all the things she wanted to do and read and see and, very importantly, what to wear on every occasion.

Swimming remained, however, her prime passion and preoccupation. In January 1938 she was totally focused on her training for the Empire Games in February. However, she had contracted a debilitating streptococcal infection in her throat that she couldn't seem to shake off. These were the days before sulphur drugs, or even penicillin, and no matter how hard she tried she could feel her strength daily draining away from her. She had always been prone to colds and as a child had regularly contracted bronchitis, as well as bouts of pleurisy and pneumonia. She is still susceptible to these infections, even in the age of antibiotics. Swimming so constantly had also made her very vulnerable to middle-ear infections.

Her father was distraught. He even resorted to taking her out and buying her oysters and asparagus, in the hope that they would build up her strength. They were considered by Margaret to be very big treats. But nothing, it seemed, not even her father's best efforts, would cure her. Finally, as the big competition loomed closer, the doctor advised her that she was not well enough to swim. Margaret simply refused to believe that she could not recover in time. She kept training and hoping that she would get better.

The day before the games began she remembers her father desperately searching for medication that would provide some relief, but to no avail. She was disallowed from marching in the opening ceremony because she had to swim the next day.

On the night of the race, with the lights sparkling into the blue lanes of the pool, her mother and father and all her friends sitting in the stands to cheer her on, Margaret stood on the blocks ready to dive into the water for the 220 yard (50 metre) breaststroke. She felt so sick she was afraid she would sink like a stone to the bottom of the pool as soon as she hit the water. Once she was in and the race was on, every stroke seemed to drag her backwards. Her arms and legs were dead weights, but she forced herself to push them through the increasingly heavy water.

She didn't sink as she had feared. She willed herself with every last ounce of energy in her aching body to finish the race. She succeeded, but she didn't get a place. In fact, she came last. The gold medal was won by England's Doris Storey, the silver by South Africa's Carla Gerke, the bronze by Canada's Joan Langdon, with Australians Valerie George from Victoria and Joan Thomas of New South Wales coming fourth and fifth respectively.

Margaret says now, 'The English girl was always going to win, but I was the Australian champion and I was expected to come third.'

White-faced and shaking with exhaustion, she dragged herself out of the pool, overcome with shame, disappointment and embarrassment. In retrospect she agrees that she should have withdrawn from the race as it took her body a long time to recover its strength from the ordeal, but Margaret is not someone who likes to cancel anything. She thought then, and she still thinks, that opting out of something you have promised to do is letting yourself – and more importantly – the side down. And she hates to let anyone down. Besides, she also hates to miss out on an experience.

Even now when she talks about her failure to win a medal at the Empire Games she winces at the memory of coming last. She admits, though, that nothing short of being strapped to her bed would have stopped her from competing. She is not a quitter. She is a firm believer that there's nothing shameful about trying and failing in life – she stands firmly in the Aussie tradition of always 'having a go'. She knows that at least she gave it her best shot that warm night in February under the stars of the Southern Cross on behalf of her country. Her spirit was strong and willing, but her poor stricken body failed her.

By March of that year it was well known and indeed reported in the social pages of the *Herald* that Margaret Dovey, who had swum for Australia in the Empire Games, was about to commence studying economics at Sydney University. Still upset that she didn't have the necessary prerequisites to enrol in arts, she had chosen economics as a poor substitute, but insisted on studying German and English as well as her first year economics subjects.

As the year progressed it became very clear to her that she found economics boring and was really only interested in her arts subjects. But studying was not high on her list of priorities. Life at university really suited her. She simply adored it. Shedding her old skin, the blushing, awkward, adolescent school-girl found herself blossoming, just as her mother had promised, into a socially confident young woman. She also discovered flirting. Serious flirting. What's more, she was very good at it. Flirting with good-looking 'sorts', as she calls them, is still one of her favourite occupations.

At a Melbourne Cup lunch a few years ago at the Bellevue Hotel in Paddington there was a handsome young blond actor at our table who offered to place Margaret's bets for her to save her standing in the queue at the TAB. She was wearing a blouse with a floppy tie at the neck and halfway through the lunch she returned from a visit to the loo and said, 'Good God, I just looked at myself in the mirror and decided I look like Oscar Wilde. So you, my dear,' she said with a wicked twinkle in her eyes to the blond young man, 'you can be my Bosie.' Not a bad line for an eighty-year-old flirt, I thought to myself.

In Margaret's first year at university she joined SUDS – the Sydney University Dramatic Society – and with relish resumed her range of minor roles and voice-overs. She knew that her height would always prevent her from playing female romantic or dramatic leads, but she didn't mind as long as she was involved in the theatrical production. She loved everything about the stage and even took to wearing pancake theatrical make-up and eye shadow in the evening for a more dramatic effect, replacing the light powder and lipstick her mother had recommended.

Mostly she wore twinsets and strands of pearls to university, and cotton dresses in the summer and a little light make-up. Cocktail parties meant short but pretty dresses. Margaret had two favourites. One was a black and pink checked taffeta and the other a plain black crepe with a square neckline and short sleeves, lined with blue taffeta. After she had worn it for a year her mother replaced the taffeta with a pale pink crepe which, as Margaret said, made it a new dress. Gloves were always worn. If you forgot them on your way to town then you would simply have to buy a new pair. Margaret tended only to wear hats to the races but berets in the winter were considered terribly smart.

Her father's success at the bar meant the family had moved from Bondi to the more exclusive eastern suburb of Vaucluse where their semi-detached house was replaced by a bay-windowed villa, which they first rented and later bought, set in a beautiful leafy garden that overlooked Sydney Harbour. Margaret had a front bedroom opposite her parents. Her brother, Willie, also lived there. He was studying at Sydney Grammar, his father's old school, and, like Margaret, was very involved with sporting activities.

Margaret would still go to the latest musicals with her parents and when they arrived home her mother would immediately sit down at the piano. Margaret loved to join them in singing the songs from the show as the theatre programs always had the words at the back. Whenever her parent's friends came over for bridge there would be a break for tea and cakes, or biscuits and cheese, and they'd all stand around the piano and sing. This was a popular form of social entertainment at the time, which Margaret's parents were particularly keen on.

Margaret was also taking private singing lessons with a woman she'd met several years before at a musical society – Margaret says her mother was always 'the queen of some musical society or other'. The teacher had the exotic name of Lute Drummond and she lived as an independent single woman in a flat on top of a building in Bridge Street in the city. It had originally been a janitor's flat and Lute had a bedroom at the back, a little kitchen and bathroom, and a studio at the front where she'd teach students individually. Margaret thought it was all very exciting and bohemian.

On Wednesday afternoons Miss Drummond would teach

them all Italian in order that they might sing opera. Margaret adored every aspect of it and continued to take lessons during her second year at university, until war was declared and Lute gave up teaching for war work. Among her students were a young Joan Hammond and Kenneth Neate, and Margaret was very chuffed when she heard later that Miss Drummond had told another student that she had real talent and was in fact potentially a young Kirsten Flagstad, who was considered 'the tops' at the time. Margaret would have loved to have continued with her singing lessons and still secretly dreamt of a career on the stage or the concert hall, but the war interfered with her plans.

Often she would have so many activities on the go that she could not be home for dinner so her mother would make sure that a sandwich and a small thermos of warm milk would be waiting for her on the dressing table. They were a thoughtful and generous family to each other, with everyone's individual needs respected.

The worst thing Margaret says she ever did to her mother happened during this period. She was still living at home, but her parents were away and she had invited some friends over for a party. The living room had a high shelf around the walls on which Mary had placed her favourite plates and Toby jugs. Margaret decided that she hated the look of them, so she took them all down and dumped them in her father's billiard room. Of course she forgot to replace them before her parents returned. Her mother was hurt rather than angry and didn't even remonstrate with her, which only made her feel worse.

Not that her mother was incapable of being angry. Her parents had arguments like any other couple. She said she always knew when they were having a serious row because the bedroom door would be closed. She'd often put her ear to it to try and hear what they were saying.

My mother was usually having a go at my father about how late he was coming home from lodge. He drank as much as most chaps at the time, but he wasn't a drunk. He loved the races, but he wasn't a big gambler. Later on in life, when he was vice-chairman of the Australian Jockey Club, he leased some horses.

Mother was very prim in her use of language and Father was not. He'd call her a bitch in an argument and I can hear her now intoning, 'I am not a female dog.' My father was both a man's man and a woman's man. When he died my aunt said to me, 'He was a wonderful man, but there were times when he was very naughty.' I assumed from the word 'naughty' that she meant there were little dalliances. I don't think he would ever have risked being seen out at lunch – they would have been nocturnal adventures.

When Margaret was a little girl and was asked what she was going to do when she grew up, her standard reply was, 'Oh, I'm going to be a social butterfly and go on moonlight exertions.' Trams at that time were always advertising 'moonlight excursions.' She admits that she did indeed become a bit of a social butterfly at university and did go out on moonlight exertions, 'with the emphasis on the exertion'.

Neither of her parents had ever spoken to her about sex and, like most young women of her class and era, she'd had to work it out for herself. She said there had been a little bit of 'you show me yours and I'll show you mine' when she was eleven at the back of the Presbyterian churchyard, and she was always a great reference reader, occasionally looking up something that she thought might be naughty. She remembers looking up 'adultery', which was defined as 'the violation of the marriage bed'.

'I did a bit of experimental masturbation as a kid but there was no reality to it except thinking, well, I like that.'

When she was at university there was 'a tremendous lot of foreplay but no real play' between her and the young men in her group. The fear of an unwanted pregnancy was ever-present.

> People I knew mostly didn't do it or, if they did, they seemed to get themselves into all sorts of strife. For instance, one of our contemporaries went off one night after a party and was never seen again. She disappeared. The speculation was that she was pregnant, that she had an abortion that didn't work, and that she died. She was a lovely, good fun girl. We didn't actually know for certain that she was pregnant, but that was the assumption. We were all very unsophisticated.
>
> Georgie [Swift] and I used to talk to each other in French on the tram just because we thought it was sophisticated. We had a lovely lot of chaps that we used to go out with, all of us in a group. My mother never said anything to me about my sexual attraction to any of them, she would only comment on whether they were 'acceptable' or not. I remember one of my beaus, Lyle, coming to pick me up and when he arrived he was wearing tails. As I was keeping him waiting, as usual, Mother called out, 'Oh, you must come and see Lyle, he looks so lovely in his tails.' I said, 'I'll be out there shortly,' and when I presented myself and clearly didn't say enough glorifying things Mother stepped in and went on with, 'Doesn't he look good?' and all that sort of rubbish. I was always more keen on a couple of his mates and eventually went out with them a few times.

Sex, of the intercourse variety, was never expected to be part of the evening. You only ever went 'so far'. Margaret, however, found herself eager to go as far as she dared. It was never she who called a stop to it.

'You never expected to be raced off totally because the chaps would always stop. They were apprehensive of going too far themselves.'

Margaret says she liked it so much that she would have been game, but that was probably because she was so unsophisticated. 'One bloke actually stopped and said, "I can't do it to you. You're too nice, we're too young". I was thinking, go ahead, I'd love it.'

Sex and romance were always on her mind and she was very keen to find herself a man with whom she could fall hopelessly in love.

As for lesbianism, she says they all knew it existed but it was never spoken of.

> I never felt tempted to try it because I never met another woman whom I felt I could fall for. Frankly, I really didn't think about it. The urge to have sex with another woman would have to have been very strong for anyone to act on it. Nowadays, everyone is interested in everyone – mix and match – but in my day it just didn't happen openly. The only lesbian I can remember knowing from that time was a top sportswoman at school. She was a fencer and a tall, handsome blonde. They didn't discuss her sexuality at school, they just thought she was 'different'. When she left school and never married then they did discuss it, as that was considered 'a sign'.
>
> Gay men, or men whom you suspected were gay, were called 'the brown suede brigade' because if they wore suede shoes they were a bit 'suss'. They were called 'pansies'; the term 'poofter' came later. I met a number of really nifty, charming young men who were undoubtedly homosexual. They were very

attractive to women but not sexually attracted by them; they were caring and lovely, and if you were in strife they'd always help you. We never talked about their sexual orientation.

They were great dancing partners at balls. In those days every faculty had a dance or a ball, and so did all the sporting clubs. We often didn't really know or care what these men's sexual orientation was, as long as they were good dancers. If someone was really keen on someone we might say, 'You're wasting your time there,' but that didn't happen very often.

It was the era of Noël Coward, and Margaret and all her friends were very familiar with his songs and adored his plays. Coward was the perfect model of charm and wit and sophistication as far as they were concerned. Margaret had read Christopher Isherwood's *Goodbye to Berlin* and W. H. Auden's poetry and was well aware that all these writers were homosexual, but that knowledge didn't really mean anything to her.

When she was eighteen Margaret always used to announce to anyone who cared to listen that if she wasn't married by the time she was thirty she was going to 'take lots of lovers'. Looking back on that statement now she thinks she was stretching it a bit because in those days you were well and truly on the shelf by the time you were thirty. She says, 'By then the only available chaps would have been gay, or leftovers.' In fact, she believes that it's almost impossible to apply today's standards or expectations to when she was a young woman because sexually it was a different world.

She won't have it said, however, that life was dull in Sydney in the late 1930s. 'It was a very stupid thing to say that you had to go overseas to get decent theatre. There were lots of decent plays and good playwrights, like Oriel Gray. There were plenty of so-called "little theatres" – Gilbert and Sullivan, comedies, operettas – and of course for vaudeville there was the Tivoli.'

As much as Margaret loves to go to established theatre and has had a long-standing subscription to the Sydney Theatre Company, she still loves the other end of the spectrum: amateur theatre. She is a long-time member of a club called the Glugs of Gosh, which is a group of people involved in various aspects of the theatre, although most of the members are now her age or older.

In 2005 Margaret asked me to join her as her guest at the annual Glugs of Gosh Christmas lunch. In the name of research I agreed and it was here that I saw a side of her I'd not previously witnessed. She has never taken any member of her family to this club – her daughter, Catherine, says that she can't begin to understand what her mother sees in it and her sons are not even aware that she attends it. Margaret doesn't care – she loves it.

On our arrival she insisted that everyone at the table open their Christmas crackers, put on their paper hats and read out the excruciatingly bad jokes on the little strips of paper.

Margaret began by reading hers aloud, in dramatic fashion, to the table.

'What's the difference between a sick cow and an angry crowd? One moos badly, the other boos madly.'

She threw back her head and chortled. 'I like that,' she said, to my somewhat incredulous face. And then she added, 'I'm such a child, aren't I?'

And there it was, still evident in her face and her demeanour: a childish innocence, a delight in being silly and amused simply for the sake of it. She was enjoying herself and if I wasn't then it was my bad luck.

When the turkey arrived she was reminded of what she described to me as 'a wonderful phase in our lives when we lived in Cabramatta and the local Italian baker would cook and deliver the Christmas turkey. He'd also bring sough-dough bread every week. This was long before it was fashionable.' Next, the trifle arrived. It was sitting in a coffee cup. I thought to myself that the hotel must have run out of dessert plates. Margaret on the other hand said, 'Isn't this marvellous? I've never thought of serving trifle in a cup – it's great, isn't it? Makes it look more. I love trifle, don't you?'

Suddenly it was announced over the microphone, 'Margaret Whitlam, one of our youngest members, will pick the winning ticket for the Christmas hamper.' She did so with great flair and I could see the young schoolgirl show-off enjoying herself.

Then someone standing in front of her while she was attempting to take a photo said, 'Hello Margaret, remember me?' I thought to myself, 'If she had a dollar for every time she's heard that line, she'd be a millionaire.'

Margaret smiled patiently, looked the woman in the face and said, 'I'm trying.'

The woman said, 'I went to SCEGGS.'

Margaret replied, 'Good for you,' unwilling to be drawn into a conversation about which year because it would inevitably preclude the other people at the table. She always makes an effort to involve everyone in the conversation.

Suddenly a bell was rung loudly for the MC to announce, 'Some people did not get their nomination forms.'

'Nomination for what?' asked Margaret in her louder than usual voice.

The lady sitting next to her tapped her hand and said, 'Don't bother. He's deaf.' Someone else came around selling a book about their experiences in the theatre and Margaret immediately bought one.

I noticed there was a queue of old blokes waiting to talk to her. One by one they kissed her on the cheek or the hand and told her how well she was looking. She flirted back like a teenager. Suddenly she turned to me and said, 'Where's my book? Someone's nicked it.'

I lifted her table napkin and there it was. She laughed and said, 'I suppose you're going to put that in the book. You think all this is silly, don't you? Well, I don't care. I love it.'

And I thought, why shouldn't she have an opportunity to let her hair down and be a bit silly, be an amateur performer again among these old timers? It must be a relief to be away from endlessly shaking hands and sitting through boring branch meetings and lugubrious Labor Party dinners, where she is always on show as the dutiful wife, the living national treasure or the matriarchal icon of the Labor Party. Not that she resents it, not any of it, but this is a different sort of party, one where she is there solely for herself, to enjoy herself, to have some innocent fun. I realise it's the young Margaret Dovey I am sitting next to, not Mrs Whitlam, wife of Gough, former PM and mother of Antony, Nicholas, Stephen and Catherine.

In her first year at university Margaret Dovey was keen to play any part in a SUDS production that she was offered, either on- or offstage. Her height was still a limitation for the major female roles, but in 1938 she played the part of Emilia, a hand-maiden in *Lucrèce*, André Obey's play translated by Thornton Wilder. In this play it did not matter that she was tall because whenever she was on stage Lyndall Barbour, the leading lady, was either prone or seated. In the review of the production the university paper, *Honi Soit*, said, 'The second act of *Lucrèce* is the most daring SUDS has ever attempted and the most convincing act in the whole play. Lyndall Barbour has almost entirely overcome the nervous mannerisms which for so long marred her work. The support, with the exception of Margaret Dovey, showed a lack of understanding.'

It was only small praise but at least she was named and noticed favourably. It must have frustrated Margaret, who was clearly talented and had trained in acting, singing and dancing, that her height prevented her from claiming centre stage. However, it is indicative of the approach she would take to other problems in her life over which she had no control that she refused to let it depress her or plunge her into a well of self-pity. She never bemoaned her fate, but simply made the most of what she could do rather than dwelling on what was barred from her.

Moreover, she enjoyed whatever part she played. This was not a simplistic Pollyanna, 'let's always play the glad game' stance on her part, but rather a practical approach to what could be done to solve the problem. For Margaret the glass is always half-full rather than half-empty, not because of any philosophical or psychological attachment to optimism but because, quite simply, life is more enjoyable and fulfilling if you approach it that way.

In March 1938 Margaret Dovey made her debut into society at an exclusive event called the Imperial Services Ball, held in Sydney Town Hall. Margaret attended with her own party of friends, and each of the eight girls who were being presented, first to the governor of New South Wales and then to the Administrator of the Commonwealth, had been allocated a partner for the formal presentation. Margaret's partner was called Leo Cook. She was delighted because he was both tall and handsome, and was one of the young chaps from the army stationed at Victoria Barracks. Margaret is still friends with Leo, but hasn't seen him since his first wife died. He'd be around ninety now, she thinks.

Having officially 'come out', as it was then called, she was even more eager to throw herself into the social whirl. However, her academic results at the end of her first year were not as good as her social life. While she enjoyed the subjects she liked, she failed half her economics subjects.

Even though Margaret didn't like economics, she repeated

the failed subjects in 1939 and also, at her mother's suggestion, attended a business college in order to learn shorthand and typing. She spent that year in her usual whirl of sporting, artistic and social activities and continued to enjoy herself. She felt, quite simply, that 'the whole world was my oyster'.

In September 1939 the Prime Minister of Australia, Robert Menzies, declared that it was his melancholy duty to inform his fellow Australians that as Britain had declared war on Germany because of Germany's persistence in the invasion of Poland, Australia was now at war.

Margaret does not remember there being any discussion about politics or the war at home. This could have been because her parents didn't wish to blight her life and wanted to protect her from what they feared lay ahead so things could continue to be as normal as possible. Or it could have been because Margaret was living in a romantic haze where dreams of a stage, or a singing career, or being swept away by a sophisticated young man resembling Noël Coward were uppermost in her mind.

Or it could have been that when confronted with the harsh realities of an ugly world, she resorted to her aunt's dictum of changing the topic of discussion by saying, 'Enough of that. Let us speak of fruit and flowers.' Even now when a conversation about political or social issues becomes heated, especially if her children are voicing harsh judgements against people they view as political enemies, Margaret will interrupt with, 'Let us speak of fruit and flowers.'

One hot December night in 1939, Margaret went to a SUDS cocktail party at the house of Alice Jackson, who was the editor of

The Australian Women's Weekly, and whose daughter, Hazel, was a friend of hers. Margaret was wearing a light green ensemble that matched the colour of her eyes, and her hair was still wet from swimming earlier in the evening. At the party she caught the eye above the crowded room of a dark-haired, handsome chap. He was 6 feet 4 inches tall and she thought he was 'quite the most delicious thing I'd ever seen'.

His name was Gough Whitlam. She noticed that he even had exactly the same widow's peak hairline as the film star Robert Taylor to whom, when she was at school, she had written her one and only fan letter, receiving a signed photograph in return.

Each of them had been told about the other by mutual friends and when their eyes met on that balmy December evening there was an instant chemical reaction. The words of a popular 1934 hit song rang in her ears:

> Are the stars out tonight?
> I don't know if it's cloudy or bright
> 'Cause I only have eyes for you, dear.

For Margaret, 'It was love at first sight. He was the most gorgeous thing I'd ever seen in my life. Sometimes he still is.' Gough said he'd felt the same chemistry. They danced and talked with each other the whole evening. Margaret remarks that even now 'he's a pretty good dancer, though he talks all the time and doesn't listen to the music'.

In 1939 Oscar Hammerstein wrote a song called 'All the Things You Are', whose refrain begins, 'You are the promised kiss of springtime' and ends with, 'One day my happy arms will hold you / And some day I'll know that moment divine / When all the things you are, are mine.' This is still Margaret's favourite 'swoon' song and when she hears it she will poke you in the ribs and whisper, 'Isn't it simply heaven?'

The next morning at breakfast when her father asked her, 'Was there anybody nice at your party last night?' she replied, 'Oh, yes. I met Gough Whitlam.'

Her father said, 'Would he be related to Fred Whitlam?'

Margaret said, 'Yes, he's his son.'

Gough's father was the Commonwealth Crown Solicitor, and a successful and well-known barrister. Gough quickly managed to wrangle an invitation out of Margaret for Sunday lunch at the Doveys', claiming that the food at university was not like his mother's home cooking.

For Christmas 1939 he gave Margaret a copy of James Joyce's *Ulysses*, which was acquired with some difficulty because there was talk of banning its sale in Australia. Although he didn't write an inscription in it, Margaret was impressed with his choice of present. Not only was he gorgeous-looking, but he took her seriously.

Books were very central to the education and upbringing of Edward Gough Whitlam, first-born on 11 July 1916 to Martha and Frederick Whitlam of Kew in Melbourne. Their daughter Freda followed four years later. In 1918 the family moved to Sydney, then in 1927 Fred's job took them to Canberra. Eventually appointed crown solicitor by the Lyons government in 1936, Gough's father became one of the nation's most senior and highly paid public servants.

Fred Whitlam's relaxation was reading and he had collected a huge library with its emphasis on history, sociology, English literature and especially Greek and Latin classics, all of which he encouraged his son to read and absorb.

According to Laurie Oakes' biography of Gough, his father strongly believed that only a classical education developed the qualities essential for leadership and public administration. Bedtime stories for Gough and Freda came not from *Grimm's Fairytales*, but largely from a book called *The Myths of Greece and Rome* by H. A. Guerber. At an age when most children are fascinated by the stories of Hansel and Gretel and Snow White and the Seven Dwarves, Gough's world was peopled by characters such as Prometheus, Persephone, Orpheus, the nine muses, Oedipus, Odysseus, Clytemnestra and Perseus. When he was not much more than two years old, his mother found him sitting at her dressing table, a book open in his lap, weeping over a picture of Persephone, the daughter of Zeus and Demeter, being abducted by Hades while gathering flowers.

From the time they could read, whenever the Whitlam children asked the meaning of a word, they were instructed to look it up in the latest and most comprehensive dictionaries on their bookshelves.

Fred Whitlam followed strict standards in his personal and professional life and had little interest in material things. The family never owned a car, even though Fred could well have afforded one. There was no radio in the house until 1934 because Fred and Martha believed it would distract the children from study. Money was never spent frivolously and the family's only extravagance was books, says Oakes.

Gough's mother, Martha, was almost totally deaf due to a childhood accident and contracting encephalitis after Gough's birth, but she was a warm and witty woman who, unable to take much part in conversation, spent her time in the kitchen preparing delicious meals. Gough explains his lifelong interest in and passion for good food as the result of his mother being such a fine cook. If she couldn't contribute to the conversation because of her deafness, she could envelop him in the home-cooked food she so lovingly prepared. She was always the first to bake cakes and biscuits for guests in the newly developing neighbourhood of Forrest in Canberra, and during the Depression she gave food to the daily stream of unemployed men who knocked on her door. Not only that, but every day she prepared nine cut lunches: one each for Gough, Fred and his brother George, and six to be given to the needy.

Even now, in her late eighties, Margaret still makes Gough his lunchtime sandwiches to take to his office. When I asked her why he didn't just send someone down to buy him sandwiches, she said, 'He says he likes mine best, and why should I change a habit of a lifetime at this stage in his life?'

One day I stayed for lunch with Margaret and she had made extra sandwiches for us as well as Gough. I can now understand why he prefers her sandwiches – ours were generous servings of chicken, walnuts, cucumber and mayonnaise on fresh multigrain bread. However, unlike Gough who doesn't drink much, Margaret and I knocked off a bottle of good red wine with ours.

Unlike the cosmopolitan nature of Bondi in Sydney, where Margaret grew up in a semi-detached home, Gough's early life in Canberra was spent in a big mock Tudor house in whose bare backyard his father toiled daily to convert into a productive garden. Canberra, populated by public servants and politicians, was very much a city in embryo and his parents took seriously their contributions towards the making and building of a community. Fred was deeply religious but not narrow-minded, and both he and Martha had attended a variety of Protestant churches before they had moved to the national capital. They had met at the Murrumbeena Baptist church in Melbourne but Fred's theological reading and his friendships spanned all denominations. 'There was nothing wowser-ish or sanctimonious about Fred, nor did he try to force his beliefs or way of life on others, even his children,' Oakes writes in his biography.

From 1950 to 1954, after Fred retired, he was Australia's representative on the UN Human Rights Commission and was an outspoken advocate for the fair treatment of minorities, individuals, and for a liberalised migration policy.

Laurie Oakes tells of Kurshed K. Lalkaka, a Parsee, and a regular guest of the Whitlam household in the 1920s:

> Racial tolerance was not one of the more fashionable virtues in Australia in those days, but Lalkaka was at home with the Whitlams. Fred would have been horrified if either of his children had shown any sign of racial or religious prejudice. On one occasion when Lalkaka was dining with the Whitlams, young Gough asked his father, "Is Mr Lalkaka's god the same as our god?" Without hesitation his father replied, "Of course."

To those steeped in the class warfare of the old-style Labor Party, Gough Whitlam was seen later in his life to have been born to a life of plenty and privilege and was therefore 'Not one of us'. To conservatives he was and is still seen as a traitor to his class. They cannot understand why he chose to become 'One of them'. Clearly his father's influence, his values, his belief in equal opportunity and human rights, together with a deep interest in foreign affairs, steered Gough towards the Labor Party.

As a child Gough was, 'tall, willowy with rosy cheeks, a clear complexion, wavy hair and large, luminous blue-grey eyes'. The sensitivity in his make-up was evident in his appreciation of literature, his response to it and in his reaction to criticism and teasing by other children. His father's interest in correct language and grammar inclined Gough towards early pedantry. 'His high-school magazine said of him that he could not repeat a limerick without adjusting its diction and metre,' says Oakes.

Before his family moved to Canberra, Gough began his education at Mowbray House and went on to Knox Grammar School, both private schools popular with well-to-do Sydney North Shore families. His father was concerned that the style of classical Greek education that he wanted for his son was not readily available at public schools. In Canberra, however, he attended the public Telopea Park High School. In 1928 the school register shows him as enrolment number forty-three. The onset of the Depression meant that in public schools children of senior public servants sat alongside the children of the unemployed, and Gough would have been well aware that some of his fellow students were less privileged than himself, through no fault of their own or their parents.

Young Gough was not only meticulous about language, grammar and history but also about his personal appearance. Apart from the fact that he physically towered above children of his own age, his manner was sometimes aloof, he played no sport and he preferred to walk or swim for exercise. He spent most of his spare time reading rather than mixing with his school fellows. He was teased for being an oddity. Oakes says, 'According to people who knew him during his first months in Canberra it was because of the teasing that he learned to use his tongue like a whip.'

In 1931 Gough was the treasurer of the Telopea Park High dramatic society and played the title role in a short play called *The Man in the Bowler Hat*. The review in the school magazine described him as one of the outstanding players. He also began to write satirical verse in the style of the eighteenth-century poet Alexander Pope. This poetic ability was further developed when he transferred to Canberra Grammar in 1932 and edited *The Canberran*, the school magazine in which he included his translation of the classics. Oakes reports that Gough once told his parents that it was his intention to translate the whole of the poet Horace's works. He has the kind of memory that stores a huge range of facts and general knowledge, and to this day if you ask him a simple question you will get an avalanche of historical information on the subject.

In 1972 in a television interview on the ABC program *This Day Tonight*, Freda said of her brother when he was a teenager, 'He always knew so much. Anything you asked Gough, he knew the answer, but he'd never do my homework for me because he'd always explain things at such length and I'd want a quick answer.'

The talk around the family dinner table focused on current affairs, history and books. Gough's designated dining-room chair backed onto the bookcase where the encyclopaedias were kept (Freda says there were books in every room but the bathroom) and if something came up that he didn't know about in the course of a conversation, he would tilt back his chair and select the required encyclopaedia.

Margaret and Gough's apartment in Darling Point, where they have lived since Gough left politics, is very small, particularly the living room. The table that sits between their two comfy chairs is always piled high with Gough's reference books, much to Margaret's annoyance. Whenever she places a vase of flowers on the table he asks, 'What are these doing here? You know I need room for my books. They need to be at hand.'

She understands that this is a habit of a lifetime, having his books at hand, but that doesn't stop her regularly placing a vase of fresh flowers smack in the middle of the table, just to remind him that two people live in the apartment. Fortunately, he has a large ex-prime-ministerial office nearby in William Street in Darlinghurst, to which he still goes every day from 10 am until 6 pm, and which houses a huge reference library. Nonetheless, he continues to bring home material for the endless speeches he is still invited to give. He works hard on making them perfect and when he is particularly agitated about something he is writing Margaret will say, 'Well, why do you accept these invitations to speak? People will understand if you refuse. For God's sake, you're ninety.'

Inevitably his response is something like, 'No, Margaret, these are good people who did good work for the party and I can't let them down,' and he returns to his reference book.

When he was away from the endless shelves of books at home, Gough spent many hours in the library of Old Parliament House, in which students of Telopea Park High were given free rein to browse. Not content with studying French and Latin at school, he learnt German after school and had Greek lessons in his spare time.

Entertainment for teenagers in Canberra at that time consisted of organised dances held in private homes. His parents encouraged him to attend and ensured his manners were perfect and he understood that male guests were expected to ask the host's daughter to dance.

On Sundays his father would play the piano to entertain the family, with everyday popular tunes of the time included among the classical pieces. Like Margaret, Gough has a wide taste in music, from opera and ballet to Hollywood musicals. He took his own children to see *South Pacific* four times. Bob Hope was another performer to which he took the family, not so much for the jokes as for the timing and the way Hope told them. The performer in Gough is always present and to this day he is meticulous in his presentation and his timing of lines. Unfortunately, some people have always taken his theatrical bent and his sense of humour literally, without distinguishing between the performer and the man. Sometimes Gough allows one to parody the other. Margaret admits it took her a while to understand his sense of self-parody.

In 1933 he won a scholarship worth £120 a year to pay for his university fees. However, he remained at school in 1934 because he wanted to study Greek and his father believed that anyone under the age of eighteen was too immature to attend university. Fred expected his son to follow him into law but Gough had made no plans other than to study arts. According to Oakes, everyone thought he would become an academic, teaching classics, and many of his school friends thought he'd go into the Church because at Canberra Grammar he topped divinity. 'However, the headmaster, the Reverend W. J. Edwards, who was the divinity teacher, refused to give him the prize because he wasn't convinced that Gough had faith in what he had written in his examination paper. The unfairness of being deprived for purely subjective reasons of a prize he had earned still rankles with him.'

The campus at Sydney University when Gough arrived in 1935 was a hotbed of political debate and activity, mostly due to radical philosophy professor John Anderson, who had been openly censured by the state parliament and the university senate. Anderson was considered a left-wing anarchist and his followers were engaged in heated arguments with the Labor people, who took a traditional communist line.

Socialism, communism and the Spanish Civil War were the hottest topics at all student meetings. Debates were passionate. Gough Whitlam, however, was not a participant. He certainly attended the meetings addressed by Anderson and other notorious campus agitators, but he preferred to remain on the sidelines. He joined no student political clubs or societies and was not openly vocal about his political sympathies.

Oakes surmises that his reluctance to join the Anderson stirrers was linked to the fact that he lived at St Paul's College in Newtown, among largely privileged conservatives. The students at Paul's had a 'stand them up against the wall and shoot them' attitude to strikers. Gough did, however, once suggest to Margaret with his characteristic irony that he was thinking about standing for election 'as the intellectual Labor candidate for Newtown'.

Most of his university acquaintances remember him either as good-humoured, witty and smiling, or 'an aloof, smart-alecky kind of bastard'. He dressed as most college men did at the time in grey slacks and well-cut sports jackets, but he was said to aspire to a high level of sartorial elegance and style. When he left the college, the student newspaper, *The Pauline*, said, 'Divinely tall and more divinely dark and handsome, it is unfortunate that Gough could not claim direct descent from Olympus.'

Prior to meeting and courting Margaret Dovey, the Sydney *Daily Mirror* reported Gough's attraction for a visiting violinist from the United States, twenty-two-year-old Guila Bustabo, who toured Australia as a concert artist in 1938. He attended all her concerts, sent her flowers and held a sherry party for her and her mother at Paul's. Once her tour was over, however, they didn't maintain contact.

Oakes says that the incident was not typical of Gough; that he was not known as a womaniser. He seemed far more interested in good food than young women – when David Jones opened their continental food section in the city, 'He looked around with obvious glee, gave a sigh and remarked, "Isn't civilisation wonderful."'

In his arts course he studied English, Latin, Greek and did a year of psychology. He wasn't interested in gaining honours in exams, did not take his lectures very seriously, but read a lot and for his own erudition. 'For quite a time Fred Whitlam was concerned that young Gough was "kicking over the traces a bit,"' says Oakes.

Apart from the liberating aspects of university and the freedom from his parents' simple home life and high educational expectations, Gough spent a lot of time partying with a group of students from Paul's. After he met Margaret at the SUDS Christmas party their courtship, at times haphazard, is best followed in a private Nancy Mitford-style journal that Margaret began on 2 January 1940.

From Margaret's point of view Edward Gough Whitlam, three years her senior, son of the Commonwealth Crown Solicitor, 6 foot 4 inches tall, handsome, witty, interested in music, opera, ballet and musicals, would seem the perfect fit. From Gough's point of view Margaret Elaine Dovey, the tall, attractive daughter of well-known barrister and man-about-town Wilfred Dovey, champion swimmer and Australian team member of the Empire Games, actress, singer, dancer, lover of all art forms, accomplished social mixer and conversationalist (described in the social pages as a socialite), and former student of the prestigious SCEGGS, was also a perfect match. But, like most forms of match-making, such deductions are too simplistic. Neither Gough nor Margaret fitted the clichéd archetypes of socialist and socialite. The underlying truth of their erratic courtship was that even though both had experience of being treated as 'different' because of their height, and both had felt a very strong physical attraction for each other, they were both innately shy. Margaret was waiting to be swept off her feet by a confident, sophisticated man of the world, not an intellectual, epicurian aesthete.

Anyway, according to her private journal, Gough quickly dropped out of the picture because only three weeks after she met him he disappeared on a regimental student training camp.

Despite her strong feelings about him at that first meeting she was subsequently captivated by other men, starting with the Russian dancers and writers of the Ballet Russe, whom she met at a stage party after the first night of the ballet *Paganini*. Excerpts from her journal reveal her state of mind.

> 2nd January 1940
> Champagne was flowing – indeed in my view I was so excited I think I drank a little too much. Somehow men – foreign men especially – make me behave in a most peculiar manner and when Lichine offered me his seat I nearly died of embarrassment.

Despite this attraction to foreign men, she is, however, mostly looking forward to a trip from Adelaide to Perth, sponsored by the university swimming club for the inter-varsity races. She had decided that it was to be her last season of competitive swimming. And, of course, there is always present the heady power of music.

> 7th January
> Music has become a necessary part of me. Whether it's combined with ballet or just comes over the radio I find I am happiest when sensing music. Listened to a recording of Rachmaninoff's *Rhapsody on a Theme of Paganini* this afternoon. Conducted by Stokowski with the piano part played by R. himself. Have seen the ballet *Paganini* three times already and am seeing it again Wednesday.

She expresses some misgivings about going to the ballet with her mother and wonders if she'd rather go alone.

Something is missing with her. Perhaps she just doesn't understand the intricacies of theatrical enjoyment.

In the same entry she expresses the constant yearning of the young to find the thing that they really want to do with their lives.

My mind is very mobile. One minute I'm positive I only want to write and then it's act on the radio. The only part I'm sure about is that it will have to be something artistic or even just 'arty'.

Lurking behind any of her vocational wishes is always the urge to be desired by men. She has a very clear image of who she aspires to become and it fits exactly the heroines in Noël Coward's plays.

I want to be smooth and witty, elegant and attractive to men with an easy approach to life. At twenty I thought these things would have come but I can see that all my life I'll be waiting for them to come to me if I don't make the first move.

For, always present in the mind of a young woman in this era and of this class is the need to make a good match, not to end up an 'old maid'. Overlaid with this need is the desire for an all-consuming, all-devouring romantic love affair.

Soon, a rather heavy love affair, one that means something on both sides regardless of the eventual outcome, would be a good thing. While not actually thinking of being an old maid, there seems to be the need for some soul satisfying episode.

Ever present for Margaret regarding her choice of men is, however, the harsh reality of her height.

> If ballet men weren't so small they'd be ideal – but even if I did actually fall in love with one, were I to get the chance, I would probably start thinking, 'Isn't this silly, when he's so small.'

As she goes through a rollcall of all the men in whom she is or could be interested, Gough gets a mention, but at this stage she doesn't even know how to spell his name. She is also suspicious that it's only her height that attracts him.

> Why can't John Murray ask me out, or Goff Whitlam? I wonder if Goff really likes me a lot or just thinks he does because I'm tall?

The entry on 13 January finds her preoccupied by what clothes to pack for her forthcoming visit to Adelaide and Perth. Women were very much judged by what they wore in this era and if people were going to stare at Margaret because of her height, she wanted them to see a smartly outfitted young woman.

> 13th January
> Have decided to wear on the train the grey suit and yellow blouse with new glass buttons and my yellow coat – with black shoes and bag and God knows what gloves. As yet I haven't found any that are both whole and clean – other than the two pairs I washed at lunchtime. Seem to have thousands of blazers – my pet aversion.

Books to take are also a prime consideration.

> Am taking Romain Rolland's *Jean Christophe*; Thomas Wood's *Cobbers*; Noël Coward's *Sketches and Lyrics* and a cheap edition of Igor Schwezoff's *Borzoi*. A propos – this morning's Patricia Penn [a social column in the *Herald*] had me in the same paragraph as Igor Schwezoff. I was so thrilled because I saw him at the ballet last night and I think he recognised me – any hopes in that direction must be shattered, however, as we will probably not get back until just before the last night of the company in Sydney.

Patricia Penn's social column in *The Sydney Morning Herald*, titled 'Round the Town', has the following item on 15 January:

> Confusion in the Dovey household on Saturday night. At twenty-three minutes to nine it was discovered that the clocks were an hour slow and the Melbourne express on which Margaret was booked to leave with the university swimming team for the championships in Adelaide was due out of Central at ten minutes to nine. Literally hurling themselves into the car the family made it to Strathfield, hoping to pick up the express there. Their chagrin knew no bounds, when, as customary, it sailed through the station. Needless to say, Margaret was in plenty of time for the express last night. History does not relate what her team-mates said when they left Sydney without their champion. No doubt they're hoping her times in the events will be a bit faster than the family clocks.

It was these references to her life in the social columns that led people to call Margaret a socialite, but while such entries amused her and she was present at many social events, she was never susceptible to social snobbery. Nor has anyone ever accused her of it.

Although she was travelling with her mother, her next few journal entries are full of outings, drives, dinners and lunches with people in Melbourne, Perth and Adelaide. She was particularly impressed with the style of the receptions, and by a chap called Nugent.

7th February
Have been in Adelaide since the night of the 5th. Feel very excited and don't know whether or not I want the feeling to go away – it's marvellous to live this way. Nugent was at the station and drove Mother and me to the hotel. We were received by the Lord Mayor and his lady at midday yesterday in an infinitely more pleasant atmosphere than Perth or Kalgoorlie. The rooms were attractive and there was decent sherry as well as the usual beer. Nugent has been wearing a super smooth suit since we've been here.

The first entry of 9 February is concerned with the fact that Nugent was expecting her to go to the Saturday evening dance with him but hadn't actually asked her formally. But 'things' with Nugent are definitely progressing. Such 'things' are too exciting even to commit to paper, and her next entry betrays a simmering sensuality as well as a secretive sense of humour.

Because of my ecstatic experience last night – there was much holding of hands – I don't want to write of anything else although there is much to write about. The very garrulity of this last sentence tells a tale.

The second entry talks of a marvellous dinner at friends of her father's, the Villeneuve-Smiths, whose house she describes as a 'small edition of an English country house or estate'. Again she is impressed with Adelaide because everything is done 'in a most distinguished style'.

> We had lobster cocktail, jellied soup, chicken roasted with bananas and corn and cunning sweets of jelly, peaches and little 'jobs' made to look like a duck. Glasses set out in proper array – I think my first private dinner where it has been so and we drank sherry and sauterne wine with the food.
>
> Conversation afterwards was most invigorating and by no means one-sided. To tell the truth all the wine and cocktails went to my head for a while and I couldn't see straight, let alone hear what was being said to me. If I'd had any more I would have been completely pie-eyed so I refused liqueurs and afterwards only drank fruit cup. At one stage I was offered a whisky and soda – must look a bit sophisticated these days.

This entry reveals the seeds of the woman who blossomed into the fully mature Margaret. Even though she still loves to have a good time and has always loved to eat and drink, no matter how much she is tempted, she is in control. Even at twenty, young and impressionable, Margaret is realising the importance of knowing where to draw the line in every sense.

While she loves to have a good time she nevertheless believes in maintaining a sense of decorum – not in any snobbish or pretentious manner – but simply in terms of a sense of one's dignity as a human being. Manners were always and are still important to her, because they facilitate the graceful ease of living. Addressing people in a respectful fashion, setting a table in the right way, waiters serving food from the left and taking it away from the right, are all aspects of civilised living that she still comments on and thinks are important. These are attitudes inculcated by her upbringing, particularly from her mother. But even her father, while not banning her from smoking, for example (which was very fashionable when she was a young woman), would not allow her to smoke in the living room as he did not think it was dignified behaviour for a young woman.

On 11 February Margaret's journal entry begins: 'Why do men act in such an uncertain manner?'

She was extremely annoyed with Nugent because he had messed up the evening's arrangements by turning up to take her to the trots when she had assumed he was taking her to the boatshed dance and had dressed accordingly. However, he saved 'the usual terrible boatshed hop' from being a disaster by later having what she describes as 'the most divine dance' with her. She goes on to write: 'We even trucked for a time – I can still feel it.'

'Trucking' was a form of dancing where you rock back and forth in rhythm with each other. It was a very popular dance style in the era of swing, so this entry is not, after all, describing her first lover.

Margaret, however, goes on to admit in her journal that 'things might have happened if I'd been with him all night'. She also notes his clothes.

> He had on a marvellous suit – double breasted, lounge grey with a pale blue tie. The whole time we've been here he's worn the most perfectly tailored suits – really smooth.

She is determined to pursue him and admits on 11 February:

> By fair means or foul I got down to Moana [an Adelaide coastal beach] in Nugent's car. We surfed and enjoyed ourselves very

much indeed – helped, no doubt, by numerous flagons and bottles of beer.

It's hard to imagine Margaret as the original 'surfer's moll'. She goes on:

Nugent had so much in the end that the others wouldn't let him drive his car home – he really was quite all right and was just putting it on. I sat up on top of the seat and cut a very dashing figure – dark red and white sun frock on an ice blue car assisted by fishnet on the head and supplemented by black sunglasses. A bit good?

And then further down she confesses:

There is some strange bond between us and I feel that once it is discovered all will be well.

However, by 12 February she is writing:

Have come to the conclusion that Nugent doesn't like me – at least I had until I heard that he noticed how smooth John Seppelt thought I was – ha ha ha!

They'd had lunch at Château Tanunda and the John Seppelt mentioned is one of the sons of the great Seppelts' wine family enterprise. She continues:

A wonderful time with John Seppelt. I don't think I've ever drunk so much as I have in the last two days – beer yesterday and sherry and hock today.

Despite a terrible hangover she gave a swimming exhibition of her prowess at the intervarsity carnival on 14 February 1940:

> Swam especially well over 100 metres to annoy Nugent who is very keen on stylish breaststroke. John Seppelt arrived and attacked me like a vulture – it seems he really is coming to Sydney soon.

Another addition to what she describes as 'her fold' is Bob McKay, who was a reporter on *The Adelaide Advertiser*. Unfortunately he was short, only reaching her waist, but he sat and talked for hours with Margaret, much to the annoyance of Nugent, who finally kissed her: 'First casually, then very firmly. He knows something is in the air.'

And all this was going on behind her mother's back.

The entry for 16 February finds them in Melbourne doing the shops and having wonderful dinners: oysters, soup, corn on the cob, boiled chicken, strawberries with marshmallow, French sauterne and coffee. At nights they went to see the musical comedy *The Student Prince* and the film *Ninotchka* with Greta Garbo and Melvyn Douglas. Margaret thought Garbo looked 'positively haggard'.

There is, of course, always the question of how Margaret funded her activities. Usually she relied on her darling Daddy to slip her extra money.

> 8th March
> Daddy has gone to Melbourne for a few days and left me in Mother's power as far as money is concerned. I wonder how I'll get to the ballet tomorrow and Wednesday afternoons.

And then on 24 March there is this entry:

> Gough Whitlam (have discovered the spelling at last) took me to a dance at the Australia last night. Vodka was the highlight of the night. I had two glasses. We also drank 1930 hock at 7/- a bottle. Wonder whether I really should drink when out at such parties – none of the other women did and I felt most depraved. Gough insisted that I looked imperial and regal. Funny that he should suddenly turn up like this – but after all he's only out of camp a week. My new brocade coat impressed him.

By 23 April she is back at university. She had sworn nothing would get her back there, but eventually she forged a compromise with her mother, who wanted her to get an All Australian Blue in swimming, which so far she had missed. Even though she enrolled in economics II, economic history, German I, and psychology II, her mother agreed she should enjoy herself and not worry about exams. Margaret's real interest, however, is literary and her journal states:

> Must achieve something before I am 21 – am trying to work on a radio programme, have ideas for a couple of novels and plays but nothing seems definite enough.

The date of 20 May finds her in Gough's company again. She reports:

> This is not the usual, elated feeling. I think it goes deeper. I don't 'tremble at his touch' but I feel a certain concern and interest in everything he does. We shall see.
>
> A rather dreadful, but amusing thing happened on our way

up to the night club. When we got into the taxi Gough said, 'The university,' and the driver said, 'University Hotel (pause) or the university.' I was speechless.

I might ask him out to dinner during the vac – have discovered that he lives in Canberra – not often tho' as he's with Sly and Russell [Solicitors]. Asked him why no one ever called him 'Edward' as it is his first name and he said, 'I'll let you call me Edward.'

There is a sentence at the end of this entry that reveals Nugent's girlfriend is engaged to another bloke. Margaret says, 'I don't know if I'm glad or not.'

29th May
Gough came to dinner last night and both impressed and was impressed by the family. I never feel at all embarrassed or uncomfortable when I'm with him.

She goes on to detail her other two interests – one literary, the other gastronomic. The novel that she has begun to write in 'a sort of David Copperfield way titled *The Other House* is about me – fictionalised'. She also reports that she had lunch in a new Italian café in Martin Place and for 1/6 had 'some excellent spaghetti, fruit salad and cream and coffee, together with nice crunchy bread'.

Her June entries contain for the first time concerned references to the war and she notes that she had been elected secretary of the university's war effort. There is also an anecdote about her ringing Gough up at work and saying to the solicitor who answered, whom she thought was Gough, 'Hello goon, it's Dovey.' This love of special names or words has lasted their entire lives and they still have funny little rituals, like speaking in French whenever they greet each other.

The date of 10 June finds Margaret still in bed at nearly midday writing up her journal about the members of her group of friends.

> Drank far too much at SUDS sherry party last night and am beginning to feel really remorseful. Had hoped G. would be there but he was not. Barbara [Glasgow] was getting off with another bloke so Johnny and I got together – tho' we only went so far. That was far enough – I've got a bruised foot from where we fell down some steps at Double Bay, whence we walked from the Arabian [a coffee house in Kings Cross] – and a bruised mouth from many places. Perhaps a heart too, for I learned that G. has asked Pat Chien to the informal. As I thought – he doesn't want to go too far with me as he's rather scared of the consequences – how could any children of two tall people be anything but taller?

It is interesting to note Margaret's underlying fear about their future children. All her worries and insecurities, however, disappear when – finally – on 9 July, Gough kisses her.

> I got quite a shock last night when it happened that I intended to ask for an explanation tonight – but the same thing recurred. It's almost as though everyone were decided. Tho' today I thought how funny it would be if we were the first to announce our engagement when the others – John and Barbara and Mickey and Haggie – have been at it much longer. Am undecided whether to write him a letter telling him my views in full – there seems to be no explanation to our present behaviour and it might go on thus uncomfortable for a long time.

Johnny and Mickey go into AIF [Australian Imperial Force] camp tomorrow and Gough rang and asked me to a farewell party at Romano's. I wonder why he doesn't join up too?

During this month Margaret starts her training with the VAD (Voluntary Aid Detachment) at Sydney Hospital, but she writes that she is worried about not being able to attend as she is playing in *Twelfth Night*. She is also knitting balaclavas for Mickey and Johnny before they leave for the war. By September she has been to the SUWANS (Sydney University Women's Army National Service) training camp in Castlereagh as part of the University Women's Unit.

She has also crashed her parents' car into a gate at the Ritz Hotel in Leura in the Blue Mountains. She used to write to Gough on the Ritz letterhead, because under its name was inscribed, 'The House of Distinction', which he found highly amusing. He always printed it on the front of his letters to her when he replied.

By now she is getting to know him very well:

He is being very difficult – at times so marvellous and others a beast.

On 19 November Margaret turned twenty-one. She wrote that, 'The day was hysterically full of pleasure.' The night before, for the birthday celebration, her parents had taken her and Gough and some of her friends to dinner at Romano's, where Noël Coward was performing. The Bollinger flowed. Margaret was so besotted with Coward that her next entry records a romantic dream she had about Noël and herself.

1st December

He was sitting on one of those cushioned seats that we have at Cahill's and Romano's. When he saw me he beckoned wildly with his arm and vacated a seat on his right. We then proceeded to play in the 'chopsticks' manner, then some of his compositions as duets with much singing and romanticism. This was broken by Noël saying, 'Can you swing it?' And we did.

Perhaps the Bollinger was still flowing through her veins.

At the end of 1940 Margaret was a big hit in the university revue, in which she sang 'The Girl with Pigtails in her Hair' in pigtails and a little frock. It was a send-up of Deanna Durbin as a child star. In that same revue, her popularity was matched by that of Gough, who performed a satire on Neville Chamberlain in which he produced a 'peace in our time' document that was reams and reams of lavatory paper. He also drove the audience wild (especially Margaret) with his imitation of Noël Coward. Margaret's plans for her own plays continued.

2nd December

George-ette [Georgie Swift] is coming home today. We might be able to begin our play – only when we're together can we think of our snappy dialogue.

Georgie Swift was a year behind Margaret at university. They met through Barbara Glasgow, a friend whose mother was dying of cancer and therefore had more freedom than either Margaret or Georgie. She had read Marie Stopes's book, at that time considered a wicked guide to sexuality and contraception, and she subsequently went away for a risqué weekend. She was having an affair with Guy Manton, who was a lecturer in Greek at Sydney

University and a group of them, including the poet A. D. Hope, used to go for weekends down to the South Coast.

Margaret and Georgie weren't involved in such racy scenes as Barbara. Indeed, one afternoon when they were sitting on a tram on their way home from university they confessed to each other that they hadn't 'done it' yet. They were both in SUDS and together performed in *School for Scandal*, with Margaret (6 foot 2) playing the male lead in the minuet and Georgie (5 foot 2) playing her partner in the female role. No reference was made between them about their difference in height (and still isn't), unless they were walking down a street, in which case Margaret would say to Georgie, 'Let me walk on the low side.'

Margaret thought Georgie was a gorgeous-looking girl. 'She had lovely shoulder-length dark hair that bounced. She was the only girl I knew who wore a Lamotte suit to university.' Georgie and Margaret both fancied everybody in their group, and Georgie said, 'Margaret always had fellows around her because she was such fun and used to laugh a lot. But when Gough came on the scene he was so handsome and dressed so beautifully we all told her to grab him, because who else could she dance cheek to cheek with? And he was also very funny.'

They all went out together to concerts and dances and to Romano's afterwards, unless the chaps didn't have any money, in which case they'd have a hamburger or a pie at Harry's Café de Wheels. Those were the days when men paid for everything, young women wore long elegant evening gowns and wrapped themselves in furs in the winter, and fellows seemed to be permanently attached to their dinner suits. Margaret and Gough were considered to be a particularly handsome and impressive couple.

When the war started and men began to enlist Georgie decided she wanted to work on a newspaper. One day her Aunty Helen was at the races and she saw Ezra Norton, then editor of *The Daily Mirror* in Sydney. She called out to him, 'My niece, Georgie, wants to be a journalist,' and he called back, 'Send her in.'

So, unlike Margaret, who had only been offered social rounds by Frank Packer, much to her chagrin, Georgie started on police rounds.

Georgie still vividly remembers Margaret's twenty-first birthday party.

> Her birthday night was really special. Her father picked up me and Barbara – looking sexy in a blue lamé dress she had made herself – Pip Street and some other friends and took us all to Romano's. Noël Coward sang 'The Last Time I Saw Paris' and we all cried. It was wonderful.
>
> Her dad adored her, worshipped her really. He was very proud of her swimming achievements and the fact that she was intelligent and so at ease with people. Everyone knew Bill Dovey, he was a very distinguished man. Margaret's parents always took her out with them to theatre, ballet and concerts, where she met lots of people and was always laughing and chatting with them. Her mother made all her clothes and dressed her very well. She was very easy with all Margaret's friends. Going over to her house was always good fun – her grandmother was often there and all sorts of aunts and of course the maid, Bottle. It was jolly and no one stood on ceremony or anything like that.

In December 1940 Margaret took off with eight other passengers in a De Havilland plane bound for New Guinea. A friend from

SCEGGS, Jeanette Best, had married Mick Leahy, one of the prominent Leahy brothers who were goldminers in New Guinea. Jeanette had invited Margaret to stay with her over the Christmas and university vacation. Her parents offered to pay for the trip – her father was particularly keen for her to go as he had served there during World War I. Even though the war in Europe had been going for over a year, they thought she would be quite safe. Margaret was terribly excited as it was her first overseas trip and a grand adventure.

They stopped overnight in Townsville. Prior to that the furthest north Margaret had been was the Barrier Reef on a school trip in 1937, so she was amazed at how the topography was so different. Jeanette met her at Port Moresby and after a couple of days they went on to Salamaua and then Wau, which was the nearest town to the Leahys' property at Surprise Creek. Dressed in shorts, a shirt, a big hat and sandals, Margaret added to her freckles, which she hoped would all join up into a glorious tan.

As their property was in the highlands the heat was not unbearable and provided a wonderful excuse to drink gin and tonics. Together with their house-boys Jeanette and Margaret spent their days visiting a farm several kilometres away and another goldmine, where they had a 'slap-up' lunch consisting of barbecued pork and salads. The house-boys were most impressed with Margaret's stature and called her Mrs Allasame Mountain.

Margaret had been planning to stay in New Guinea until February but in late December German raiders shelled the tiny island of Nauru and all visitors in the vicinity were ordered back to their places of residence.

Back in Australia Margaret writes in her private journal that she is glad to be home. But she does mention several 'diversions' in New Guinea in the form of a BP sub-manager and a beautiful curly-haired goldminer. However, even though she had tried hard to be broad-minded, she found 'the morals of the tropic dweller rather shocking. Conclusion reached is that anyone can do it – simply anyone – and I'm so glad I did not succumb.'

Her virginity still intact, she goes on:

> Darling Edward [Gough] will be out on Sunday. I am so excited – his sweater will be finished and I have a new photo in which I achieve a certain degree of intensity. I hope so much that he will ask for one.

And then she adds: 'And I think I want to become engaged too.'

Everyone else in their group, it seemed, was getting engaged or married. In her journal Margaret reports that Nugent has just announced his engagement to Joy Minnett ('It didn't last,' says Margaret in a somewhat triumphant tone) and Pip Street has confessed to her that she is secretly engaged to Jack Fingleton. Her parents wouldn't let her announce it, although she intended to be married before Christmas. Sonya and Cedric were to be married on New Year's Eve and Barbara Glasgow intended to have Johnny marry her when he came back from the war (in fact, she abandoned him for Guy Manton, the Greek lecturer).

The intimate musings of Margaret Dovey end mid-way through 1941. Her final entry in the journal is dated 19 July 1941.

> Mother is sponsoring a dreadful dance at home. I would not ask Gough but relenting I rang him and because of the jazz band we couldn't hear each other.

Margaret says that she doesn't remember why she stopped writing her diary – she was probably just too busy doing other things. She spent that year studying a social-work course to which she had transferred from economics. Now Gough was out of his training camp, he was keeping up with his law studies at Sydney University and had begun work as an associate to Supreme Court Justice Victor Maxwell.

Labor came into power in October 1941 under John Curtin. On 8 December Australia awoke to the news on the wireless that overnight the Japanese had attacked Pearl Harbor. The entry of Japan into the war was for Gough and for many others the realisation of Australia's worst fears. He took himself off immediately to enlist in the RAAF. He was told it would be several months before he was actually called up, but in the meantime he was asked to learn Morse code and undergo other preliminary training. Three nights a week he trained in preparation to join the air force, while continuing to study law.

Prior to this Margaret had been continuing her work as a commissioned officer in the VADs. During the year she had also been off to several camps with them to be trained in basic military manoeuvres. It seemed to her that they did a lot of marching in platoons and moving around from place to place. She had also contributed to aircraft watches and learnt first aid and Morse code. Their uniforms were khaki and consisted of trousers, shirts and a cotton hat known as a giggle hat. Not very fetching, Margaret thought, but practical.

Over Christmas 1941 and January 1942 Margaret's mother rented a holiday house at Terrigal on the Central Coast and invited many of Margaret's friends to stay at various times, among them Gough Whitlam. While they were on the beach one day a friend of Margaret's nicknamed Tiddles said to Gough, 'When are you going to hang the rock?'

'What do you mean, hang the rock?' he replied.

She pointed to the third finger on her left hand and said, 'On Margaret's finger.'

Gough laughed, but clearly he took the hint because after the holiday, together with another couple of their friends, Margaret Dovey and Gough Whitlam finally announced their engagement.

Margaret now says in her droll fashion she chose Gough 'because he was there'. This, of course, denies the fact that he was there because she had asked him to be and that she had decided that he was 'the one'.

Margaret recalls that Gough's actual words to her when he proposed were, 'I wouldn't mind if we got hitched.' The man who was twice dux of Canberra Grammar, a graduate of arts and law and a distinguished scholar of Latin and Greek was, at heart, when it really came down to it, just another bashful Aussie bloke asking his girl to 'get hitched'.

They had a small engagement party for relatives and friends at the Dovey home in Vaucluse. Georgie gave Margaret a green bowl which miraculously she still has, although, knowing Margaret's capacity for hanging on to things, it's probably not so amazing. In fact, Georgie stayed at Margaret's for the engagement party and one of her aunts said to her, 'Isn't it wonderful – Barbara has given Margaret the book.' Georgie assumed that given Barbara's usual proclivities the book she had given Margaret was Marie Stopes's book on contraception, but in fact the book was Mrs Beeton's *Household Management*.

Gough's version of these events is almost entirely concerned with the practical and financial aspects of supporting a wife.

> In those days one used to think of getting married, but of course one could never afford it. When I joined the air force I had, by the standards of those times, sufficient income to support

a wife. During 1940 and '41 I used to go for lunch on Sundays at the Dovey home in Hopetoun Avenue, Vaucluse. I saw a lot of Margaret over Christmas 1941 and New Year '42 at Terrigal. I had become an associate to Justice Maxwell in the Supreme Court through Margaret's father, Bill Dovey. He'd recommended me. He was a good bloke. I liked her parents and we all got along very well.

After they came back from Terrigal I was there for dinner on the Sunday and it had been arranged for me to meet Bill Dovey in the dining room while the rest of them were out on the verandah. Except the aunt was hovering when I sought permission. Which was graciously accorded. There was nothing pre-nuptial – that was usual. Certainly, proper girls didn't.

MARRIAGE

With the onset of the war in the Pacific it seemed to Margaret that all her friends were getting married. On New Year's Eve 1941 she had been bridesmaid to her best friend, Sonya Johnston. One of the traditional duties of the bridesmaid was to pack the bride's going-away case. Margaret filled Sonya's suitcase almost entirely with nightdresses which, as Sonya told her laughingly when she returned, were the one item of clothing that she was most unlikely to wear on her honeymoon. Margaret was very amused at her own naïvity.

Then there was her speech. The wedding was small and held at Sonya's home but nevertheless followed all the usual formalities. During the speeches when it was Margaret's turn to give the bridesmaid's response, she caused great mirth among the guests when she stood up and said, 'This wedding is all very new and exciting because I am the one who usually sleeps with Sonya and shares her room.' Even now she hoots at the recollection.

Three of her close friends had been married in the preceding months and her attitude was pretty much, 'I'm going to be one of them.' The family seemed much more excited about the forthcoming event than she did. Both the Dovey family and the Whitlams were pleased with the match their children had made and considered them to be eminently suitable for each other.

Margaret's parents were very keen on Gough and knew him

well from his regular attendance at family Sunday lunches. He was well read, well dressed, had perfect manners and came from a legal and highly respected family. Margaret knew Gough's parents less well but Gough's father was acquainted with Bill Dovey through legal circles and Gough's mother so adored her son that she thought he could do no wrong. She would have trusted his choice whomever he had decided to marry, but she genuinely liked Margaret.

Freda, his younger sister, remembers that after the engagement Margaret and her mother visited the Whitlam family home for the first time in Canberra for afternoon tea. She thought that Margaret was relaxed, warm and completely at ease with them. She was obviously very skilled at conversation and socialising, which Freda thought would make her an excellent wife for her brother.

And so it was that on 22 April 1942, in St Michael's Anglican church in Vaucluse, Margaret and Gough were wed. Her mother made Margaret's dress, of course. It was satin, off-white, heavy and elegant, with French lovers' bows around the heart-shaped neck and on each sleeve, long gloves and a bouquet of gardenias and camellias. Her aunt, who was a milliner, made the veil, which was a generous frothing of plain white tulle with a few gardenias sewn on. Her only jewellery was the single strand of pearls she had received from her parents as a twenty-first birthday gift. Underneath the gown she wore a blue garter for 'something blue'. She can't remember whether she wore elastic 'step-ins', as they were called, or just a suspender belt for her nylon stockings. Her bra was a Kesta, which she says was made from a crepe material. It had thin straps that you could cross at the back depending on the dress you were wearing. (Describing the bra she couldn't help making a crack that young women today seem to wear their bras on the outside of their clothes, not to mention their open display of the belly button.) The shoes were 'silver strappy affairs, like sandals', which she had specially made.

Her bridesmaids were Sonya and her sister-in-law, Freda, both of whom wore sapphire-blue velvet dresses. Her mother chose the wedding bouquets, which were radiant roses – yellow with red tips – shaped like tulips. Margaret thought at first the choice was a bit odd, but the whole effect was a gorgeous deep blue and gold.

The men wore regular suits and Gough's best men were Dick Harris, who was a friend from Paul's, and Rag Holmes, both doctors.

It was a traditional ceremony where they promised to love each other for better or worse, for richer or poorer, etc. Margaret thinks she did promise to obey, not that she took that seriously.

Gough's one disappointment with the ceremony was that the organist rejected his suggestions for the wedding music. He wanted the love music from Wagner's *Tristan and Isolde* and when this was knocked back he unsuccessfully asked for Tchaikovsky's *Romeo and Juliet*.

The wedding was held at 4 pm in order that members of the legal fraternity could finish their work and be there. It was a big wedding for wartime, with over 120 guests.

Her father didn't cry when he walked her down the aisle; in fact, Margaret said he was positively beaming and he seemed to enjoy every minute of it. The reception was held in a large marquee on the back lawn of the Dovey house with the harbour sparkling in the background. It was a gorgeous sunny day and everyone was smiling and visibly happy. Margaret observed that Gough was a lot more relaxed after he'd made his speech. To this day she says he is practically 'incommunicado' before a speech. She is used to it now but on his wedding day she thought it 'a bit quaint'. Gough's main memory of the speech was his enjoyment at addressing 'a full bench', as there were a lot of judges and KCs there, together with the purveyor of Johnnie Walker whisky, who was a great friend of Bill Dovey's. More than ample supplies were consumed at the wedding.

The caterers had set up a bridal table for the bride and groom, but for the guests it was a buffet. Margaret didn't want to sit at the table like a bride doll, so she spent the afternoon mixing and mingling and chatting with all the guests. She says she went through it all in rather a trance, just 'wafting around having a lovely time with all my mates'. Her mother swirled around, giggling and socialising with everyone.

Wedding presents were displayed on the table and the back verandah. The most humorous wedding present from Margaret's point of view was from her brother, Will, who was eighteen and repeating his final year of school before going into the navy. He had gone to town on the morning of the wedding and bought them some silver nutcrackers. Margaret thought the whole notion of giving them nutcrackers was very funny, but she says they were nevertheless lovely ones, with toothpicks at the end of the handle that you unscrewed. Of course she still has them, just as they are still using the silver cutlery given to them by her parents. Her grandmother gave her a camphorwood chest as a glory box and it still sits beside their bed, on his side.

For her going-away outfit she wore a mid-blue dress and jacket in a wool fabric called *tissus michel*. The skirt was slightly pleated and just below the knee, the neck was round, and the dress had a belt made from the same material. The jacket was semi-fitted with long sleeves. Her dark brown hair was braided, with one plait wound across and one behind her head. She had started growing it when she was ten and always wore it in two plaits, only ever having it out loose when she washed it. Gough liked it long and she didn't cut it until she was forty. They left for their honeymoon by taxi, caught a train to Glenbrook and then another taxi to the Lapstone Hotel. Margaret had packed practically every item of clothing she possessed into two huge suitcases. They didn't arrive until midnight and by the time the suitcases were deposited in their room they were both absolutely exhausted.

Margaret described the honeymoon as 'good fun' and Gough said it was 'rapturous'. They spent, not surprisingly, a lot of time in bed and Margaret says matter-of-factly, 'I just expected an orgasm and I got it.'

As far as contraception was concerned, her mother 'fixed her up' with some pessaries. Margaret thought they were messy and described them as rice bubbles. 'You inserted one and it made you feel like a rice bubble. Everything was snap, crackle and pop.' Gough was a very romantic lover and read Margaret poems from Keats, Shelley and Byron in bed. 'I suppose you'd call it foreplay and I just thought it was lovely.'

In order to wear as many as possible of the clothes that she had packed, she insisted that they always got up and dressed for dinner. A lot of friends of her father's were holidaying there and, she recalls, several young couples they knew didn't want to recognise them as they were having what used to be called 'a dirty weekend'.

After four days of newly wedded bliss they returned to a little first-floor flat they had rented in Roslyn Street, Elizabeth Bay, near Rushcutters Bay Park. It was in a red-brick building called Woodlands and their flat had a bedroom, a sitting room with a kitchenette off it and a bathroom that came off the bedroom, in which you could just get a glimpse of the harbour from the loo seat.

'We furnished it after a fashion. Gough wouldn't have a double bed because he knew he had to go away and he said we'd both be too lonely. So we had twin beds pushed together. One of them had to be right under the window and I used to say to him, "You've got me under the eaves."'

As they lived overlooking the harbour every window in their house had to be covered. There was rationing but Margaret thought it was generous compared to what they had in Britain. Everyone had a ration card and an identity card which you had to show wherever you went, particularly in hotels where you might go for lunch or a drink.

His parents paid the rent of £4.50 for the flat to help them out. Gough was a judge's associate and earned about £6, £3 of which he gave to Margaret for housekeeping, and as she was still at university her father gave her his usual £1 a week for fares and pocket money. Margaret was learning to be a good manager of money and said that they lived quite well.

Neither of them ate much breakfast, just tea and toast; Gough would have lunch in town and Margaret at the university, where she usually had macaroni cheese or something similar. Dinner was always spent together and she would cook chops, or steak and vegetables, sometimes spaghetti and always a pudding. Her speciality was a bought swiss roll, cut up and sprinkled with sherry and then covered with some custard-powder custard. Her bibles were Mrs Beeton's cook book, which Gough used to read aloud for laughs (though it did teach him how to boil an egg properly) and *The Australian Women's Weekly*. Recipes like those for 'veal birds' from the *Women's Weekly* were very popular – rolled veal with stuffing out of a Tandaco packet, secured with toothpicks. Casseroles were cooked a lot, too, and dishes like cauliflower cheese. They didn't drink wine with their meals but always had a sherry before dinner. Sherry parties were very popular.

In April 1942 another wife by the name of Elsie Curtin

was celebrating her twenty-fifth wedding anniversary with her husband, John Curtin, the Labor Party Prime Minister who was to steer Australia through the war. While Margaret was learning how to run a home and balance a budget Elsie Curtin was delivering 'austerity hints' to the nation. In her book *Prime Ministers' Wives*, Diane Langmore writes:

> She explained how she had simplified housekeeping at the Lodge by closing many rooms and serving simple, wholesome meals. She advised housewives to buy only what they needed, to use cheaper cuts of meat and dress them skillfully, and to use fruit, vegetables and honey instead of potatoes and rice, which were in short supply. She encouraged them to use fresh rather than tinned food, to release more industrial labour for war work, and to use wool for clothing so that valuable shipping space was not used up by imported cottons and silks. She urged women to be enterprising in renovating clothing, furniture and carpets, to hand-knit socks and go without stockings. In these ways, she said, women could feel that they were contributing to the war effort, just as were their men at the front.

When Margaret read about Elsie's advice in the newspaper she thought to herself, 'What a sensible and inspiring woman. How refreshing to have a prime minister's wife who speaks out.'

Margaret was a totally conforming wife of the period. She said there was an unspoken contract when you married. The woman did the cooking, housework, had the children and minded her ps and qs. She accepted it all, except minding her ps and qs – she wasn't so keen on that.

Margaret liked being married. 'The best thing was the fact that you didn't have to compete with anybody when you went to parties. You didn't have to think, "Now, who can I pair off with? Is there somebody here that I really like?" You didn't have to worry about being left on the shelf.'

She loved the fact that when she went to a party she had a permanent partner and that when they danced he didn't reach her shoulder. However, besotted though she was with her tall, handsome, clever husband, she made it clear very early on in the marriage that she was not going to be taken for granted now that she was his wife. 'There was one occasion when we went to a party and he spent more time with another woman than me. I looked for him and he was about to have the next dance with her, so I sounded off to him in very firm tones. We didn't have a row, but I made my expectations of how he was to treat me very clear. I accused him of being a lazy lover. It never happened again.'

Having been adored by her father, Margaret would never have settled for anything less than first place with a husband. She had also witnessed her mother not hesitating to read the rule book to her husband when she felt her needs were being ignored. Gough may have had a greater bank of intellectual knowledge, he may have achieved more academically, but he had met his equal as a human being in Margaret Dovey.

Beneath the fanciful, romantic journal writer who dreamt of glamorous parties, sparkling conversations and intimate encounters with Noël Coward, she had a strength of character, an innate confidence and a rock-solid resilience that belied her sense of fun and her bubbly giggle.

Six weeks after they were married Gough received his call-up from the RAAF and began his training as an aircrew navigator. He travelled to a succession of training schools, spending three months at the Air Observers School at Cootamundra, one month at the Bombing and Gunnery School at West Sale in Victoria, one month at New South Wales' Parkes Air Navigation School and three months at the Operational Training Unit at East Sale.

When he was training at Canberra's Fairbairn air base he would regularly bring members of his bomber crew and others from his squadron home to dinner. Having lived away from home for so long he had missed his mother's fabulous cooking and he knew that his mates in the squadron would really appreciate a splendid home-cooked meal. As his parents didn't drink and even Gough wasn't much of a drinker there was no wine or beer with the meal. And once dinner was over, as was his usual family practice of an evening, Gough handed around encyclopaedias and they all sat and read until it was time to go. Gough was blind to the stunned reaction of his RAAF mates. This was the standard family ritual after dinner and he had no comprehension how eccentric it appeared to the RAAF men, because to him it was entirely natural.

Margaret travelled to Melbourne to meet him when he was on leave from the camp in Sale. 'I came back by train and sat next to a very sick soldier, though I didn't know what was wrong with him. He was feverish. Twenty-four hours later I had scarlet fever, which wasn't very nice. The practical work that I had planned to do at the end of the year in order to complete my diploma was postponed. I went home to my parents in Vaucluse to recover.'

Gough enjoyed the training, and subjects that had held no interest for him at school, like trigonometry, now had an obvious application: 'They were very practical and interesting subjects in the air-force context. Your life depends on things like the influence of wind on flying objects and it is quite fascinating to work out.'

In fact, Flight Lieutenant Lex Goudie, who was Whitlam's pilot during the war, is on record as saying, 'Gough's navigation was carried out with pinpoint accuracy and I can't remember ever returning from long sea patrols more than a few miles off-course.'

Gough's squadron patrolled the Arafura and Timor Seas, protected convoys over wide stretches of ocean and took part in strikes on Japanese ships, barges and ports.

So much had changed in Margaret's life in such a short time. She'd married in a swirl of satin and tulle and, with her head spinning from champagne and speeches and toasts, she was suddenly on her honeymoon. It was the end of virginity and only going so far and wondering and hoping and fantasising. She'd had four days of sex and passion and romance; four intense days of exploring the limits of her own sensuality and learning the rhythms and contours of a man's body. Suddenly she was in a hotel room with her husband, a handsome, charming man – a naked man, who read love poems to her.

For the young woman who had written her longings and yearnings in a secret journal, this was the real thing, and yet it had flashed by in what seemed to her a brief swoon. Now the war was a harsh but undeniable reality for her and all Australians and an RAAF uniform was hanging in the wardrobe. By the end of 1942 even the ABC had stopped playing 'The British Grenadiers' before its evening news bulletin in favour of 'Advance Australia Fair'.

Despite the war, Margaret was optimistic about the future and content to get on with her life. She tried not to give into a fear of the unknown and the fact that her husband was flying around in a war zone. However, shortly after they were first married and he was on leave they went to see the film *Waterloo Bridge* in the Wintergarden at Rose Bay.

The film stars her favourite actor, Robert Taylor, who plays a British army colonel who has fallen in love with a ballerina, played by Vivien Leigh. Before their relationship has a chance to flower he is called away to the front, and is unaware that she is subsequently fired from the troupe and forced to work on the streets. It is a classic MGM tearjerker.

When it was over Margaret found herself sobbing uncontrollably. Such was her distress that she found she couldn't get up from her seat. She just sat there and continued to sob and sob. It was a sad and romantic film and she thinks that the reality of Gough sitting next to her in his air-force uniform about to leave again for the war was all too much. Unable to deny the reality of her situation any more, she felt overwhelmed. Gough put his arm around her and was very gentle and caring. He kept saying, 'We'll just sit here until you're calm.' And they sat there for some considerable time. Eventually Margaret pulled herself together and they went home arm in arm.

Now, whenever she and Gough see anything really sad, he'll just quietly say two words to her – 'Waterloo Bridge' – and they both remember vividly their younger, newly married selves in the dress circle of the Wintergarden: one sobbing, one comforting. (Sad films can still make her cry and so does the music of the romantics like Rachmaninov, Tchaikovsky and Chopin. She says that now she no longer cries in concerts. 'By the time you're in your eighties, you have learnt how to calm yourself down. It's time to give yourself a rest.')

As well as finishing her social work diploma Margaret continued with her VAD work and became commandant of the university detachment. She was totally committed to her training, which was run by the Red Cross in hospitals. Mostly it was probationary nursing duties and she was attached to Sydney Hospital in the middle of the city. The long wards had forty patients with no divisions between them. Margaret's protected and somewhat limited background was soon obvious, even to her.

'The first time I was asked by one of the blokes to get him a bottle, I went outside and brought him a bottle of lemonade. He said, "I need a bloody bottle, I want to have a piss."'

She had to watch over the men and assist with dressings, which she was never revolted by. The work was voluntary but a cooked lunch was provided – usually steak and kidney pie or corned beef followed by bread and butter pudding. Margaret, who had never eaten institutional food before, thought it was exotic and wonderful.

After graduating in social studies, her first real job was with the Family Welfare Bureau whose offices were in Martin Place in the city. She shared an office with a fellow social worker, Margaret McNamara, which she was aware sometimes caused embarrassment to the clients, who had to give their personal reasons for assistance. Most of her clients were unsure of where to go for help and her job was to provide that knowledge and help them organise it with both government and non-government organisations (NGOs).

Margaret was aware of the popular perception that social workers were 'do-gooders', but she was trained to avoid that approach. For the most part she didn't have money to give them. The aim of the job was to tell them where they could earn some money, or find shelter, or legal or medical advice. For the first time in her privileged existence she was made aware of the lives of some of the people that her father, as a criminal lawyer, was in daily contact with. Her clients were also often the victims of the criminal classes.

Many servicemen and their dependants came to her for help and she would put them in touch with Legacy, or the Red Cross, which were at that time virtually government-funded. The NGOs were mainly run by the Church. For someone like Margaret, who had led an extremely protected and cosseted life, it was an opportunity for her to really get to know the broader community. She found it very rewarding to help them help themselves. She loved the fact that what she was doing was useful and made a real difference to their lives.

She would always make an appointment with clients before she visited them at home in order for them to feel they were prepared. No matter how poor they were, and some of them might only have had threepence to spare, they would spend that on some biscuits to go with the tea. At first Margaret was embarrassed that they would spend their much-needed money on her visit, but she realised that it was important to their pride that they provided a morning or afternoon tea. She also witnessed things she had never imagined, like a visit to a house where a handicapped child had been living in a pram his entire life because his parents had nowhere else to keep him and no knowledge of how to get the help they needed.

One day a woman who needed to have an operation which would require her to be hospitalised for some time came to Margaret to ask her advice on a placement for her children. When Margaret recommended a Church home the woman looked at her and asked, 'Miss, would you send your baby there?' That question really struck a chord. Margaret said that from then on it was the one question she always asked herself. She never sent anyone to a place that she hadn't inspected and would have deemed suitable for her own family. She worked long hours, but enjoyed it while she waited eagerly for Gough to come home on leave to their little flat.

A lot of their friends were pregnant and as it was wartime the air was full of *carpe diem* urgings. Margaret said that once she got over the shock of being married she thought to herself, 'What are we waiting for – let's get stuck into it.' So, on one of his leaves she announced, 'Let's forget about the rice bubbles and declare open season.' Gough didn't need any persuading and five months into her first job she realised she was pregnant.

When she first found out she rushed to ring her mother from a public phone at the GPO. She said, 'Guess what, darling – you're going to be a grandmother before you're fifty!' and there was a strange silence at the other end of the phone until her mother seemed to recover herself and offer her congratulations. Her father was absolutely delighted with the news.

From the beginning of her pregnancy Margaret experienced what is commonly called morning sickness, except she describes it as morning, noon and night sickness. Five months in she was hauled over the coals by the chief social worker, who said, 'Margaret, you seem to be coming in later and later every morning. This really won't do.' Margaret responded, 'Well, I think the way I'm feeling, soon I probably won't be coming in at all,' and she explained why.

The sickness never receded and it wasn't long before she found it all too much. 'So I just stayed home and threw up a lot.' As Gough was in the air force she collected what was called the 'wife's allotment' from the post office every fortnight, and as their rent was paid for she managed to get by without working.

Even though her family's income had continually increased through her father's success as a barrister and then a judge, Margaret had always been taught by her mother to be frugal. She is careful with money, not mean. She still can't bear to waste anything. The only distinction grade she gained in her entire academic life was for a course called nutrition and family budgeting, and it still gives her great pleasure when questioned about her housekeeping to recall that.

When Gough came home on leave they would stay in the flat, but the rest of the time she lived at her parents' house in Vaucluse. Her mother was on hand for dressmaking and advice, and Alice was ready to help with the baby when it arrived.

Antony Philip Whitlam was born on 7 January 1944 in St Luke's in Elizabeth Bay, a building that had previously been the family home of Patrick White. Margaret arrived at the hospital just before midnight with her mother and her brother, Will, home on leave from the navy.

The pain of childbirth, she said, 'wasn't too good', and she didn't really understand what was happening. The labour took eight hours. 'They'd say "push" and I'd say "push what?" But I did get better at it with each birth.'

Antony was 9 pounds 10 ounces and a bonny, healthy child. Gough managed to see him a few hours after his birth and he was absolutely overjoyed with his first-born, as he was with all his children. (After every birth he would always say, quite seriously, to Margaret's mother, 'Mary, have you ever seen a more beautiful child?')

After Antony was born Margaret's life revolved around looking after her son and writing letters to her husband every few days about his progress.

> The weekend papers had lots of articles on bringing up children and, of course, there was the inevitable Dr Spock. Baby health centres were very big. Once you had the baby it was obligatory to make your visit. I went to one in Rose Bay. You'd bundle the baby up, get on the bus and away you'd go. And you had your

little book. We weighed in every week and there'd be hell to pay if the baby hadn't put on the right amount of weight. Also hell to pay if he had put on too much weight, then you'd have to do a test feed to see if the baby was a gobbler.

As often as she could organise it, she would take the baby to the beach. He would happily sit on the sand and play while his mother went for a quick swim, always with one eye on the child. When Tony was around eighteen months old, a radio announcer described on his program having been at Parsley Bay that morning and observing an amazing sight: he had seen a young woman with a baby on her back swimming out to sea. When it was reported to Margaret she realised it had been her and baby Tony, who was quite happy to climb onto his mother's back and hang on while she breaststroked them through the water and then back safely to land.

Gough wrote letters to his wife every two days, addressing her solely as 'darling'. They mostly consisted of descriptions of daily occurrences, articles or books he was reading and requests for articles of clothing, or toothpaste, or food. Sometimes there were cryptic references to where he had been, in order to avoid wartime censorship. He would sign off with one word – 'all' – which was their code for 'all my love', or with lines such as Noël Coward's message to Gertrude Lawrence on the occasion of her wedding – 'On this, as every other day, I love you.'

In one letter he noted the end of a marriage of a couple they both knew, concluding, 'Pity the poor souls didn't and don't know such continuous and constant bliss, such unmitigated and unperturbed romance as has been ours.' And on the eve of his last Christmas away at war he wrote, 'This will probably be my last letter to reach you before Christmas. I hope you have a very happy one, the last without me for up to half a century at least.' (He has kept that promise, and more.)

There were also constant references to 'the bub' and how pleased he was that Tony was eating ice-cream, though Gough confesses that he had hoped to be the one to introduce him to that particular pleasure. He did, however, begin to sound less like the doting husband and more like the federal politician he was to become when, in one letter, he lectured her on why she must vote 'yes' in the 1944 referendum, which was an attempt to alter the constitution to grant the federal government increased powers for post-war reconstruction. Curtin had hoped that the states convention would lead to the states referring some of their powers to the Commonwealth, but only two states passed the legislation. Curtin then called for a referendum on the issue and Gough campaigned vigorously in his squadron for a 'yes' vote.

In his letter to Margaret on the issue he stated it thus:

> I now approach a moral which I feel I must point out with as little show of impatience as I can when I consider your own general attitude at times. I see no hope of having cheap money in this country unless we pass the referendum. The states can control such matters even without the referendum, the Commonwealth mightn't control them even with it, the nation might be able to do nothing about them in the face of the world, but if we are to try and control them, I see the only real hope of doing so, as far as we can do it as a nation, is through the national parliament. I urge you and for you to urge all our friends to vote 'yes'.

Margaret did as she was urged by her husband, but the referendum was not passed and the powers of the states versus the

Commonwealth was to become one of Gough's great preoccupations as prime minister. Indeed, it was Curtin and his leadership who had stimulated Gough's interest in politics and in particular in joining the Labor Party. He told *The Financial Review*, 'When Curtin got his chance, his dignity, his eloquence, were so much better than anything we'd ever had.'

When Gough returned home from the war he was twenty-nine and had a law degree to finish on a not very large salary as a judge's associate. Margaret was by now pregnant with her second child and as the flat in Elizabeth Bay would be too small for them and two children, they moved back to the Doveys' in Vaucluse, where they took over the huge billiard room downstairs and turned it into their private space. The advantages for them were financial and pastoral – Margaret's mother often offered to baby-sit.

Gough quickly became a member of the ALP: his first ticket was dated 8 August 1945. Within two months he'd become minute secretary of the Darlinghurst branch. Given his parental upbringing, the principles of his father, his war experience and his admiration for Curtin, it is clearly understandable that the ALP would be his political choice. Despite rumours to the contrary he never even thought of joining the Liberal Party.

Margaret had never taken much interest in politics, nor heard many political discussions at the Dovey dining-room table. Her only recollection of any mention of a politician was when her father came home and announced 'Old Lang's gone,' which referred to the dismissal of the Lang government of New South Wales in 1932 by Governor Philip Game. Bill Dovey, as a leading

KC, had many contacts on both sides of politics and had at one stage contested a preselection for the conservative United Australia Party, losing to the sitting conservative. He was also a member of the Waverley Council for one term on the conservative ticket with Jack Hickie, who was a solicitor. Margaret remembers her mother loathing the council meetings because afterwards the members stayed on for beer and sausages, which she thought most uncouth. She was, however, a Labor voter, true to her father, who had been pre-selected as a Labor candidate just prior to his tragic drowning.

Margaret had cast her first vote for New South Wales Labor candidate Jessie Street, because she was the mother of her school friend Pip. Margaret would often go to the Street house in Darling Point after school to play tennis and have dinner. The Streets were considered very posh because they had a cook, a nurse and a housekeeper, and yet they were openly left-wing in their political beliefs, particularly Jessie. Margaret knew that Jessie Street stood for a fair go for women in terms of employment and she remembered that a lot of the children she had been to Bondi primary school with had mothers who were forced to work in low-paid jobs.

In March 2006 Margaret invited me to the annual Jessie Street Trust Luncheon in the Strangers' dining room in Parliament House in Sydney. The Hon. Mary Gaudron, a retired high court judge, gave a spirited and inspiring address with an intensity I had not heard since the heady days of the 1970s, and was applauded with a standing ovation. As always, whenever Margaret attends an event, an endless stream of people came up to talk to her. This time she was most taken with Tom Uren, who had been a minister in her husband's government. He kissed her and then he said to me, 'Her husband was never crazy about me but I was always crazy about this lady, she was so charming and lovely to me.'

Margaret, ever the flirt, flashed her eyes at him and purred, 'That's because I always fancied you.' Tom was quite overcome by this admission and didn't seem sure how to deal with it, so he kissed her hand. Again and again. Much to her satisfaction. Sex and romance will always beat politics as far as Margaret is concerned.

Nicholas Richard Whitlam was born on St Nicholas Day, 6 December 1945. He weighed 8 pounds 6 ounces and was a strong and healthy baby.

Now that there were two extra adults and two young children in the Dovey–Whitlam house, Alice decided it was time to leave and get married herself.

Margaret thought it was harder for Gough to be living with her parents than it was for her.

> He had to more or less dance to the tune they played. So did I, but if I didn't like it I'd speak up, whereas he was disinclined in that direction. He loved the competitions they would all have at the dinner table over pronunciation, or the meanings of words. Gough has always gone on and on about how to correctly pronounce words like 'kilometre' and when he'd get carried away Pa would say, 'Look, lad, I prefer such and such,' and then they'd get out the dictionary. Gough didn't always win.

CRONULLA

Gough's grandfather had left him money to study at Oxford University, but Gough decided to use it to buy a block of land at Cronulla in Sydney's south. In 1946 he took out a mortgage from the Rural Bank to build a two-bedroom house at 2 Wangi Avenue. His father, Fred, guaranteed the loan.

The land cost £100 and the house £650. Margaret and Gough had chosen Cronulla because they wanted something near the water and they could only afford that by moving south. The southern fringes of metropolitan Sydney were a far cry from the exclusivity of the eastern suburbs and their proximity to the city where they had previously lived, but they were so excited about owning their first home they didn't care.

As Nick Whitlam writes in his memoir *Still Standing*, 'Cronulla is part of the Sydney suburban railway system and then, as now, it is the only beach you can reach directly by rail. Wangi Avenue was near the end of the Cronulla peninsula, a short walk from the bus stop where the two roads that provide a circumnavigation of the peninsula meet. They were the only two paved roads in our neck of the woods.'

To Margaret's parents it was practically the end of the earth. When her mother was told where they were going to live her first comment was, 'But, darling, is there a doctor there?'

They couldn't wait to start building their own home, especially one in a pretty street surrounded by bush, and a short stroll to the beach. They hired a fashionable architect of the time, John Mansfield, to design the house, but it took a year longer than expected to complete because the first builder went broke. Almost every weekend Margaret would pack a picnic basket and the family would go down to Cronulla to inspect the progress of the building. They were thrilled when they finally moved in November 1947, just after Margaret's twenty-eighth birthday.

Gough had been admitted to the bar in February and now had the letters BA, LLB after his name. He had also been selected to run for the Labor team for the Fitzroy Ward in the Sydney City Council elections 1947. But unfortunately the elections were postponed and when he moved to Cronulla he was not successful in his run for the Sutherland Shire Council in 1948. While he was working hard to build up a law practice, including taking briefs on Saturdays, he joined the Miranda branch of the ALP and then transferred to the Cronulla branch when it started. He was then elected to the Werriwa federal electorate council of the ALP and the state electorate council for Sutherland.

Meanwhile, Margaret was really enjoying living in her new home, which she describes as a charming, pretty white cottage with a blue tiled roof.

> When you walked in the front door it had a nice little foyer, where I could put a divan for when my grandmother came to stay. On the left of that was a big living room; straight ahead was a dining room with the kitchen; and the laundry was behind, leading to the back garden. To the right down the hall were two good-sized bedrooms and the bathroom. Our bedroom looked out onto the garden. The home was considered to be terribly modern because it had glass louvers in the entrance

hall, which were very chic and unusual then, and they gave a view to the bay.

Margaret took great delight in furnishing her new house. The living room had a beige carpet over polished boards and the three-piece suite was covered with a Sanderson's fabric that had soft green and pink flowers. The kitchen was laid with blue lino, and had white cupboards and yellow and white checked curtains.

Their neighbours were all young couples like themselves with children. Many were families living in garages while they saved the money to build their house. Very few of them, apart from the doctors, had cars and it was an hour's trip on the train to the city. By the time the Whitlams moved, Tony was four and he attended the pre-school next to the primary school at South Cronulla. Whenever Margaret delivered him there in the morning, Nick, who was two, would cry because he wanted to go as well. She spent a lot of time with them swimming, playing on the beach and climbing the rocks, all of which were accessible from the end of their street. She quickly made friends with the neighbours and they all took turns to mind each other's children.

Gough soon involved himself in community affairs. He was active in the RSL and was made president of the Cronulla Committee of the Children's Library Movement, and president of the local Parents' and Citizens' Association. He also became a radio quiz champion on an ABC program called *Australian National Quiz,* sponsored by the federal Treasury in an attempt to encourage people to buy government security loans for postwar construction.

One night when the family had been listening to the program he announced he was going to audition for it. He sat a long general-knowledge examination with dozens of other hopeful applicants, was selected and took part in the quiz from 1948 to 1950. The programs were live and there was a special hook-up for international contests. The prizes were government bonds and Gough's general knowledge won him about a thousand pounds' worth, which he used to buy the vacant block next to their house.

On one of the occasions when the quiz was held in Melbourne, Margaret, Tony and Nick accompanied Gough. They stayed at a very respectable hotel and were about to have dinner in the large dining room when both boys decided to demonstrate their somersaulting skills in the long aisles between the tables. Everyone was thoroughly entertained by them and all Margaret and Gough could do was laugh at their antics.

Prime Minister Ben Chifley was the program's sponsor and he always listened to the quizzes and discussed Gough's performance with Fred Whitlam when they met in Canberra. Gough, however, didn't meet Chifley until he was a delegate to the 1949 New South Wales state conference of the Labor Party.

Gough caught the 7.30 am train to the city every day, including Saturdays, leaving Margaret to deal with the household chores and the children. Being so close in age the two boys fought. A lot. Even when Nick was a baby, Margaret says, 'Tony used to say "I love bubba," and then put his hand over his face as if to suffocate him.' When Margaret was breastfeeding Nick, Tony would try to climb up and sit on her lap. By the time they were both at primary school they had rival gangs who fought it out in the reserve below the houses.

In his memoir Nick writes, 'As children [Tony] was the leader of one pack and I was the leader of a younger one. Images of *Lord of the Flies* would not be out of line; fights in Darook Park always finished in tears.'

Despite this, Nick's memories of childhood are of an idyllic place. 'For us kids South Cronulla was laid-back, uncomplicated and quiet. The fathers would get the train to the city for work, leaving the children behind with their mothers. We'd play and swim on Gunnamatta Bay where, at low tide, if it were not for the ferry channel you could have walked across to Burraneer. Darook Park was wild then – no cleared or cultivated open spaces, as now – and we played cowboys and Indians in the caves and the bushes. There were two other families with whom my parents were close, the Glovers and the Hampshires. To be fair, it was probably the mothers – Coralie Glover, Greta Hampshire and Margaret Whitlam – who were the real pals, because it was they who were left to handle and entertain the children.'

Meanwhile it had been open season in the Whitlam bedroom and Margaret was pregnant again. Stephen Charles Whitlam was born on 4 April 1950, weighing over 8 pounds. But within three weeks of being born he was constantly regurgitating his food. Diagnosed with hypertrophic pyloric stenosis, he had a blockage in the pylorus that prevented the milk from going into his stomach. Margaret and baby Stephen went into the Children's Hospital at Camperdown for an operation to correct the problem. She expressed the milk and it was fed to him intravenously. He was a very sick baby and Margaret spent the whole time in the hospital crying at the prospect of his death – she says his milk was always mixed with tears.

Mothers like her were encouraged to visit the other wards and the sight of little children dying of cancer only added to her fear and trauma. Her tears continued to flow. One night when Stephen had taken a dramatic turn for the worse the nurse asked Margaret if she wanted to ring her husband to come and see the baby. Margaret refused on the grounds that he was bringing the boys in to see them both tomorrow, but in reality she simply refused to believe that her baby would die. Fortunately, he recovered and has led a very healthy life ever since.

Meanwhile her husband was working hard at building his political career. In 1950 Gough was selected to contest the state seat of Sutherland against a prominent Liberal, Mr C. O. Joe Munro, who was known as the 'King of Cronulla'.

In Whitlam's biography Laurie Oakes says, 'Even at that stage Whitlam was a controversial figure within the ALP in the area. He attracted quite a bit of animosity from the old die-hards of the party for some of his radical ideas.' Gough hardly fitted the standard image of the loyal ALP member. Many regarded him as a pompous academic who took every opportunity to lecture them on his opinions and show off his vast knowledge. There were also those who dismissed him as a 'silvertail' – a person from the right side of the tracks who is, therefore, not to be trusted. In 1950 you still needed to be a bona fide member of the working class to be accepted in the ranks of the ALP.

Gough, therefore, had to work hard to convince them of his integrity and his sincerity. He didn't own a car so he did all his door-knocking on foot or using public transport. Most of the local roads were unmade, there were no gutters and street lighting was sparse. In the winter he trudged around in his raincoat and his gumboots, knocking on doors, trying to make himself known to leading citizens. He would chat to families about their children and their dogs, give out lots of free legal advice and drink hundreds of cups of tea. He was really doing the hard slog.

He and Margaret attended endless local dances, balls and fêtes, and every kind of social function to which they were invited. Gough even drank lots of beer just to appear to be a regular Aussie bloke. To have admitted to being practically a non-drinker would have been political suicide in the local ALP. Margaret liked a 'noggin' so she rubbed along famously with everyone.

All Gough's hard work did not translate into winning the Sutherland seat, but he increased the vote for the ALP. Margaret said that he didn't seem too upset about it because he knew that having been asked to stand he couldn't turn it down or he would never be asked again. He had shown his dedication to the task and his next goal was to gain preselection for the federal seat of Werriwa when the local member, Mr H. P. 'Bert' Lazzarini, retired. He and Margaret maintained their increasing involvement with activities in the local community and he campaigned enthusiastically for other Labor candidates.

In early 1951 Margaret slipped on some water in the laundry and broke her hip. For two weeks she stayed in bed at home while the doctor did various tests and decided what to do. Her mother came to stay to look after the children. It was no mean task for a woman of her age to take on the care of two young boys and a one-year-old baby. At the end of the day they both needed a stiff drink and this became known in family folklore as 'having a Cronulla'.

Eventually it was decided to send Margaret to hospital and pin the hip. Mary stayed on with some help from the regular baby-sitter until she returned from hospital. Many a Cronulla was needed.

Later in 1951 Lazzarini did finally announce that due to ill-health he wouldn't be seeking re-election. Gough knew this was his chance and like a heat-seeking missile he aimed himself at winning the Labor nomination, which meant winning over as many ALP ticket-holders in the electorate as he could.

That meant impressing members of both the middle-class and working class in Cronulla, as well as miners in the southern mining towns towards Wollongong. As 1952 began, once again Gough used all his spare time to walk the streets and catch public transport to visit the constituents. The family had put their name down to buy a new Holden over twelve months before but post-war restrictions meant they had to wait.

Gough's upbringing, though sheltered and academically privileged, had never encouraged him to 'put on side' and he felt totally at home sitting down with people in their makeshift garage homes and having a cup of tea. He confessed to one neighbour that he liked having tea with her because she didn't mind if he dunked his biscuit, whereas Margaret would not allow it. One of his household chores as a boy in Canberra was chopping wood and he impressed another woman with his speed and skill at chopping her wood.

Although not good at small talk, he always asked questions about each family's children and chatted about domestic issues in a way that showed them his family was struggling with many of the same problems. Meanwhile he was receiving some well-timed publicity by appearing as junior to his father-in-law – the counsel assisting a controversial Royal Commission inquiry into the liquor trade, which involved the exposure of some of Sydney's more notorious underworld figures. When Bill Dovey fell ill Gough stepped into his shoes and had a chance to strut his stuff. His supporters made the most of having a well-known barrister as their local representative.

The preselection ballot for Werriwa was held on 19 April 1952 and after preferences were distributed Gough defeated eight rivals by 249 votes to 163. Margaret was pleased for him, but prior to the preselection ballot she'd had a miscarriage. She had been three months pregnant and was extremely upset at the loss of the baby. She was also very shocked as she had never had any problems with her other pregnancies. The doctors assured her that whatever went wrong, it was probably a good thing that it had happened sooner rather than later and she tried to console herself with this knowledge. Nothing like this had ever gone wrong in her life and she had to learn how to deal with it.

She said that she cried a lot but never blamed God and never resorted to 'why me' self-pity. She just cried for the poor little person who hadn't made it into the world. There was a dull ache inside her that she had never experienced before. Following the miscarriage she had to go to the local clinic for a curette, which also upset her. Her newfound friends and neighbours rallied round and despite her mother's drama-queen pronouncements such as 'Margaret will not have any more children,' she was determined she would.

It was at this time that she also decided to join the Labor Party. It was clear to her that even though she had married a lawyer, Gough was passionate about politics and, knowing his determination when he set his mind on a goal, she realised it would not be long before she was the wife of a politician. Whatever he had decided to do she would have supported him, not only because she loved him but because that was what she understood she had committed herself to as part of the marriage contract.

Gough certainly hadn't pressured her into become a member – he would never have tried pressuring Margaret into anything she didn't want to do. Firstly, it wasn't his personal style, and secondly, it would have been a waste of time. Gentle persuasion will always get you much further with Margaret than overt bullying. She wasn't fascinated by the inner machinations of political parties, nor was she a convert to the ideology of either political side.

With her trademark understatement she says that she thinks party meetings are 'a bit dreary', which is why she always took her knitting to any meeting she did attend.

All Gough ever said to her was, 'If you want to have anything to do with politics, you should choose the party that has the most things with which you agree, with which you're in accord. There's no way you are ever going to be in accordance with everything that the political parties put up.'

Margaret thought that was a fair and practical method of assessing her political choice and she made hers, not unsurprisingly, for the ALP.

She didn't have to wait long for some political action. In October 1952 Bert Lazzarini died and Gough was launched into an immediate by-election. And as if on cue their car also became available. A brand new, pale blue Holden with the numberplate AGK 999, which they used to pretend stood for attorney-general, was parked on their front lawn.

Now that they had a car, Gough had the means to cover a far greater area to secure votes. His driving, however, left a lot to be desired. Nick recalls, 'Father was a terrible driver, always crunching the gears, a danger to himself and everyone else. It was kept from us until we were adults that one night he had flipped the car in the rain outside the Gunnamatta Bay baths.'

The Whitlam children made it very clear that their mother was definitely their preferred driver. In fact, one night when Gough was driving, in his own intrepid style, up to the Blue Mountains and the other boys were asleep in the back seat, Margaret turned around to see young Stephen sitting firmly upright with his eyes wide open. 'Why aren't you asleep like your brothers?' she asked. 'Because I want to be awake when I die,' was his reply.

No doubt the car was an asset to Gough in 1952 as he did his electoral rounds, but other assets in the Labor Party's favour were the credit squeeze and high unemployment. Doc Evatt, the ALP leader, took part in the campaign and called on voters to censure the Menzies–Fadden coalition government for its employment and financial policies.

On 29 November 1952 Gough Whitlam more than trebled Lazzarini's previous majority and became a member of the House of Representatives. He had gained a 12 per cent swing to Labor. He was thirty-six years of age. His was the perfect example of an electorate to which young couples had moved in order to start their homes and found themselves hampered by government restrictions on home finance and loan money to build the necessary schools and hospitals. His victory must have been partly a result of the fact that he not only lived among them but was attempting to pay off his own mortgage.

On the day of the by-election eight-year-old Tony and six-year-old Nick helped to hand out 'how to vote' cards for their father, while their mother slaved in the kitchen, together with some supportive neighbours, cutting sandwiches and preparing food for what they hoped would be a victory party. The keg was in the backyard and everything was ready when the results were announced. Party members, workers on the polling booths, Labor MPs and their families poured into the Whitlam home to eat and drink and celebrate. It was the first of many such nights, which were to become a tradition in their household. Margaret became very skilled at feeding increasingly large hordes of people and there were always plenty of neighbours and friends eager to help her cut up the fruit for what became literally buckets of fruit salad.

Such celebrations were very different from those they had previously enjoyed in the plush red velvet booths in Romano's, but Margaret had a great capacity to make the most of any party or entertainment. Besides, she was very proud of her husband.

When all the flurry and excitement of victory had faded and Gough was away from home in Canberra from Monday to Friday, Margaret realised that she was alone in the house now and, like most political wives, it was her sole responsibility to raise the family. It was a daunting prospect, especially for one so unprepared. The day-to-day routines of domestic work were not exactly the stuff of her adolescent dreams. 'Desperate housewife' would be more accurate.

The two older boys were growing taller and heavier by the day and were not always easy to control.

> I thought they were monsters, but they probably weren't. Although I remember one afternoon I simply couldn't cope with Tony, so I locked him out of the house. He was running from one window to another bashing on them, crying out, 'Mum, let me in.' I didn't give in. He and Nick fought a lot and I wouldn't put up with it. I hated fighting, disobedience and rudeness. I simply wouldn't stand for it.
>
> Gough had set them all chores to be done on the weekends, which included getting up on the roof to scoop the leaves out. Tony loved getting up there but Nick would say, 'Please, Father, no, Father.' Tony was a bully and Nick was a sook. I used to whack them with my hand. The sound was worse than the sting. Nick would cry, but Tony never did. I tried threatening them with their father's wrath when he came home on the weekend, but he wasn't going to be forced into being an ogre. I think Tony missed him a lot and so he tried it out on me.
>
> Once, when Tony was about eleven, I had to ring up the husband of one of our friends to come around and discipline

him, but he didn't want to be an ogre either. Gough felt guilty about being away from them so he would spoil them rotten when he came home. He always read them Greek and Roman myths, the same ones his father had read to him as a child. Once, when Stephen was having a disagreement with Gough over some domestic chore and Gough was literally chasing him to make him do it, Stephen suddenly stopped, turned around and shouted at Gough, 'Who do you think you are? Apollo?' Gough just dissolved into laughter.

Nick remembers how they would cheat on their chores. 'Tony and I were set weed quotas. These were categorised as so many buckets of weeds from the couch grass on the front and back yards and so many barrow-loads from the buffalo grass on the extra block, and they had to be shown to Dad for inspection. We'd cheat him by putting rocks or earth at the base of the bucket or barrow. As with some public servants when he was prime minister, it took Dad a while to wake up to the fact that some people he trusted were up to no good.'

The boys, however, all admit that they placed their father on a pedestal, and still do to some extent. They are well aware of his deficiencies and because of his age would never mention them, or disagree with him in company. They all still demonstrate a great respect and fondness for him.

Margaret had been determined to have another child after the miscarriage, and she and Gough were really hoping for a daughter this time. As if by mail order, on 2 February 1954 Catherine Julia Whitlam was born, weighing 8 pounds 2 ounces, at the Jacaranda Hospital in Caringbah. 'Catherine was my pink and white child – very bonny. She was the cutest thing as a baby. She wasn't fat in any way but her limbs were nicely rounded and she had pretty curly hair.'

Gough was at the Smithfield RSL with some supporters when he received the news, and by the time he arrived back at Cronulla he was so tired and full of celebratory beers that he slept in the car. When the baby-sitter found him there the next morning there was no time for him to nurse his unaccustomed hangover as it was the day of the Queen's visit and he had to get all the boys ready, take them to the hospital to see their mother and then ferry them to Farm Cove to see the reigning monarch. A photo shows Tony and Nick in white shirts and shorts, and Stephen, who was only four, looking very smart in his little sailor suit. As it was outside visiting hours Gough lined them all up at the window of their mother's hospital room so they could wave to her and see their new baby sister. Margaret held up Catherine to them and blew them kisses through the glass, before Gough bundled them all in the car and took them off to see the Queen.

The boys, of course, were innocently unaware of the political jockeying that had gone on over who should greet Her Majesty first. Joe Cahill, the New South Wales premier, thought it should be his duty, but so did Prime Minister Menzies. The problem was solved by building a floating pontoon on which Menzies greeted the Queen and then, when she stepped onto state soil, Cahill had his turn to shake the royal glove.

When the Queen arrived, the young Whitlam boys were more interested in waving to their grandfather, Bill Dovey, who had just been appointed to the Supreme Court as Chief Judge in Divorce. Judge Dovey was standing head and shoulders above all the other dignitaries on the pontoon, resplendent in his morning suit. They were so excited to see him that they caused quite a commotion trying to get their grandfather's attention.

'There's Pa! Pa, hello Pa! We're over here, Pa!' they all shouted, jumping up and down and waving frantically in the hope that he could see them above the crowd. Both the elder boys had close relationships with their grandparents. 'Pa' smoked and drank and taught them both to play snooker and billiards on the full-size billiards table he had in his basement. He also had cases of Coca-Cola in plentiful supply, which was a great treat for them.

Nick has a special memory of his grandfather: at the age of sixteen he was in a taxi waiting for Pa to come out of the Bayswater Hotel, where he had gone to buy a bottle of scotch. The taxi driver turned to Nick and said, 'That's Judge Dovey, isn't it?'

'Yes, it is. How do you know him?' asked Nick.

'Great bloke,' said the cabbie. 'He got rid of the wife.'

Tony remembers that by the time he was at high school he often saw his grandfather's name in *The Sun* or *The Mirror* newspapers, either because he was the judge in some salacious case, or in his guise as vice-chairman of the Australian Jockey Club. He was quite a character and the boys were very aware that he seemed to know a lot of people involved in cricket and football, too, in which their father had no interest. After he retired Tony would often go to the local bowling club with him and Pa would jokingly introduce Tony as his younger brother.

The children also loved to visit Gough's parents whenever they were in Canberra as Gough's mother cooked them fabulous meals, with freshly grown vegetables and fruit from their grandfather's garden. Nick loved spending time with Grandpa in his book-lined study filled with the warm aroma of his cigars. Grandpa Whitlam gave him his first taste of travel by sending him postcards from all over the world when he was Australia's representative at the annual meetings of the UN Commission on Human Rights.

The boys all thought their baby sister was very sweet and they used to take her out in her pram like a little doll and show her off to the neighbours. Margaret's mother was delighted to finally have a granddaughter to make pretty dresses for and, on Catherine's first Christmas, she made her little white dotted muslin dresses threaded with red ribbons. Gough was particularly delighted with his little daughter and often said sentimentally to Margaret, 'Now I'll have someone who'll love me all of my life.'

After Catherine was born Margaret made the decision to have her tubes tied. She'd had to have what was commonly called 'a big repair job' after her daughter's birth and the doctor's advice was that she should have the tubular ligation. In those days nobody much had heard of vasectomies.

When it was over she found the aftermath strangely disorienting and disturbing:

> I didn't have time to feel different while Cathy was a baby but when she started to thrive, I suddenly thought, I can't have any more babies, and it made me feel weird. I got a bit depressed thinking about it, but the local quack told me not to be ridiculous, I was fine and healthy, with four great kids, and I should just get on with my life. The psychology of it is that you feel somehow neutered, and different. I did feel very weird for a time. Anyhow, I got over it.

The boys usually made their own way to Cronulla South public school. Nick says that none of the kids wore shoes and their feet were so tough that they could walk on the asphalt roads in summer without blinking. Margaret says they were given shoes, they just refused to wear them. Tony used to hide his shoes under the hydrangeas at his friend Richard Glover's house. Only when they attended Sunday School were they made to dress up and wear shoes. Nick and Tony hated both the Sunday School and the shoes.

Richard Glover, now a Sydney lawyer, remembers wonderful

days running wild in the bushland with the Whitlam boys, but he says none of them were in any doubt that Margaret was the disciplinarian.

'Whatever Margaret said, went. You weren't going to argue with her. She'd give us a clip under the ears and if we still played up she'd report us to Gough who, when he came home on weekends, would make us weed the lawn for hours.'

But he also remembers with great fondness her legendary Sunday lunches, when she would gather together local families, neighbourhood kids and the party faithful.

'She ruled those lunches. She was famous for her spaghetti bolognese. There was a long table with Margaret at one end and Gough at the other. She treated everyone as equals, no matter who they were, and was always at home in anyone's company. She was never in Gough's shadow, always her own person, as she had already achieved her own sporting eminence. She taught us all how to swim.'

On really hot days Margaret would meet the boys after school, take them to the Oak Park pool and give them what they called 'arvo tea' – a big buttered bun or home-made cake. On weekends the whole family walked down to the bay and had a picnic supper on the beach. Margaret would pack up sandwiches or salad and bottles of red cordial and home-made cake for a treat.

'They'd play on the sand or among the boats that were moored there. They were very lucky kids to have been brought up in such a lovely place. Life there was so open and free. I'd leave the back door open and while we were at the beach people would deliver the groceries, or the fruit and veg. They'd even put it in the fridge for me.'

Gough's salary was not high, even with the additional money from the legal briefs, for which he would travel into chambers every Saturday morning. Margaret devised ways of making the money stretch to feed a growing family. Her close friend Coralie Glover, Richard's mother and Catherine's godmother, had three boys roughly the age of hers, and they would buy half a side of lamb and share it. They also had a friend who had entrée to the markets, and four of them would buy cases of fruit and divvy them up. Whenever Margaret went to the city she would buy two pounds of peas – one for Coralie and one for her – and on her journey on the train back to Cronulla she would shell them.

In Gough's maiden speech he talked about the pressing problems of his constituents, making detailed references to the difficulty they had obtaining home loans, the fact that there was no local hospital or high school, and that they had 'more unsatisfied telephone applications than any other electorate'. At the end of his speech the Labor member for Hindmarsh in South Australia said, 'You've just heard a future prime minister.'

Yet, despite his close connection with the problems in his electorate and the fact that he was living a similar suburban life to his neighbours, the label of 'silvertail' was still used against him by many in the party. Rather than embrace his qualifications, his erudition and his verbal skills, they were suspicious of them. Consequently, he spent his early years as an MP in Canberra working alone in the parliamentary library, or at his desk in the caucus room, rather than hanging around the members' bar.

Members of the Liberal Party were even more hostile, accusing him of being a class traitor. The rumours that he had once been a member of their party persisted, even though he denied them and challenged the perpetrators to produce some evidence, which they couldn't. Such pernicious rumours spread by his political enemies on both sides of politics were to dog him all his life.

Just before his political career began, Margaret and Gough were asked out to what they realised later was a 'seduction' dinner, where a young henchman of Robert Menzies' who was the same age as Gough let it be known that Menzies was very keen for him to change parties. They kept asking him, almost incredulously, 'Why are you with "them"? You are both one of "us".'

Gough's reply, to their amazement, was, 'Because the Labor Party cares about the less privileged in our community and the Liberal Party doesn't.'

So Margaret and Gough had a very nice dinner, but rather than being seduced they were amused at the approach and the attitudes of the Liberals, who were acting like the proverbial woman scorned.

As the wife of a member of Parliament and someone who was involved in many community meetings and activities, Margaret took herself off to the Penguin Club, where they taught you how to chair a meeting, how to be a secretary to a committee, how to speak spontaneously, how to give constructive criticism of other people and the whole gamut of public speaking. The skills she was taught there she claimed gave her the confidence she needed to contribute to any organisation for the rest of her life.

'I learnt that if you are asked to speak at a gathering or a meeting you don't say, "Oh no, not me, I'm so inadequate," you stand up and say what you've got to say, or confess that you have nothing to add. You don't carry on about being inadequate.'

At first she found it difficult to adjust to the fact that Gough was away all week in Canberra and then on Saturdays would go into his law office and not return until two o'clock. It wasn't much fun for her and she let him know it, but she also knew that it was a financial necessity for him to work on Saturdays and that it was mean of her to complain about it.

During the week she always listened to *Question Time* on the radio and so did the children – it made them all feel connected to their father and his work. Once she had been to Parliament and seen where everyone was sitting she was able to picture it like a theatrical play and she soon became engrossed in the drama of the speeches and the power plays. They were the days before television coverage and spin doctors and many of the speakers, especially her husband, gave free vent to their theatrical aspirations.

Gough ritually rang her once a day and always tried to speak to the children. Every Friday night there was a local ball to attend – balls were very popular in the 1950s – and sometimes they'd have to go to three different social events. Saturday night was the same. These were hardly the kind of events she had been used to attending on the exclusive eastern suburbs social circuit. They certainly never made the social pages. But Margaret couldn't have cared less and threw herself into them with gusto, never complaining about having to attend, not because she was a long-suffering politician's wife, but because she loved to go out, she had a genuine interest in other people and she always had the ability to make friends wherever she was. Her mother was still making her clothes so she knew she looked good, and she made sure she always had a jolly time by seeking out like-minded people:

> I was very happy. We had such fun. I can remember us coming out of a ball at the Cecil ballroom in Cronulla and together with a group of local doctors and their wives we went to the fair that was on in the village. We all got on the ferris wheel, all the women in their long evening dresses and the chaps in their

dinner suits, had a couple of rides and then went back to the ball. It was a good community. We'd have lots of dinner parties where we'd all bring a dish and we'd share the baby-sitters.

A year after Catherine was born the family went to Coffs Harbour for the summer holidays, where Margaret contracted hepatitis. She began projectile vomiting and felt so wretched that she insisted they came home early. She says she thought to herself, 'If I'm going to die, it's going to be at home.'

On the trip back she had a raging thirst and was drinking constantly out of a bottle of lemonade. Nick grabbed the bottle and had a swig too. So when they diagnosed Margaret with hepatitis it was no surprise to find that Nick was infected too. He was very upset because it meant he missed out on his school's swimming championships. They were both ordered to have bed rest, lots of liquids and no fats. The local woman who came to help with the housework took Catherine home to look after her, Tony went to stay with Gough's parents in Canberra and Stephen stayed with one of the neighbours. Gough looked after Margaret and Nick until Parliament resumed.

Gough always enjoyed holidays with the children as it gave him a chance to spoil them in compensation for his absences. In 1956 the family travelled by car to Melbourne to visit Gough's relatives, one of whom owned a bookshop opposite Pellegrini's, which was one of the first Italian restaurants in Melbourne. Nick remembers it as the first proper restaurant he ever ate in and they all marvelled at the new flavours of the pasta, the fish and veal and the cassata ice-cream. Tony and Nick were amazed that there was more to pasta than macaroni cheese, and they worked their way through the spaghetti, the rigatoni and the lasagne on the menu. Eating well is still a shared family passion, although Stephen has always had 'eccentric taste in food' according to his mother.

On holiday they also loved staying in motels along the way and having their breakfast delivered through a hatch in the motel room. Margaret was delighted not to have to feed everyone three times a day, especially growing boys.

Their visit coincided with the Olympic Games in Melbourne and Gough obtained tickets for the opening of the games because even though he had never been a sports competitor, the rest of his family were all keen swimmers and sport lovers, particularly Nick, who was to go on to win various state swimming championships.

According to Nick, '[Gough] was not the sort of father to kick a ball around with us and he certainly didn't have the free time to come to my swimming carnivals, but I never felt neglected in any way. We were proud of him. He made us feel good about ourselves and what he was doing. We knew that he looked after the migrants and was on the side of the workers.'

He does remember being hurt when other children accused his father of being a communist – he didn't know what the word meant, but he knew it was intended as an insult. Mostly he ignored the criticisms and instead boasted about having a father who had three jobs – member of Parliament, barrister and father. His mother he simply took for granted, like all children of that era who had mothers who shopped and cooked and baked and were always there when you came home from school.

The children never thought of their parents as 'famous'. Like all children, they felt their mother and father were simply there to service their needs. Tony remembers, 'I didn't think about what my parents thought about me. I never really thought much about them, they were just my parents. I expected to get a meal when I came home, to do the bloody chores my father had designated, and basically get on with my own life.' It wasn't until Gough became deputy leader that he started to appear on television or in the newspapers and while they knew their mother had been a champion swimmer, to them she was just a housewife and a mother. Theirs was a simple childhood where there was love, security, good healthy food and not a lot of money for extras. Books were plentiful and their only real luxury: libraries always played a large part in Margaret's life. She was a regular user of the municipal library in Cronulla and the Book Stall library in the city, for which her father had given her life membership on her eighteenth birthday. She also belonged to the Pickwick Club, which had a good lending library where she would often go for lunch on her weekly jaunt into town.

In Cronulla Margaret was soon invited to join local WEA (Workers' Educational Association) discussion groups, which a dentist's wife, Mavis Gates, had initiated. Six or seven of them would take it in turns to meet in each other's houses and do the WEA courses together – on literature, history, comparative religions or art. She also belonged to a tennis group, and swam regularly in the sea – with or without the children.

It was a full life, very much along the lines of her own mother's. Mary, too, had always hated to waste time. She and Gough also managed to squeeze in visits to the ballet, the theatre and symphony concerts. If they couldn't go together they would take it in turns to baby-sit and each would go with a friend.

Although Margaret had a household rule about the children sleeping in their own beds, whenever Gough was baby-sitting she would come home and find one or more of them in their double bed. This came back to the fact that he felt he had so little time to spend with them he indulged their every wish.

Margaret was a good mother and a well-organised wife and housekeeper. She didn't find the work onerous or boring and took on the challenge of running a smooth and efficient home for every member of the family with energy and enthusiasm. The 1950s were the so-called halcyon days of family life, when men were the breadwinners and women were the homemakers. Of course, there were many women who worked outside the home, but that was because they needed to economically; few of them would have chosen to. A woman was expected to wave goodbye at the gate to her husband as he left for work, and her children as they left for school, each carrying their freshly packed lunch prepared by her that morning. She was also expected to be there with a glass of milk and a healthy snack when the children returned from school, and to have a cooked dinner ready when her husband returned from work.

Margaret fulfilled all these expectations happily, except that she had a husband who worked away from home during the week, which placed extra responsibilities on her. She simply took these in her stride and organised herself and her duties in such a way that she could incorporate her own activities, duties and pleasures into her routine.

She was never bored or depressed or dissatisfied with her role. Nor did she question it. She never looked back to her privileged and cosseted life in Vaucluse with her parents and the maid Alice, nor forward to Gough's ambition to be the leader of the party, and ultimately prime minister.

She just enjoyed every day in the best way she could, dealt with the tasks at hand, organised her life as a mother and a wife, and found time to indulge her own interests.

She thinks of this phase of her life as neither better nor worse than her previous phases. It was just different.

CABRAMATTA

In 1955 Gough's electorate of Werriwa had become so populous that it was divided into two and its boundaries were redistributed. When the redistribution proposals were debated Gough made a statement: 'Since Mr Lazzarini's death I have represented the sub-divisions of Liverpool, Cabramatta and Fairfield. These represent 65 per cent of the electors found in the western half of my old electorate and I propose to seek selection for it.'

He took the name of Werriwa with him and in 1956 he and Margaret looked around for a house to buy in the new electorate. When they couldn't find anything suitable for their now large family they bought a block of land on what had been a vineyard in Cabramatta and decided to build another new house to suit their needs.

Number 32 Albert Street, Cabramatta was only the second house on the block when they moved in there in November 1957. Built of brick, unlike most of the small fibro houses nearby, it was larger than their Cronulla house, with four bedrooms. It was split level, architecturally designed and, like their Cronulla house, for its time it was considered very modern, with its peacock-blue front door, huge blue and white awnings, and big glass windows. Margaret loved it. (Years later it was suggested that 32 Albert Street should be preserved as a Whitlam museum. Margaret dismissed the proposition as 'utterly ridiculous and inappropriate'.)

Yet again, she set about making a garden from scratch. They were allowed to select plants from the government nursery in Canberra and so many trees were planted. Margaret decided against flower beds and instead opted for geraniums and creepers out the back, and a climbing pink Lorraine Lee rose over the front door.

It was totally different from their first house in Cronulla but Margaret loved it just as much and it was more suitable for her growing family.

The two older boys were very reluctant to leave Cronulla and their friends, particularly Tony, who loved to surf. Cabramatta was rural, not coastal, and he never really adjusted to the move, spending most weekends hitchhiking back to Cronulla and surfing with his old crowd.

Nick was the most gregarious of the boys and threw himself into the new social activities in the area: having joined a local athletics club he was soon happily flirting with the girls and eager to practise his dancing skills.

Stephen was only seven when the family moved and soon his two older brothers started to pick on him because he wasn't forced to do nearly as many chores in the new house as they had been required to fulfil in Cronulla. Their father was much busier and had many more demands on his time by now, and he could spend even less time with Stephen and Catherine than he had with Tony and Nick.

Catherine was only three when they moved and has no memories of Cronulla.

And as for Margaret – just as she had enjoyed school, but not wept when she left it, so too she had loved Cronulla, but was looking forward to the next chapter of her life. She says that initially, moving to Cabramatta did seem a bit like 'going to the ends of the Earth', but she soon became used to driving the hour or so into the city for meetings of the Ladies' Auxiliary at the boys' school.

She started up another WEA women's group like the one she had joined in Cronulla. The boys used to call them 'Mum's culture evenings' and Stephen in particular would sneak into the room to listen to the discussions. When Margaret queried his presence he'd say, 'I like the convos, Mum.'

She maintained contact with her old friends from Cronulla and continued to invite them to her celebrated Sunday lunches. Richard Glover remembers one lunch for twenty-five when Gough read something in the paper that really upset him:

> He went ballistic. He was pacing around and shouting. It was a serious Gough eruption. Margaret suddenly emerged from the kitchen, the spaghetti ladle still in her hand and said firmly but calmly, 'Gough, we can't have this behaviour in front of all these people. Now settle down, darling, and go back to your seat.' And Gough went quietly back to his chair, suitably admonished. She just had this amazing controlling, calming influence.

By now Tony was attending Sydney Boys' High, one of the top selective schools in New South Wales. Nick joined him in 1958. Only three boys from South Cronulla Primary went to a selective school and that year was a record.

At the end of Tony's first year there his Aunt Freda had just been appointed headmistress of PLC Croydon in Sydney's west and offered to pay for him to attend Sydney Grammar so he could follow the tradition set by his Grandfather Dovey. Tony thanked her but refused the offer because he was proud to go to a school where the rich couldn't buy their children a place. In fact, that is what Sydney's Boys' High told them when they arrived there and

Tony says it remains a very powerful argument for the existence of state-funded selective schools.

'My parents were always interested in my education and my mother is a great joiner of things, particularly in relation to her children. As Nick and I were both at Sydney High she joined the Mothers' Club and became the president in 1959. Most of the students came from the eastern suburbs and for her to drive from Cabramatta was quite a commitment.'

Stephen attended the Cabramatta public school, and so did his sister as soon as she was old enough. They loved the freedom of the open spaces in Cabramatta, especially the stables across the road with the huge mulberry tree, and the massive gum trees on the edge of the creek, where they tied ropes to swing out over the water.

Gough had grown up in Canberra when it was an unfinished country town, the streets were unsealed and there were clusters of houses surrounded by paddocks, so Cabramatta felt familiar to him. Margaret's upbringing in cosmopolitian Bondi and exclusive Vaucluse could not have been more different, but it was that very difference that attracted her. Adventures do not usually spring from familiar places, and she always loved a new adventure.

Cabramatta was very much hotter than Cronulla, not having any of the coastal breezes from the beach to cool them down in the evenings. The first Christmas after they had moved, Margaret's parents came for Christmas Day and her mother found the heat so oppressive she spent the entire afternoon lying in the bath. She declared there were to be no more family Christmases spent in Cabramatta and instead they would all go to her parents, or her brother and sister-in-law's house in Rose Bay, which had formerly been their custom.

Margaret's brother had finally left home and married, at the age of thirty-two. Margaret's mother had relinquished him to a small, quiet girl from the country. Known as Willie to the family, but Bill once he attended Sydney Grammar, he had, like Margaret, loved sport more than academic study. Having served in the school cadets, he joined the Royal Australian Navy, and when he finished his officer training he went on exchange with the navy during the war, and was part of the force that was sent to liberate Norway. After the war he returned to Sydney University and studied law. Unlike Margaret and his parents he had no interest in the arts but he was very social and handsome and, according to Margaret, had lots of girlfriends.

He became a barrister, like his father, resembling him, too, in his ebullience. He met his wife, Susan Fane de Salis, at a country ball. His mother approved, and he and Susan were very happy, going on to have two daughters. Like many brothers and sisters who fight when they are children, Margaret and her brother became very close and she is godmother to his eldest daughter, Fane. They never, however, had another scorching hot Christmas at Cabramatta.

Despite the seasonal heat there was no swimming pool in Cabramatta, so in the summer Margaret drove herself and the children to the pools in Bankstown, or Granville, and then Liverpool. Together with the well-known feminist social reformer Edna Ryan, who was on the Fairfield Council, Margaret joined the group that established the Cabramatta pool and soon became the president of its swimming club. Catherine remembers her constantly having a timing watch around her neck, organising the running of the races.

The block on which the Whitlams had built their new house overlooked what eventually became Warwick Farm Racecourse. The majority of the migrants who had established themselves there were Yugoslavs and Italians. The Yugoslavs tended to build two-storey brick houses, often leaving the lower storey unfinished until more of their relatives arrived to live with them. The Italians lived further out and established market gardens, which provided fresh produce for the locals and fresh flowers for Whitlams' closest neighbour and friend, Aunty Betty, who had the second brick house on the block and ran the florist shop and real estate agency in John Street.

When Margaret and Gough visited events in clubs they would be held in the German-Austrian Club or the Polish White Eagle Club, the Club Marconi or the RSL Diggers Club. The history of Cabramatta is the history of its different waves of migration. With the huge influx of Vietnamese migrants John Street today is unrecognisable from the main shopping street of the 1950s and 1960s that the Whitlams knew. Now, most of the shops are Asian or Vietnamese, and most of the Anglo faces you see are those of tourists, who come on special bus trips to purchase the bargains and lunch in the restaurants.

On one of our research and recreation trips, Catherine drove me and Margaret to Cabramatta and we too had lunch in one of the Vietnamese restaurants in the main street. Next to us was a long table of women tourists in Cabramatta for the bargains. Margaret noticed that one of the women sitting behind her was trying unsuccessfully to scratch her back, so she casually leant across and scratched it for her. When the woman turned around to thank the stranger who had relieved her itch she recognised her immediately. She giggled and blushed and didn't know what to say. Margaret smiled and said, 'There's nothing worse than not being able to reach a scratch, is there?'

The woman nodded and thanked her profusely. I could just imagine her at home that night saying to her husband, 'You'll never guess who scratched my back today . . .'

Earlier, when we had driven past the house that the Whitlams had built and lived in for many years, Margaret was visibly upset at how dilapidated and unkempt it had become. 'Oh dear, they've taken down my blue and white awnings – how upsetting. But look, there's the Lorraine Lee rose I planted myself. Poor thing, they should have pruned it properly – it's been so neglected. At least it's still flowering.'

We drove through Catherine's high school, which is now an accurate reflection of what Cabramatta has always been: an historical record of the latest wave of immigrants. The tiny fibro house of her best friend, Eileen, was still there. Her father was a brick carter and Margaret remembered them as 'really good, warm people'.

Walking back to the car after lunch, it was obvious that Margaret's back was causing her real pain. At one stage she visibly paled and had to stop and lean against a building. Catherine fetched her a drink, she took some painkillers and once in the car with a warm pad on her back she relaxed. Most women of her age would have called it a day. Not Margaret. She was on for gelato and coffee as she had been promised. We stopped in Leichhardt, she ordered her favourite gelato and insisted I share it with her.

Whenever you are with Margaret you instantly feel like family. She has a genuine talent for inclusiveness.

Margaret was happy in her new home and her new suburb and even though it was a long drive from Sydney, she remained in very close contact with her parents, particularly her dad.

> My father knew I was really looking forward to turning forty and so on the eve of my birthday he called me up and said, 'What are you doing for lunch? I'll take you to Ushers.' So we had a lovely lunch and at the end I said to him, 'This has been very nice, darling, but what have I done especially? I know it's my birthday, but I've had other birthdays.' He said,

'It's your fortieth and you told me you were looking forward to it, so I thought I'd make it a really good one.' And I had to tell him, 'I've got news for you, old boy, I'm thirty-nine today.'

In November 1959 Margaret did finally turn forty, and she celebrated it by having the long hair that she had worn since she was a child cut. She remembers she rang her mother and told her, 'I'm so sick of my hair, it's all wispy and horrible. I'd like to cut it off.' They arranged to meet in David Jones in the city, where a hairdresser called Antoine cut off her plaits and gave her a 'long bob'. She was very pleased with the effect. Her hair seemed immediately to rejuvenate itself and the grey bits on the side disappeared. She bumped into her father in the city on the day she had it cut and he said, 'Good God, girl, what have you done?'

Margaret replied, 'I've had my hair cut'.

He said, 'And you've had it dyed too,' to which she could respond, 'I have not. Absolutely not.'

Gough, however, was not pleased. He had always liked Margaret's long hair, and he was even more upset that she had cut it without discussing it with him. But, after the initial shock of seeing her with short hair, he soon got used to it. He had bigger things on his mind than the length of Margaret's hair.

In February of that year his hard work and ability had been rewarded by the party and he was elected to Herbert 'Doc' Evatt's shadow cabinet. It had taken him six years on the backbench to serve his apprenticeship, but he knew this was the first step in the plan he had been formulating. He had kept to himself and worked hard but, apart from when he was so pleased with a speech he had given in the House and had insisted on buying his backbench colleagues drinks at the bar, he had made few friends. He was basically a loner. Lance Barnard, who had represented the Tasmanian seat of Bass since 1954, however, was one of his admirers. It was he who suggested to Gough that when Doc Evatt resigned as leader of the party, Gough ought to put himself up for the deputy leadership. When he told Barnard he was prepared to give it a go, Barnard worked quietly on his behalf, getting the numbers behind the scenes.

Evatt's leadership ended with his appointment as Chief Justice of New South Wales on 15 February 1960. Arthur Calwell was the hot tip to succeed him and Gough simply sent a letter to all caucus members informing them of his intention to stand for the deputy leadership. Others, organised by Barnard, worked on his behalf and on 7 March, at forty-three years of age, Gough Whitlam became the deputy leader of the ALP.

The Canberra Times' assessment the day after was, 'On the debit side Mr Whitlam would appear to have difficulty in interpreting the phrase self-discipline and his impetuous remarks and offensive terms directed at some government members in debate have reduced him in stature in the eyes of experienced politicians on both sides of Parliament.'

He was quick, witty and lethal with his tongue. He also had a very quick temper, which would flare up and then be over. Margaret had often been reduced to rage or tears by his verbal swordplay. Afterwards, he could barely remember what he had said in the heat of his outburst and sometimes he would apologise and say he hadn't meant it. Margaret, however, has never believed that excuse and freely admits that while she doesn't have a temper, she's a sulker. Often she would barely speak to Gough for several days after one of his hurtful outbursts.

John Menadue joined Gough's staff as his private secretary after he became deputy leader, and he met Margaret almost immediately. He says, 'His temper was a thing she lived with all her life.

Basically, at least in public, she tried to ignore it because in ten minutes he didn't know he'd done it.'

In his book *Things You Learn Along the Way* Menadue recalls, 'With some of the staff, Whitlam was tough. Tears were not uncommon. He drove himself hard and sometimes expected too much of others.'

He saw Margaret as 'an enormous help in stabilising and sustaining [Gough]: calm, sensible, her feet always firmly planted on the ground. Even when irritated by her good advice he would say, "She's a good wife to me."'

When he first met Margaret, Menadue was impressed by how genuinely friendly she was. 'She always asked after my family and remembered the kids' names, where they were and what they were doing.'

Gough, on the other hand, was ill-at-ease with small talk and could be awkward with ALP members. 'He was shy. Painfully so at times . . . We all project a public persona to protect our private self. For politicians it is even more important. Gough Whitlam was no exception. His confidence on the public platform was often at variance with the diffident private person.'

Nevertheless, Menadue found Gough 'inspiring to work with, iconoclastic and with big-picture ideas tumbling out all the time'. He said it was 'like working in a power house'.

Words were Gough's strength. He had an encyclopaedic store of knowledge and could quote *Hansard*, the classics, acts of Parliament, the Bible and list most major historical events at a moment's notice. At parliamentary lunches or dinners he outperformed every other leader, except Menzies. His childhood, his home background and his education had taught him the power of knowledge and words, and when asked to give an example of his view of equality he said, 'I want every kid to have a desk with a lamp and his own room to study,' recalls Menadue.

Menadue described working with Gough as like being part of an unending seminar or tutorial. His weaknesses, even in 1960, were also on display for everyone to observe: his pedantry, his impatience, his lack of character judgement and his inability to restrain his tendency to show how clever and erudite he was. His sense of humour is very dry, usually dripping with irony or self-mockery. Even today when he sets off the security alarms at airports he proclaims, 'I think you'll find that's my aura.'

Gough knew that his natural support base was the increasingly large sector of white-collar workers and middle-class employees, and he knew that the ALP had to broaden its support base and could no longer just rely on its blue-collar trade unionists.

As early as 1960 he addressed the issue of feminism and at the New South Wales ALP Women's Conference he said that Labor's failure to nominate a woman for the Senate was a disgrace. He was a vocal supporter of equal pay.

Gough's mother had died in 1958 and his father lasted only another three years without his close, lifelong companion. Fred died the day before the federal election in 1961, which the ALP lost.

Nicholas had just turned sixteen and couldn't understand why he was considered too young to attend the funeral when his older brother was allowed to go. These days children much younger than sixteen not only attend funerals but speak at them. Margaret remembers making that decision on the grounds that she was protecting her children from a sorrowful occasion. It just wasn't the done thing to subject your children to death at an early age. In fact, Anglican women traditionally never went to the grave. She didn't attend funerals as a rule and still doesn't go to them nearly as often as Gough, even now, when they are outliving so many of their friends.

Margaret describes Fred Whitlam as a true gentleman, a pillar of the Church, a very competent and modest man.

'I wouldn't say he was self-deprecating, but he was a very modest man. Not like his son in that respect. His mother was much more aggressive in her opinions of people and had no hesitation in describing them unattractively if that was her judgement. I was a very obedient daughter-in-law. I admired her, but I thought she led a cloistered life because she never seemed to get out of the kitchen. She just loved cooking.'

Gough's father loved his garden equally, where he grew wonderful vegetables and fruit. His only concession to flowers was a patch of violets. He would pick one every day for his wife and she would place it in a vase next to the others. She always put two cups of tea on the window-sill for him, just in case he was really thirsty.

Gough's parents clearly adored him and always had very high hopes for their only son, who returned their devotion. As the subject of a documentary when he was eighty, Gough's eyes filled with tears when he was asked about his parents. 'My parents meant a great deal to me . . . and their memory still does,' he said.

Parenting was very important to both Margaret and Gough, and although Margaret was a sole parent for much of the time, she never complained or whinged. It's not her style. She just became super-organised.

'When I'd got them all off to school and there was nothing to do that had to be done within a certain time, I'd sit down and read a book. I wouldn't go to town unless I'd done the washing-up and made the beds, although they all made their own beds when they were old enough.'

All her children attest to her organisational skills, her ability to get a lot of food on the table fast, her involvement in whatever they did and her encouragement of their sporting activities, especially swimming. She really had two sets of children. By the time the two elder boys had left Sydney High and were at university, she only had the younger two to look after.

Tony called his mother Margaret from the time he left home to study at the Australian National University in 1961. He considers her to be 'absolutely a good mother', and, regardless of his father's absences, he never had any sense of being neglected. However, as in all families, there was sibling rivalry.

The one thing Margaret couldn't control in her family was the older boys picking on Stephen. They used to call him a weed, or 'the puny one', and tell him he'd never reach thirteen. Stephen was not madly keen on sport as they were – like his father, he preferred to spend his spare time inside reading books. To Tony and Nick this was most peculiar, and they let him know it by constantly having digs at him.

Margaret says, 'It was bullying and disgraceful behaviour, but they were both bigger than me and if I took Stevie's side too much they made it worse for him. They didn't seem to care that it upset me. They referred to both Stephen and Catherine as 'the brats' because they said they had more privileges as younger children than they had. It was probably true because when they were little we didn't have much money.'

Tony says:

> Nick was Mum's favourite. Because he was a swimmer he was always getting out of chores. I did bully Stephen a bit, but he was such a weed. He is entirely different from the rest of us: he isn't interested in sport, he doesn't drink, he doesn't entertain. Physically, Catherine and I are most like Margaret. In personality, I don't think any of us are much like her. Margaret is a lot more sentimental than any of us. She wants everybody

to be happy. Her sentimental view of people is quite genuine: she instinctively wants to see the best in people and really tries to be nice about them. The only person I've ever heard her really criticise is Janette Howard.

She's very rarely likely to be repelled by people's views on issues. I guess that's allowed her to get along with everyone, and it's probably a strength given that she's married to Gough, because he is exactly the reverse. He really does hate some people and bear them grudges. Somebody could be a most charming host and have the most lovely manners, but if they spoke ill of his position on East Timor he'd never forgive them. Never. Whereas Margaret wouldn't have a political or ideological reference to put that into. She's a broad-brush person and not analytical.

Tony believes that Margaret gave Gough a level grounding in what normal mainstream life was like. He views his father as unusual because he came from a very disciplined Christian family in which neither his mother or father had any obvious vices and they lived within their Christian values. Gough's religion was developing the best public policy and giving all Australians an equal opportunity in education, health and employment. He, too, lived and breathed that.

Tony has always been impressed that, 'Margaret never panics or over-reacts. When Nick was about fifteen and a bit of a lad with the girls, Margaret answered the phone and some girl came on and said, "I'm pregnant by your son, Nick." Margaret didn't bat an eye and replied, "Well, just a second, you'd better speak to Nick about that." Nick got on the phone and asked, "Who the hell is this?"

'It was soon clear it was rubbish, but Margaret took it all in her stride.'

Nick says his mother, whom he still calls Mother or Margot, never really talked to him about sex, other than to say before he went on a date, 'Just remember, that girl is somebody's sister.'

For Nick the house in Cabramatta became 'almost a dormitory. I commuted to the city, went to swimming or football training [rugby union], arrived home late and on the weekends played sport.'

Margaret constantly cooked a lot of food to keep them all satisfied. Nick recalls:

> The kitchen must have been something of an industrial enterprise for our mother; Tony would have almost reached his full height of six foot seven, I grew to six foot four and Stephen and Catherine, although younger, were growing and always hungry, too. Stephen was picky with his food, so Tony and I introduced 'the equal proportions rule' to prevent him having more than his share of any preferred dish. Mother rarely observed the rule but it was regularly invoked by Tony and me.
>
> Sunday night was shoe-cleaning night, when Dad cleaned his shoes to perfection, spitting and buffing on the Kiwi and polishing to a high shine, and we all did the same.

Stephen has written a small family memoir for his children and in it he too talks of their chores, except he was also sometimes expected to cook for himself and Catherine, and do some ironing. 'I even used the sewing machine to make some trousers narrower than my mother wanted me to.'

In the early sixties Stephen and Catherine spent a lot of time travelling around Australia with their parents (their older brothers considered themselves too old for such family trips). Stephen says:

> The places we visited were often of scenic or historical interest, but we also seemed to . . . call on people who were not relatives, or even friends . . . It was only later that I realised these calls were an essential part of the process by which my father made himself known to ALP members . . . throughout the country, and familiarised himself with issues and problems of relevance to the people and the party . . . Mother never seemed to mind waiting in the car while he popped in to see someone. She's a very patient person.

One of Catherine's clearest memories of her mother during their years in Cabramatta is of her wearing thongs and a skirt above the knees, which the young Catherine thought 'was bold for an old chook'. She pictures her mostly standing in the garden with the hose.

> Cabramatta used to get very hot in the summer and Mum was always trying to revive the garden. She used to let me and my best friend, Eileen, romp around on the lawn in our bathers while she sprayed us with the hose. She was always in the kitchen cooking up a storm and she spent a lot of time at the swimming club. Dad was away a lot and I used to get very irritated when he came home because our routines changed and Mum suddenly had to become available for electoral commitments that involved him.

In 1962, due to the looming entry of the United Kingdom into the European Common Market, Gough Whitlam was included in the tour of Europe that Prime Minister Menzies had approved for Opposition leaders. Gough was deputy leader at the time, and took Arthur Calwell's place on the trip when Calwell was unable to go. Margaret accompanied him.

In spite of his detailed knowledge of European and in particular Roman and Greek civilisations, Gough had never visited Europe. Their first port of call was Athens and he thought he was in heaven. As they were walking up to the Parthenon, Margaret wondered if he would faint away, he was so ecstatic. Being far more practical she couldn't help noticing that you were charged to see the Parthenon, so why couldn't they 'restore it a little – corral all the bits lying around? Apart from that it would stop little old ladies from breaking their ankles.'

Gough was forty-six before he actually saw these countries first hand and he became a self-appointed tour guide for Margaret and private secretary John Menadue (who was only twenty-seven). It was the 'first time' for all of them. Menadue described Margaret as 'a wonderful companion, warm and easy to be with, a tower of strength'. He was amazed at Gough's detailed knowledge of the places they visited, right down to which paintings were in which salons in which galleries. Gough physically leapt from painting to painting, talking and enthusing. He was unrelenting in his excitement and his detailed examination of each one. After six or seven hours when Menadue said his mind and his legs were numb and aching, Margaret would say, 'Gough, John and I have had enough for today. Leave something for tomorrow.' Menadue said Gough would 'grind his teeth, mutter to himself and obey'.

Gough was very much at home in Europe, and totally relaxed with meeting and talking to diplomats and leaders of European parliaments, as there was a purpose to the discussions. They met a seemingly never-ending pageant of famous and powerful people, from Pope Paul VI, to President Johnson, to Billy Graham and the Black Panthers.

Once they were back on home territory, however, it was all hard slog. The election losses for the ALP in 1961 and then in 1963 were dispiriting to everyone but Gough. Calwell was no match for Menzies, and the ALP had failed to tackle the party reform that was desperately needed, in particular the split between the ALP and the Democratic Labour Party. Whitlam said openly that the DLP was neither democratic, Labor nor a party, and in fact had no real power base outside Victoria.

Whitlam's ideological commitment was to equality of opportunity, not the rigid doctrine of socialism espoused by some of those in the left wing of the party. In all the meetings in which Margaret sat in the audience knitting and listening to her husband's ideas, there was one section of the constitution that he repeated like a mantra, and that was Section 96 – the charter of public enterprise. Almost all the new and radical programs that Whitlam ultimately enacted were dependent on the ability of the federal government to make grants under Section 96.

Thus Gough had found a chink in the constitutional armour whereby a federal Labor government could fund its reform programs. He used their overseas trips to find precedents in other federal systems in order to implement Section 96 grants, and in speech after speech, he referred to what other countries were achieving through their federal funding of programs. However, Gough never discussed such matters with Margaret. He had a clear division between home and Parliament, and when he was at home, apart from all the constituents who constantly rang or called by with their problems, he focused on home and the family. Politics were not discussed unless one of the children asked a question. In that case the answer could take up to an hour.

In 1963 Nick was accepted to study at Harvard. His contacts and friendships with a number of champion Australian swimmers who had attained scholarships to study at American colleges had inspired him to apply to all the top American universities. This was entirely his own initiative. Gough confessed to Catherine much later that when he saw the letter arrive from Harvard he contemplated tearing it up because even though Nick had won a scholarship he knew there would be so many other expenses and he was concerned that they could not afford them. Nick was very excited at being accepted and so they found a way to make it happen. Gough had some limited corporate connections, including one with P&O in Sydney, and he arranged for Nick to work his passage to America as a supernumerary on a steamer ship.

In August 1963 Nick sailed out through the heads, 'A callow youth – seventeen – with tears cascading down my face, not knowing when I'd come back, but thrilled with the adventure.' He was his mother's son.

By now Tony was studying law at the ANU in Canberra. His girlfriend at the time was another student, Kate Shea (later Maclaren), and when Kate was taken home to Cabramatta to meet the family in 1962, she became smitten not just with Tony, but with Margaret, too.

> The house at Cabramatta had mirrors I couldn't see into and cupboards I couldn't reach. Everything was so high, even the beds were longer. When I stayed over, Tony and I used to have sex in his bed and then I'd duck back into Gough's study to sleep on the divan. Margaret knew what we were doing but nothing was ever said. At about four in the morning Gough would come in to make international phone calls. He'd sit on the bed

totally oblivious to the fact that he was also sitting on my legs. He always seemed to be talking to someone called Harry Lee. I remember lying there quiet as a little mouse, getting pins and needles, and thinking, This is probably history I'm listening to, and I'd thank God I'd got back into the bed in time.

I was totally in awe of Margaret's skill in feeding this house full of giants. She had an enormous Sunbeam frying pan and in it went all the eggs and bacon and tomatoes. Next to that was the Mixmaster and into that would go half a tin of Milo, some ice-cream and a few pints of milk. Everyone would get a huge glass of Milo and there were vast amounts of pineapple and paw-paw. I remember peeling fruit into a bucket for election nights, when Margaret would make huge fruit salads.

Kate was impressed with Margaret's calm when Gough would ring up just before dinner and say, 'I'm bringing home Fred, Joe and Steve,' or whoever, and six extra blokes would turn up for dinner. She was always so warm and charming to everyone and simply got on with it.

Nothing, it seemed to Kate, would ever ruffle Margaret. She remembers a time when she and Tony were spending their university Christmas holidays at Cabramatta. They were off to a formal dinner and Kate was attempting to tie Tony's bow-tie with a finger that was bleeding. When she failed miserably and left blood on his tailored dinner shirt, Tony lost his inherited Whitlam temper and punched the bathroom door, which clearly wasn't very substantial because his fist splintered a hole in it – the only door to the only bathroom in the house. Completely unfazed, Margaret went to the magazine rack and returned with two pictures of the fountains of Rome, which she proceeded to tape over the hole. She says, 'They were probably still on the door when we sold the house.'

Kate admits that she kept her relationship with Tony going longer than it should have lasted simply because she couldn't bear to think she'd lose contact with Margaret. She needn't have worried. Even after she and Tony split up and she was married and having children, exquisite little singlets would arrive that Margaret had knitted for them. 'She never just sat around, she was always knitting, or writing postcards – she never wasted a minute.'

On Saturdays constituents flooded to the Whitlam family home with their problems for Gough to solve. (Electorate offices only worked on weekdays.) Stephen writes in his memoir:

> Constituents would line up by the low brick fence at the front of our Cabramatta home for their interview about . . . family migration, pensions, etc. The interviews were conducted in the living room, which is why we eventually installed a folding door between that room and the dining room to give us family members some privacy. As the electorate was strongly working class and with a large number of migrants (mainly Italians, Yugoslavs, Maltese, Greeks, Lebanese) the load was quite heavy. My father's well-known knowledge of and interest in many of the cultures of the migrants encouraged the numbers . . . but they usually did not come empty-handed. Many were market gardeners and . . . I believe I can trace my dislike of tomatoes to the fact that there were very few weekends when a case of tomatoes was not among the generous donations.

No doubt Margaret made lots of bottles of tomato sauce for the spaghetti.

In 1964 Gough was awarded a grant to travel to America for three months to investigate forms of government. But the grant money did not include or stretch to taking a wife, and neither did the Whitlams' family budget. Undeterred, Margaret thought, 'Blow this for a joke, I'm going too.' She organised for Catherine to stay with their neighbour and Stephen with her brother, Bill, and his wife, Sue. Nick was in the States already and Tony was living at the ANU in Canberra. She cashed in a small insurance policy she'd had and with some money given to her by her beloved father, and her own savings, she followed Gough. It took her a week to meet up with him in Washington and she did so by travelling across the States in a Greyhound bus, which to most women would be a feat of endurance but to Margaret was great fun. She loved it because it was the first chance she'd had since she married Gough to take off on her own, pleasing herself where she stopped and where she stayed. And, of course, Margaret enjoyed the adventure.

When she met up with Gough she took up once again the role of the deputy leader's wife. There were elegant dinners in Washington and New York with politicians and ambassadors, all of which she enjoyed, though she secretly missed the freedom she had enjoyed travelling on her own and staying at cheap places.

When Gough continued on to England she went to Boston where Nick was working at his summer job. Like most students at American universities he had taken part-time work during the Harvard term, and throughout his vacations. He had a flat on Myrtle Street in Boston which he shared with two Australian and three American boys. They all gave her the big bedroom, and she became their chief cook and bottle-washer for a week.

Nick was working at a community club as a swimming instructor, pool attendant and tennis companion. He travelled around

Boston on a motorbike and took Margaret for a quick trial run one night. She was quite terrified and let the neighbourhood know it.

'I was sitting on the back of this thing, yelling my head off. It was very comic. Fortunately, the bike was stolen shortly afterwards and I didn't have to endure any more of those rides.'

After Boston she met up with an Australian friend and they travelled by bus to Montreal and then on to Niagara Falls. Her next stop was Chicago. She was alone and literally down to 'my last five quid' so she directed a cab to take her to the YMCA hotel. She was being her usual friendly self and chatting away to the cab driver when, as they were approaching her hotel, he said, 'It's been really interesting talking to you. I tell you what, why don't you go in, drop your things in your room, come back down, I'll take you all around the city and then we'll have a roll in the hay.'

Margaret said she nearly collapsed when she heard the words 'roll in the hay' but, cool as ever, she replied, 'Well, I think I might take a raincheck on that.' Of course, later on she told Gough about the bloke who put the hard word on her and she said he was vastly amused.

In New Orleans she stopped overnight in what turned out to be a brothel, but she didn't mind as it was cheap and right above the bus station. When she asked the taxi driver on the rank what it would cost to take her around the city he told her and added, 'I'll even take you to see the Gordons.' Margaret asked who the Gordons were and discovered he meant the gardens, where part of *Gone With the Wind* had been shot. Being a great fan of the film and a self-confessed romantic, she readily accepted.

In San Francisco she again stayed at the 'Y', which was across the road from a broadcasting station where, she noticed, they produced television shows with live audiences. As it was free she popped over there and joined an audience, laughing and clapping on cue, having a great time. When she finally dragged herself away, caught a bus to the airport and checked in, a staff member from the Australian Consulate General was waiting for her. He was most distraught and exclaimed, 'Mrs Whitlam, where have you been? We knew you were flying out today and we've been looking all over for you. We wanted to pick you up and bring you to the airport. We thought you were lost. We were so worried that something had happened to you.'

Margaret repressed a smile and didn't tell him how she had spent the day. Instead she said graciously, 'I certainly wasn't lost and it's very kind of you to care, but really you didn't need to concern yourself.' Having now located her he insisted on escorting her safely to the VIP lounge, which she had to admit was more comfortable than the Greyhound bus station.

While VIP lounges are wonderful, Margaret treasures the memories of those little adventures she experienced entirely on her own. The real luxury for her was freedom – the freedom to be herself and do what she wanted at a whim, without having to answer to anybody, or cook a meal or three. Her taste of freedom had been quite intoxicating.

However, the trip had cleaned out her bank balance. When she returned home and was bemoaning her lack of funds, her mother said, 'Why don't you go back to work? They're crying out for social workers, I've seen ads in the paper.' It hadn't occurred to Margaret to seek work, but there was no reason not to now her two older sons were at university and Stephen, aged fourteen, and Catherine, aged ten, were both at school all day. So she applied for a job at Parramatta District Hospital, which was very close to home, and they were happy for her to work part-time – three days a week, or the equivalent. She arranged with the administrator that if she had to accompany Gough somewhere important then she could rearrange her times. It all worked out very well.

For the first time in twenty years Margaret was earning her own money again. 'Not that I'd really been denied anything, but at the same time it's nice to have your own earnings. I bought a few things that in those days were regarded as luxuries, like a new outdoor table-and-chairs setting.'

Her children were pleased that she was working and noticed how happy she was to have achieved some independence. Tony remarked, 'You'd never not work again, would you?' He thought that the world had reopened for her, and she certainly felt a new, strangely thrilling sense of being her own person and not simply someone else's wife and mother.

On 7 January 1965 her first-born son turned twenty-one and, as was the tradition of the time, Tony celebrated in their backyard at Cabramatta. Margaret made the food, Catherine handed it around and Tony deputised Stephen to serve the beer from the kegs. He was fourteen and even though he knew few of Tony's mates he enjoyed the evening very much because of the humour and the fun.

> As the evening wore on, the guests became less and less steady on their feet. I remember one in particular who held a beer in one hand and himself in the other and swayed all over the lawn emptying his bladder in a performance of waving sparklers on cracker night . . .
>
> After the party my brother gave his own bed to a friend and took mine for himself. So at 5.30 am, as day was dawning, I had to thread my way through bodies on the living-room floor to one of the vacant armchairs, which I settled into for a few hours' sleep.

It is hard not to contrast Tony's twenty-first with that of his mother at Romano's starring Noël Coward. But this was the mid-sixties, not 1940. The times they were a-changing. Australia was becoming engulfed in the Vietnam War. In May 1965 Calwell gave what Menadue considered to be the greatest speech he ever heard in Parliament, written by Graham Freudenberg, who was Calwell's speech-writer and went on to become Gough's. In announcing that the ALP opposed sending eight hundred men to fight in Vietnam, Calwell said:

> I offer you the probability that you will be traduced, that your motives will be misrepresented, that your patriotism will be impugned, that your courage will be called into question. But I also offer you the sure and certain knowledge that we will be vindicated: that generations to come will record with gratitude that when a reckless government wilfully endangered the security of this nation, the voice of the Australian Labor Party was heard, strong and clear, on the side of sanity and in the cause of humanity and in the interests of Australia's security.

Gough, too, was firm in his insistence that the best way to end Australia's military commitment in Vietnam was to elect a Labor government. He was gaining great respect in the deputy leadership role and it was assumed that he would succeed Calwell. Margaret believed in his abilities absolutely, but she remained unimpressed by his uncontrolled outbreaks of temper, such as the one that occurred at 2.12 am on 30 September 1965. Laurie Oakes describes it:

> Whitlam rose to speak on a Labor amendment to a Repatriation Bill which aimed at extending repatriation benefits to more people, including Salvation Army members who'd served in combat areas. There'd been argument about the government forcing the House to sit so late. Members were tired and tempers were frayed. Paul Hasluck, the External

Affairs Minister, was sitting at the table. Whitlam knew that Hasluck's father was a retired Salvation Army chaplain. After scornfully mentioning that Hasluck never spoke on repatriation matters Whitlam said, 'If the Minister for External Affairs is prepared to deny his parents in voting against justice for Salvation Army personnel who have served with the forces, then I suppose we need not worry about persons with less propriety and pride voting against all the principles which they so loudly espoused during the daytime and on sacred occasions.'

As Whitlam sat down Hasluck leaned across the table and said quietly, 'You are one of the filthiest objects ever to come into the chamber.'

There followed what *Hansard* coyly dismissed as 'an incident'. Whitlam took up a glass of water and hurled the contents into Hasluck's face. For several seconds a stunned Hasluck sat quite still. Then with considerable dignity he took out his handkerchief and slowly wiped his face and clothing. There was uproar. The Chairman of Committee shouted for order but it was some time before order was restored. Whitlam was instructed to apologise and did so but demanded that Hasluck withdraw 'the unparliamentary and provocative terms which he used and which were heard by several of my colleagues'. He said of Hasluck's comment, 'It was too indecent. I will not repeat it.' Hasluck, in his apology, said, 'The remark was made in a personal and direct way, it was not part of the proceedings of Parliament.' During the rest of the debate Whitlam had to endure government members shouting 'Wetty Whitlam' at him across the chamber. Water Boy was another nickname with which he was instantly tagged. When he next spoke a day later he was subjected to more ridicule. But it was the impulsiveness of it which worried caucus members.

Apart from losing his temper, Gough was also losing his trust in the media. In 1965 he spent a fortnight in New Zealand with Margaret, Stephen and Catherine and during their stay in Dunedin he gave some journalists an 'off the record' briefing. Stephen remembers being in bed when a call came through from Australia asking his father whether he had really said that when there was next a ballot for the party leadership he would win it. One of the journalists had sent his comments back to Australia. Stephen remembers pretending he was asleep in the front room while his father, having summoned the offending journalist back to the house where they were staying, sat on the edge of his bed and abused him for leaking 'off-the-record' comments.

Gough's greatest clash, however, was with Calwell and the heads of the party machine over state and independent schools. Gough supported state aid for private schools. He described his approach as 'crash through or crash'. (A bit like his driving style.) Not only did it nearly cause his expulsion from the party, but it could have resulted in Margaret becoming the new member for Werriwa. On 15 February 1966 Gough gave an interview to Channel Seven's *Seven Days* program, in which he described the Federal Executive as 'incompetent and irresponsible', unable to understand policy, and made up of 'twelve witless men'. Furthermore, he attacked Calwell's leadership by saying that only a Whitlam-led Labor Party would beat the coalition.

A month later the Federal Executive charged him with disloyalty. Calwell was quoted as saying, 'We've got the numbers to get rid of the big bastard.' The numbers at that stage were seven to five against Whitlam, but Gough's successful campaigning in a recent Queensland by-election meant that the two Queensland delegates were ordered by the president of the Queensland ALP to vote against Calwell. Whitlam was ticked off with a reprimand, but Whitlam had stared them down and the ALP Federal Conference in July adopted the policy of federal aid for independent schools. Never once when under this kind of pressure did Gough lose his cool: he exuded confidence and composure.

Menadue asked him what he would have done if the numbers had gone against him and he had been expelled. Plan B would have been his resignation from Parliament. Then Margaret was to have stood as the new member for Werriwa. He assumed she would be elected as their MP. Then, when he was re-admitted to the party, she would stand down and he would come back. Of course, he had constructed this elaborate plan without Margaret's agreement, or even a tentative discussion with her. He simply assumed she would do whatever he told her. She said that she would probably have gone along with it – firstly to help Gough, and secondly because she would have thought it an interesting experience. Obviously Gough had no doubt that she could win the party endorsement and the seat because of her established contacts within the party and her high standing in the electorate. Clearly he also thought she was capable of doing the job (certainly with his help and direction).

John Menadue is of the view that with 'her strength, her warmth and her excellent commonsense [she] would have made a better politician than Gough'.

If she had become the MP for Werriwa he might have had some resistance from the electorate for replacing her with himself but that thought would, of course, never have crossed his mind. And Plan B was never tested.

Menadue is not the only person to have publicly voiced the view that Margaret would have made an excellent politician. Dame Leonie Kramer, former chair of the ABC and former chancellor of the University of Sydney, holds Margaret in very high esteem.

She is an outstanding person in her own right. She's very intelligent, very observant and she has a great deal of enthusiasm for a wide range of things. I see her as a natural leader. So, for example, she might have been a distinguished MP herself. I've no doubt she would have been better than Gough because she's more balanced. I see her as having potentially sacrificed a very important career to be his mentor. Maybe her great frailty was marrying Gough.

She's very courteous – by that I mean she always gives the impression that she's glad to see you. It's a very rare quality and it's genuine.

She always reminds you that it's a good idea to be open-minded. Just because you disagree with someone politically is no reason to make an enemy of them, and it's that quality in her that allows her to circulate so freely amongst whole ranges of people. She's got no prejudices about class – she wouldn't care if you were the boiler-maker's illegitimate daughter. It wouldn't worry her. She's able to tune into the other person's wavelength.

When Margaret was in her early fifties, people often asked her whether she was interested in entering politics and her standard reply was, 'Good heavens, no, I'm far too old.' Now she looks back on that comment and says, 'How ridiculous of me to say I was too old in my fifties. If I'd been a man I'd never have said that.'

However, neither fate nor the Federal Executive nor her husband placed such an opportunity in her path in the end. Nor did she ever contemplate it. Margaret was content to be a housewife, a wife, a mother and a part-time social worker.

THE LEADER

On 8 February 1967 Arthur Calwell lost another election and in April Gough Whitlam was elected leader of the ALP, with Lance Barnard as his deputy. Gough immediately created a shadow ministry, the first in Australian political history. Key shadow ministers had responsibility for a particular policy area, so that when they won government they would be ready to assume the ministry. The party mood swung from pessimism to optimism as, together with his colleagues and advisors, Gough set about preparing to win the 1969 election.

Now that he was finally leader, the media spotlight turned for the first time on Margaret. Prior to that she had been photographed standing beside him, or with the children, but little interest had been shown in her as an individual. It was time for her to emerge from the shadowy role into which most political wives are cast. Now that her husband was the Leader of the Opposition and a very commanding, tall and good-looking one at that, people were interested in whom he went home to at night. What they found was an equally tall, good-humoured, friendly, down-to-earth woman, who was very happy to chat about her husband and her children.

'Do come in, Father's on the telly,' were her cheery words of greeting to one journalist who, seeking her out at home, found her an 'attractive and impressive person'. Another saw her as 'a supremely contented woman with a highly developed sense of humour'. Margaret told them her life was full and satisfying. Cathy was at the local Cabramatta high school, Stephen was at Sydney Boys' High, Nick was soon to graduate from Harvard and Tony was about to be admitted to the New South Wales bar.

On 11 February 1967 *The Age* ran the headline 'WHITLAM JNR AT BAR' with a very cheerful photo of Gough in full QC's regalia standing next to Tony after he had been admitted to the Sydney bar, his admission having been moved by his grandfather, Mr Justice Dovey.

What the journalist didn't know was that Tony had said to his grandfather, who had been retired from the bench for two years and had dressed up just to move Tony's admission, that he would not be swearing an oath on the Bible in the traditional manner, he would be taking an affirmation.

'Oh no you won't; you won't be making a spectacle of me in front of my former colleagues. If you insist on that I'll return the brief,' said his grandfather. So Tony gave in to his wishes.

Mrs Whitlam sat in the court gallery together with friends and relatives of the thirty-eight solicitors and fifteen barristers admitted. While her father, her husband and her eldest son were centre stage in full regalia, Margaret was just another woman clapping in the audience. Not that she minded. In her SUDS days she had been used to minor roles or voice-overs and she was still happy simply to be part of the play.

So when she told those who interviewed her that she was content with her three-day-a-week job as a social worker and being president of the Cabravale Swimming Club, she was telling the truth.

When Catherine first went to school she had been asked to write a composition about her mother and she began it with the sentence, 'My mother is a giant'. She then went on to say that she was also 'a cook, a nurse and a swimming champion'.

As the inaugural president of the Cabravale Swimming Club, Margaret befriended all the parents, most of whom were other mothers, timed the races, organised the swimming carnivals and even arranged to buy the team's swimming costumes in bulk so she'd get them cheaper for everyone. She was a very enthusiastic member of the community. In her spare time she played tennis and golf, read books and went to the theatre, the ballet and the opera as often as she could.

When questioned about her husband's new position as leader of the Opposition she gave the expected and traditional answer that wives of prime ministers in Australia have always given: 'I will support my husband in whatever he chooses to do.'

She told one reporter, 'Father is the head of the house and what he wants to do everyone wants for him.' However, when she was asked whether she had any influence over her husband's political ideas, Margaret, who can't resist a good line, detoured from the predictable script. 'You must be joking. But if he gets out of line I give him a good thump, although he's bigger than me.'

She loves to have a bit of a laugh and can't stay earnest for long. She does admit now, though, that at this stage in Gough's political career she knew less about politics and his policies than she should have. Not that it would ever stop her giving an opinion.

Whenever she was asked about what they used to call 'women's lib' she always said it wasn't really for her and that she supported the traditional values of the family unit, with the mother at home. There was nothing smug about her contentment with cosy, family-based domesticity. She had worked hard to bring up her children in an unpretentious, warm, secure environment. When addressing the Girl Guides' Association she said, 'I am a spectator, a supporter, a goer-alonger, a washer of socks. I don't resent it at all, I'm very happy in the service.'

Margaret was, however, careful not to say anything to the press that would harm her husband's election chances.

> The first thing they ask a political wife is always about the children. 'How many do you have? Oh, how lovely. What do they do? Blah, blah, blah. And can we take a picture? Blah, blah, blah.' And then they try and slip in a political question. I'd had no political training, no media training. Thank God for the Penguin Club, which gave me some confidence. Mostly I just answered, 'Well, of course, I'm not the politician.' Then, sometimes they'd do a bit of homework and ask me, 'Weren't you a swimmer?' And I'd say, yes, and go through my swimming history, and they'd think that was a big scoop. Gough never spoke to me about it – he just trusted me to say the right thing.

Whenever a journalist asked her what she thought about her husband becoming prime minister she'd say, 'Wouldn't that be marvellous?' (What did they expect her to say?)

'People made up their own minds about you and no matter what you said they wouldn't move from their prejudices. Gough was challenging over twenty years of conservative rule in the country and some people were very threatened by him.'

Margaret remembers a friend telling her that after she left the local store one day, a woman had said, 'Do you know who that was? She's the wife of the biggest communist in Sydney.'

She hated it when her kids told her of playground taunts about their father being a communist. Catherine was often late coming home from school and when Margaret asked her where she had been, she once replied, 'Oh, I had to fight a kid after school who'd said something awful about Dad.' As the youngest Catherine probably had the toughest time because she bore the name of Whitlam while her father was in the full glare of the media spotlight.

Once he became leader, Margaret was expected to attend more functions and to travel with him. She quite liked it but Catherine would complain, 'You're not going out again tonight, are you? Why do you have to go out with Dad?'

Margaret would say, 'Because I married your father, not you.'

She says now, 'Catherine told me recently she was quite hurt by that exclusion. She always replied, "Well, if you have to go, bring me back something lovely," which could be anything from a bag of peanuts to a balloon.'

Catherine says her mother never forgot to bring her something. She needed it as a demonstration that Margaret was thinking about her.

Now Gough was leader Margaret decided to leave her job at the Parramatta Hospital – she thought it wouldn't be fair on her employer for her to be away so much. Gough's salary had improved as deputy leader and he no longer had to supplement it with legal work on Mondays and Fridays. He was a specialist in tenancy – not very riveting law, but it was regular work and it paid the bills. Now that he was leader his salary had improved again.

In January 1968 Margaret and Gough went to Cambodia, Japan, South Vietnam and Jakarta as part of an Asian tour. Margaret's duties included visits to schools, orphanages and hospitals. They took Stephen and Graham Freudenberg, Gough's press secretary, who shared a room. After one stopover, Graham took the bags to the airport while Stephen waited in his room for his parents to pick him up. Forty-five minutes after Graham left, Stephen received a phone call from his father asking him why he wasn't at the airport. They had assumed he had left with Graham and hadn't bothered to check his room. The problem of getting Stephen to the airport quickly was solved by providing him with a police escort. Stephen thought the sirens were worth the nagging suspicion that his parents had left him behind.

In June, July and August of 1968 Gough and Margaret took advantage of the mid-year break in Parliament to introduce themselves to even more of the world and they went on a whirlwind tour of America and Europe. Margaret's diary is a directory of where they went, what they saw, whom they met, where they ate, what they ate, and, in the evenings, what plays, films, operas, concerts and dinners they attended. It is tiring just to read it.

While Gough was in various cities doing formal business, Margaret caught up with Nick at Harvard, and after he had graduated in June, they travelled through Europe on rail passes. The two of them love the same things and every day was packed with sightseeing, eating marvellous food at reasonable prices and seeing theatre performances in the evening. In order to save money they sometimes shared a room, which was fine until one day their luggage was lost. Margaret washed everything they were wearing and went to bed in a sheet wound round her like a toga. Nick slept in his underpants. When she opened the door the next morning to the young woman who brought the breakfast she realised why the girl was staring at her. She was standing there wrapped in nothing but a sheet and Nick was still asleep in his underpants.

'My son is still asleep,' she said, taking the tray from the French woman, who gave her a look that said, 'Who do you think you are kidding?' Needless to say, unlike the Frenchwoman, she was highly amused.

They went on to spend several weeks in London, where Nick was starting a masters degree at the London Business School. Margaret then flew to New York to see Tony, who was currently working there. While the trip was full of excitement and interest, she wrote in a diary of her trip:

> Leaving New York – I sit in the back of the plane, alone – I think how good it is to be Australian and to be going home. [And this was long before Peter Allen wrote the song Qantas used as its theme song – 'I Still Call Australia Home']. I ate in places NY people eat – I went to the movies ($2 for a morning session at the locals), I walked to and from the subways and buses and I saw Leslie Uggams in a Broadway show. But I like being middle-aged and looking it. I like being antipodean. I feel sorry for my age-sakes: those incredible American women who can't bear to look more than ten years older than their daughters, who don't even like their husbands. That's not for me. Here I am travelling on our national airline getting the best care I've had anywhere. The menu cards even have splendid early Australian etchings on the cover.

But, ever present, were thoughts of her children. 'Leaving one son in London was a bit of a wrench . . . Now I've left another one in NYC. At least I'm on my way to my young ones at home.'

In October 1968 Gough spoke at the Federal Labor Women's Conference, in his role as an outer-suburban family man. While it is true that he was the first Labor leader who had ever represented the outer suburbs, it was Margaret who had organised the building of two houses there, raised four children there and arranged for them to travel twenty miles to a high school and twelve miles to a swimming pool (before she helped build one in Cabramatta). Margaret, who had always loved reading, had lived where there were few municipal libraries, no paved roads within a mile of their houses and no paved footpaths.

Gough, it was true, knew of these disadvantages, but Margaret had battled with them on a day-to-day basis. Her experiences were a major factor in helping Gough emphasise the need for a federal government to take responsibility for providing these facilities as other countries had done.

In December 1968 and January 1969 Stephen, Catherine and Graham Freudenberg accompanied Gough and Margaret on another tour, which included Egypt, Europe and North America. Stephen records in his memoir that on their second night in Athens when they were all waiting for their car outside their hotel, Nick, who had joined them for the European segment, suddenly fell backwards onto the pavement. Margaret screamed, thinking he had been stabbed. He quickly regained consciousness and was taken up to his room. A doctor was urgently called and after examining Nick, explained to his parents that he had fainted from exhaustion, and that he had probably been burning the candle at both ends prior to meeting them. Margaret's travel diary says, 'Last night we never made it to the taverna because Nick fainted on the doormat, literally as we were leaving the hotel. Gough, poor dear, thought he was dead of a heart attack.' (No mention of her theory.)

In Rome, two days after Christmas, they experienced the old Italian rip-off. Gough had gone to bed, and Margaret and the boys had popped into the bar of the hotel for a last drink. The bill arrived and it was clearly a ridiculous amount for what they'd had. Nick tried quiet persuasion, Graham followed with loud protests and finally thumped the table, which was made of glass – unseen because of the cloth – and broke it in two, the shattered pieces falling to the floor with their glasses of wine.

Margaret writes, 'As a body we all moved to the bar, where there was a surface on which to base an argument, and in a few moments the bill was halved. We all backed away satisfied but still muttering, scrambled into the lift, which fortunately came quickly, and exploded into pent-up laughter.'

After the tragic drowning of Liberal Party leader Harold Holt in December 1967, John Gorton was elected as his successor. Labor should have seized the advantage of a change in Liberal leadership, particularly since the ballot had revealed deep splits within the government: John McEwen, the leader of the Country Party, had threatened to end the coalition if Billy McMahon was elected as the Liberal leader.

But Gorton, a bit of a maverick, rarely took on Whitlam in Parliament, which was Whitlam's strongest battle field. Gough was also preoccupied with trying to reform the Victorian branch of the ALP. His efforts resulted in his resignation, after which he had to recontest the leadership. The gesture backfired and he eventually only won it back by thirty-eight votes to Jim Cairns's thirty-two, failing to break the Victorians' stranglehold on power.

Nevertheless, the election campaign Gough fought in October 1969 was considered by everyone in the party to be outstanding. His theatrical experience in university revues came to the fore on the hustings, where his timing was impeccable and his jokes against Gorton were a huge success. All those visits to observe Bob Hope had clearly paid off.

The main domestic policies that he proposed to initiate were a national health insurance fund to be based on a 1.75 per cent levy on taxable income, a National Schools Commission to recommend grants for both government and independent schools on a needs basis, automatic pension increases, a subsidy to institutional lenders to reduce housing interest rates, the establishment of an Urban Affairs Department and a promise to withdraw all Australian troops from Vietnam by June 1970 and to end conscription.

Margaret was personally involved in the campaign to the extent that the party allowed. She said she had enjoyed the pre-election period because she had felt useful. She now began to flex a few feminist muscles that she didn't even know she had. She coordinated a group that called itself ALPS – a sorority for political wives and party supporters. Suddenly she was in demand to speak and she had decided to speak the truth from her own point of view.

She really thought there was a definite chance they were going to make it. She had focused on all aspects of the election and had absorbed and approved of all Gough's policy initiatives. Knowing how hard he had worked to reform the party, and how well the election campaign had gone with him at the helm, she allowed herself to believe this might be 'the one'.

On election night, as the results rolled in and the supporters ate and drank to excess in the Whitlam's back garden in Cabramatta, victory certainly seemed possible. News came that they had gained back all the seats lost in Calwell's 1966 disaster, but when the final call came through, the ALP was four seats short of winning power.

Margaret was characteristically stoic and didn't let anyone see what she was really feeling. But after everyone had left the party at Cabramatta Stephen observed her standing alone in the dark, in the backyard, crying. 'I think she just thought, After all we've done, after all we've tried to do, we didn't win. The bastards won. It's one of the few occasions I can ever remember her crying. It's very rare.'

Margaret says she thinks it was more likely that she was simply crying from exhaustion. All she remembers from that election night is Mungo MacCallum, who was at that stage a journalist in the Canberra press gallery, banging his head against the wall in fury at the result. This was the election that inspired the nation's most popular playwright, David Williamson, to write the play *Don's Party*, which was not only a huge stage success but went on to be made into a popular film.

The 1969 election in Australia took place in the aftermath of the international social upheaval that had occurred in 1968. Apart from the sex, drugs and rock 'n' roll of the youth culture that had emerged, 1968 was the year of the assassinations of Bobby Kennedy and Martin Luther King, the Prague Spring, the Chicago Convention, the Tet offensive in Vietnam, the anti-war movement, the civil rights movement, the student rebellion that paralysed France, the beginning of the end for the Soviet Union and the birth of the women's movement.

Rebellion, change and protest were in the air, and significant sections of population all over the globe refused to be silent about the things that were wrong with the world. Gough Whitlam was in tune with the times. Many pundits now argue that the 1969 election was more decisive than that of the 1972 in bringing Labor to victory.

In December 1969 newspaper posters all over Sydney announced 'DEAD . . . FAMOUS JUDGE'. Underneath the headline was a large photo of Margaret's father. He had been admitted to St Vincent's Hospital in Darlinghurst because of his advanced emphysema and Margaret had been visiting him on a daily basis. When he became very ill and was taken to the intensive care ward the nurses and the doctor said to her, 'There's no point in visiting him, he won't know you. Don't come in to see him anymore, it's only a matter of days.'

Margaret says now:

> I really wanted to go in and just sit with him, but they convinced me not to go. No doubt they thought they were protecting me from the worst, but it's the greatest regret of my life that I didn't go. When Bishop Hulme-Moir, who conducted the funeral service, came to see me after Pa died, he told me that he'd been in to see him in intensive care in the last days. He said to Pa, 'Bill, if you know I'm here, just squeeze my hand.' And Pa squeezed his hand. And I thought, Oh, God, that could have been my hand.

Her beloved Pa, her greatest admirer, her tower of strength, was gone. She was bereft and so were her children.

Her father was seventy-five when he died and Nick had just turned twenty-four. Margaret wrote to him in New York and he still treasures the letter. It reads: 'I know you will be sad that you haven't seen him over the past years but think of the good times – the grand times – you had with him as a little boy and a young man. And remember his pride in you.' As well as teaching her son how to deal with his grief and his sense of loss, she was also teaching herself.

By focusing on the good times they had shared and remembering his pride in her, she gradually came to terms with her father's absence from her life. She knew that he would never have wanted her to dwell on his passing.

Her mother, however, normally so in control, found it very difficult to get over her husband's death. Distraught with grief, she would take herself to bed with the many long and loving letters he had written to her during World War I and when they were apart on her trip to London for the Coronation. She would read them alone to herself, rationing them to one a night, and weep over them.

Eventually she sold the house in Vaucluse and bought herself a flat in nearby Rose Bay, close to shops and transport, so she could resume the various activities with which she filled her life without him.

Now that Margaret no longer worked and could spend more time in Canberra, she and Gough rented a government flat in Manuka, with two bedrooms so that any of the children could stay. Here, Margaret proceeded to make a little haven for herself and Gough, away from the public glare.

She was now more focused on her husband's political life than she had ever been, but she had become somewhat disillusioned with what she was realising were the expectations placed on a politician's wife. In an interview in 1969 she foreshadowed her challenge to the traditional role. 'I do believe that people have come to realise that wives of politicians are personalities in their own right. It's true that in earlier years we were not such outgoing people and perhaps now we are becoming a bit more brazen.'

Well, Margaret certainly was. She even began to give Gough the benefit of her advice. When he was agonising over when Papua and New Guinea should be given independence she remarked, 'You don't ask a baby when it wants to be weaned. You decide yourself and do it.'

Clearly he liked her analogy because he announced that he would tour Papua and New Guinea during the 1969–70 Christmas recess of Parliament. The government allowed him to use an RAAF VIP plane and he took four journalists from Australia's major newspapers with him. On the plane he briefed them regarding his plans to make the territory self-governing by 1973, if he won the 1972 election.

When he returned he continued his attack on Australia's role as a colonial power and outlined what lay ahead were he to become prime minister.

> We are a European nation on the fringe of the most populous and deprived coloured nations in the world. What the world sees about Australia is that we have an Aboriginal population with the highest infant mortality rate on earth; that we have eagerly supported the most unpopular war in modern times on the grounds that Asia should be a battleground of our freedom; that we fail to oppose the sale of arms to South Africa; that the whole world believes our immigration policy is based on colour and that we run one of the world's last colonies.

Australia had been governed by a conservative coalition government since 1949 and Gough's speech exploded onto the front pages of all the newspapers in the country, resulting in fervent discussion in every board room and around every kitchen table. Margaret knew that were he to become prime minister she would be caught up in the controversy that his radical policies ignited.

In 1970 Margaret joined the panel of a popular television series called *Beauty and the Beast*, where a group of well-known women

LEFT Margaret's mother, Mary Duncan, aged seventeen, wrapped in tulle, 1910
RIGHT Her father, Wilfred Dovey – a budding barrister, 1935

TOP Margaret at eighteen months in her first swimming costume, 1921

BOTTOM Cutie-pie, aged three

TOP A demure-looking Mary Dovey and her son, William, 1924

BOTTOM Margaret aged four in her fairy dress

TOP RIGHT Nine-year-old Margaret with her brother, Willie, aged five

MIDDLE The Dovey children with their proud father

BOTTOM RIGHT Margaret as house captain at a SCEGGS sports day

TOP Collecting a good haul of swimming trophies

BOTTOM The winner of a Saturday-night swimming competition

A Sunday morning sun-baking at Bondi, 1936

Skating with cousin 'Bunty' (Gordon Cheers) at the Glacierium

Margaret the jolly giant at the 1937 SCEGGS Christmas play

RIGHT Margaret and her mother shopping in King Street, Sydney, 1937

MIDDLE Star-struck at university

BOTTOM Après-ski in Kosciusko, 1928, although Margaret *(far left)* looks more of a sun-bunny next to her friends Peg King and Bet Adamson

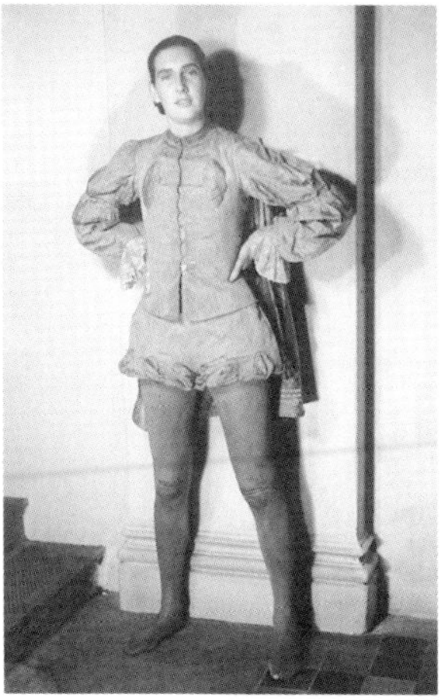

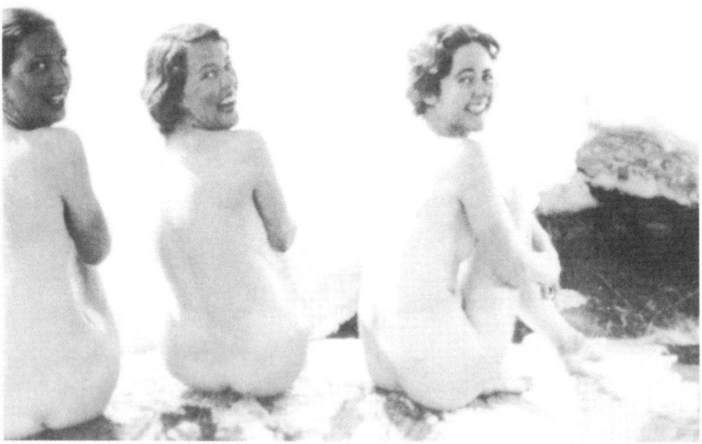

Margaret making her debut aged eighteen at Sydney Town Hall. Receiving her are (*left to right*) Lord Huntingfield, Administrator of the Commonwealth, and Lord Wakehurst, Governor of New South Wales.

A portrait of Margaret for her twenty-first birthday

Gough and Margaret sign up for married life at St Michael's church in Vaucluse with Canon Arthur Garnsey, 1942

The wedding group on the steps of St Michael's. *Front row, left to right*: Dick Harris, Freda Whitlam, Gough and Margaret, Rag Holmes, Sonya Ashton (née Johnston). *Back row*: Fred Whitlam, Bill Dovey, Mattie Whitlam, Mary Dovey

TOP Antony Whitlam's baptism, 1944. *Back row, left to right*: Margaret's Aunt Rita, her grandmother Mardi, Wilfred Dovey, Gough's parents, Martha and Fred. *Front row*: Mary Dovey, Willie, Margaret and Antony, Gough, Freda, Lex Goudie, an RAAF pilot friend of Gough's, and Aunty Dotsie (Claire Cheers)

RIGHT Margaret with Nicholas at his christening, 1946

'You're mine' – little Tony with his parents

Margaret with the boys outside their half-finished house at Cronulla, 1947

LEFT On the way to Circular Quay to catch a ferry to the zoo. Tony is two and a half; Nick, in the cuddle-seat, is six months old.

MIDDLE Stephen with his favourite bear

BOTTOM LEFT A father's treat: Wilfred Dovey takes his daughter and his wife to the Melbourne Cup.

TOP Margaret and her three sons: Stephen, Nick and Tony

RIGHT A girl at last! Proud grandparents Wilfred and Mary Dovey with Catherine, 1954

BOTTOM The back of the Whitlams' new house in Cabramatta, 1956

LEFT Margaret getting the garden in order in her thongs

BOTTOM LEFT Visiting Father Christmas: Nick, Tony, Stephen and Catherine

BOTTOM RIGHT Tony and his baby sister

TOP 'Let's have another swim': Catherine and her mother

RIGHT Catherine aged fourteen with Margaret

Another Whitlam makes it to the bar: Tony with Gough and Leslie Herron, the Chief Justice of New South Wales, 1967

acted as agony aunts in contrast to the beast, who was John Laws, the popular commercial radio presenter. The newspaper columnists described Margaret as 'zippy, zingy and uninhibited' in her approach to problems like noisy neighbours and why husbands leave home.

In an interview with *The Sun-Herald* after the first show went to air she immediately referred to the fact that her size was not a handicap on television. She was obviously self-consciously aware of the physical difference that set her apart from the other panel members. The article was headed, 'Tall Girl Makes it as Beauty' and indeed the journalist made it clear that Margaret was 'not so much large, as tall. Very tall. But,' he wrote almost patronisingly, 'her inches aren't handicapping her.'

Of course everyone wanted to know what her husband thought of her performance. Margaret explained that he hadn't seen the show as he didn't have time to watch daytime television and, she continued in her typical self-deprecating style, 'Just as well because I thought I was dreadful. I was terribly nervous and didn't know what I was meant to be doing.'

And how, they asked, did she find the so-called beast, John Laws?

'He was a surprise. He is both charming and intelligent and you don't always get those together,' she replied, revealing more about her general opinion of men than she realised.

Margaret enjoyed her early experiences on television – her love of amateur dramatics from her university days was still very much a part of her personality. Gough certainly expressed no concern over these forays into television and always encouraged her attempts to expand her horizons.

Nor was Margaret the only one in the Whitlam family to be involved in entertainment programs on television. Stephen had won a considerable amount of money from appearing on the TV quiz show *Pick-A-Box* and when his father asked him what he was going to do with his winnings he told him he was going to marry Sheena, who had been his sweetheart since he was fifteen. Gough told him he thought he was too young and was not really in a position to support a wife, and Margaret expressed the same opinion. But Stephen had it all worked out and clinched the argument by saying that it was ALP policy to give eighteen-year-olds full adult status and he was nearly twenty. And, as he reminded his parents, Gough had married Margaret when he was in his early twenties.

Neither Margaret nor Gough believed they had a right to interfere in their children's lives or their choices once they were adults and so the marriage went ahead, and a year later Margaret and Gough became grandparents to Alexander Whitlam. Stephen went on to become a trainee in the Department of Foreign Affairs in Canberra and from there took a first posting to Geneva in 1972.

On 28 June 1971 Gough took a Labor Party delegation to China. They left Australia telling the press that their general objective was 'to see how far the people of China and the people of Australia are able to talk to each other'. The anti-communists went berserk.

In the Great Hall of the People in Beijing Whitlam was invited to conduct a conversation with Premier Chou En-lai in front of the Chinese and Australian media. He knew that everything that was said would be reported, not just in Australia but all around the world.

Billy McMahon, the Minister of Foreign Affairs, was still refusing to open diplomatic relations with China and had attacked Whitlam's delegation, claiming that during Chou's conversation with Gough, Chou had shared his opinion on how President

Nixon should run his administration, and stressing how impertinent En-Lai was. A day later, Nixon announced that he, too, would visit China within ten months. Gough could not stop himself from laughing at his opponent's gaffe. Neither could the media.

Now that Margaret was free to travel with Gough, it was decided that Catherine would spend her last two years of secondary school boarding at Frensham, a private girls' school in the Southern Highlands, halfway between Sydney and Canberra. Although Catherine loved Cabramatta High and wasn't enamoured with the idea of the elitist culture of a private girls' school, she could see that it was a sensible arrangement. In fact she made several lifelong friends at Frensham. Despite her jokes with Margaret about how she was the 'neglected' child, she admits that like all the other Whitlam children she always felt very much loved by both her parents and her brothers.

Rupert Murdoch was one of the most powerful and influential newspaper magnates in Australia and when John Menadue had left Whitlam's staff in 1967 he had begun working for News Limited. Now, he was keen to get Whitlam and Murdoch together. While you would imagine that anyone aspiring to be prime minister of any country in which Murdoch had control of large sections of the press would be keen to have him on their side, Menadue said that Whitlam was uneasy and mistrustful of Murdoch.

Menadue finally arranged a dinner for the Whitlams and Murdoch in July 1971 and reported that 'the dinner conversation was polite but cool'. Then, in September 1971, Murdoch invited

Gough and Margaret to his country property at Cavan near Canberra as overnight guests. According to Menadue Gough told him that it was 'one of the most excruciatingly boring nights of his life'. Margaret's response to this comment was, 'He probably said that because he wasn't the centre of attention – perhaps people actually preferred to talk to me and listen to my opinions for a change. I've always found Rupert Murdoch to be a most charming and hospitable person.'

Once again, she was not afraid to voice opinions different from her husband's. She always made up her own mind about the people she met and no doubt her complimentary opinion of Rupert Murdoch was her own. But it was also an antidote to her husband's views, which would not have endeared him to the man who had the power to back him in his ambition to become prime minister. Gough's refusal to bow to this power was no doubt admirable in some senses, but foolhardy in others.

Despite Whitlam's dismissive behaviour Menadue knew that Murdoch wanted to support the ALP in the 1972 election because 'He didn't like McMahon and he saw Whitlam as a winner.'

In December 1971 *The Sunday Australian*, Murdoch's newest baby, ran a full-page interview with Margaret by the celebrated journalist Geraldine Pascall. Pascall spent a couple of days trailing about with Margaret, reporting on her everyday life in Cabramatta. She called her article 'Labor's Leading Lady'.

When Pascall reached 'Whitlam territory' this sophisticated Sydney journalist described what she saw as 'regulation models in fibro and brick of the new Australian dream [that] squat on their quarter-acre lots. And beyond this red-brick horizon you know they'll keep going. It's hot, at least 10 degrees hotter than the sea-cooled city and the air grazes your lips with a fine saffron dust.'

And just in case the reader didn't already know, Pascall detailed the facts of Margaret's life: 'She has lived here since 1957, is a member of the ALP and its women's conference, a branch delegate to the Federal Electoral Council, does a lot of constituent work, is a trained social worker with a practical concern for everyday problems and the sharp edge of inadequate health services and economic insecurity.'

Margaret answered her questions seriously and confirmed that at the last Federal Labor Conference she got the party to change the term 'child-minding centres' to 'child-care centres' because the difference between minding and caring for children is a huge one.

Pascall picked up immediately on Margaret's 'slight self-deprecating tone matched by a sense of humour that mocks human absurdities'. Her aim, of course, was to find out how much her opinions were hers and how much her husband's. Margaret was firm on this one. 'Gough and I agree on basics but my opinions are my own. I can see no reason why I can't express them, as an individual, here or in New York or London. Sometimes he explains things to me but he doesn't try to impose his ideas. I don't have any bandwagons, but I do want to make people aware that the alternative government is not unattractive. Gough wants to do things for Australia and the only way he can do that is as leader of the government.'

The interview covered all Margaret's interests – the ones she'd had since she was at school and still had – books, theatre, food, wine, clothes, music. Pascall summed her up thus: 'Upper-class background but a deep social conscience; strong individual personality and a traditional commitment to husband and family.'

What amused Margaret most, she admitted to the journalist, was the alarm that some people were expressing at the imminent possibility of a Labor government. 'They seem to think something frightfully obscene is going to happen. I usually tease them, "Come on now, you'll be right. We'll look after you when the revolution comes."'

Pascall was clearly won over by her and concluded: 'Whatever way the votes fall, Margaret Whitlam is the best public-relations agent Gough could have.' It was a very positive, full-page endorsement of 'Gough's secret weapon', as the media began to call her.

By the time Pascall's interview appeared on the front page of *The Sunday Australian Review*, Margaret, Gough, Catherine, Gough's sister, Freda, and Gough's staff were already in Tehran on their Christmas holiday, making the most of the parliamentary break. The highlight for Margaret of this trip to the Middle East was meeting Golda Meir, the Prime Minister of Israel. Here is an excerpt from her personal diary:

> Golda was great. Standing in the centre of the room she made a stocky figure all in black – with lace-up shoes, black dress and jacket. When we sat down, however, she assumed a commanding air. She has big, strong hands which are used a lot as she talks in her rich American accent. No artificial aids grace her face and figure, but her hair, her face, her hands, her clothes are spotless and of the best quality. We liked her. We think she liked us. She gave us more than an hour of her time and a cup of coffee while she, the only smoker, had three cigarettes.

As the 1972 election loomed larger and Margaret took on an increasingly public role, the ALP campaign organisers finally discovered that her warmth, her charm and her wit may well overcome some voters' perceptions of her husband as cold and distant.

The more she travelled around the country with Gough, the more she understood why he was so passionate about the changes he wanted to implement for his country, and the more she wanted to win. Margaret, the champion swimmer, did not want to come second in this race. Highly competitive when she chose to be, she met every criticism of her husband or his policies head-on.

Mick Young, the new ALP Federal Secretary, had taken over the coordination and planning of the election campaign. About three weeks before the election Young and Menadue suggested to Rupert Murdoch that they organise a cruise on the harbour with the Whitlams. Murdoch was returning from overseas to be in Australia prior to and during the election campaign. He was agreeable, but Gough refused. 'I'm too fucking busy to see Rupert.' When they continued to press him he said, 'I'm not going, but will Margaret do?'

Margaret, of course, had not been consulted, but Gough knew that she would fulfil any obligation that was asked of her and that she would be a witty and sociable guest. Finally, however, he was persuaded to attend with Margaret and, no doubt on her instructions, on the day was courteous and relaxed.

Mick Young also coordinated an Australia-wide series of public meetings at which Gough spoke and Margaret either sat on the stage with the local dignitaries or in the front row of the audience. The 'It's Time' theme song, chorused by all the leading artists in the country, among them Little Patty, Bert Newton and David Williamson, captured the public mood. Everywhere Gough went and spoke he received standing ovations, and wild and enthusiastic cheering. The time was right for him and he aimed to seize it in both hands.

Margaret was always by his side at these huge public events but during the day she visited many organisations and gave numerous interviews to print journalists, and on radio and television. She spoke openly about her husband, describing him as a good-hearted family man with a very dry sense of humour, who was totally committed to effecting the policies that he had taken all these years to plan and perfect. She assured them that a Labor victory would not usher in a socialist revolution and to be suspicious of such predictions by those who assumed they were 'born to rule'.

When she was asked by *The Australian* for her opinion of Sonia McMahon, the glamorous wife of the incumbent prime minister, who had recently caused such a stir by wearing a full-length sheath dress slit to the thigh, but who rarely spoke publicly, Margaret replied, 'I'm a different age, a different shape and a different person. My main decoration is, I suppose, my conversation.' It was honest, pithy and to the point.

There was a real sense that the country was on the brink of a huge change and Gough was to be the catalyst and the facilitator. He was not only able to develop radical policies, but to explain them patiently to the voters. The fact that Gorton had been replaced by Billy McMahon meant that the comparison of the two leaders – one tall, youthful, commanding; the other short, big-eared and unconvincing – was a positive factor for Labor's campaign. Television was by now a powerful political tool and while the cameras loved Gough, they were cruel to Billy.

On 2 December 1972 Gough Whitlam led the Labor Party to victory after twenty-three years of Liberal–Country Party government. Margaret, Gough and family, selected friends, staffers and journalists spent the evening in the salubrious Sunnybrook Motel in Cabramatta watching the results come in on television. When it was clear that they had won they cracked open a few bottles of champagne and then walked to their home two blocks away, where the traditional election night party, having been orchestrated by Margaret while on the trail, was in full celebratory swing. The mood was ecstatic.

Illuminated by flashing light bulbs, facing a huge bank of thrusting microphones and television cameras Gough said, 'It is clear that the majority given by New South Wales, Victoria and Tasmania is so substantial that the government will have a very good mandate to carry out all its policies . . . We are, of course, very much aware of the responsibility with which the people have now entrusted us.' He was remarkably calm and showed no obvious signs of excitement or elation, other than to thank all those who sought to congratulate him. Margaret stood nearby, laughing and looking proudly at him.

Thirty years ago she had married a law student. Now she was the wife of the Prime Minister of Australia. She couldn't really believe it had finally happened, but Gough clearly could. Already he seemed preoccupied with the task ahead. They stayed celebrating for a while, until they could slip quietly away to be ready to catch an early plane to Canberra on an RAAF VIP jet.

When the plane landed at Fairbairn RAAF base the cheering crowds were already there to greet them. Instead of going to their flat Gough went to Parliament House for a meeting with Lance Barnard, his deputy, and Margaret continued on in the car to book into the Lakeside Hotel. Twice on their journey the car had to stop because of the crush of overexcited supporters and Gough had to get out and speak to them before they cleared the road for him to pass. Margaret couldn't believe what she was seeing. All she could do was wave at everyone through the car window like the Queen. She kept laughing at the mere thought of it.

Unless you were living in Australia at that time it is hard to explain or perhaps even understand the elation and the euphoria that accompanied Gough and Margaret's arrival at the Lodge.

They knew that such high expectations, such heady idealism, are almost impossible to live up to, but they were both determined to give it their best shot.

After years of being assigned and cheerfully accepting small parts, walk-ons or even voices-off, at the age of fifty-three Margaret was now standing tall on centre stage. The eyes of the nation were upon her. When anyone takes on a public role they become the subject of both professional and amateur critics. Talk-back radio provides a voice for those who have no other outlet for their opinions, both informed and ignorant. Margaret would have to learn how to accept the praise and the adulation, together with 'the slings and arrows.'

Being seen and not heard, like Bettina Gorton, was not her style, but her main problem was that there was no prescribed role. There was not even a proper title like the Americans had for their 'First Ladies'. Without a job description, or even a series of vague guidelines, the wives of Australian prime ministers simply had to make it up as they went along, each according to her personality.

In the previous twenty-three years of conservative rule, the wives of prime ministers had seen their role merely as an extension of their existing roles of wife and mother. Dame Pattie Menzies was very firm in this belief and never wavered from standing behind her husband and supporting him in whatever way she could. She never made any political comments, at least not publicly. Yet Menzies' biographers are agreed that behind the public mask there lurked an entirely different private person who, as Langmore says, 'was his greatest debunker: she frequently took him apart, and he listened to her criticisms . . . There was a steely strength behind the starry blue eyes, the smiling face and the vivacious manner.'

Zara Holt, on the other hand, freely admitted that she knew nothing about politics, nor did it worry her, and she spent most of her two years in the Lodge redecorating it. She was constantly referred to by the press as 'bubbly', 'zany', 'daffy', 'effervescent' and generally lacking pomposity and pretension.

Zara and Margaret got along extremely well. 'Zara was very nice. Good fun. You could always have a joke with her. She never carried on with any side. And she used to wear those wonderful caftans which she initiated for formal wear.'

Margaret took me to her wardrobe and showed me the caftans she'd had for nearly forty years. Her favourite is a batik design made from very light Australian wool. She has another one from Bali in extremely solid cotton but she swears it was made from a bedcover originally. 'Look,' she said, 'it's still got all those border rings on it that bedcovers have.' She didn't care, she's still wearing it.

The press were more interested in Sonia McMahon's dresses than her opinions, not that she seemed very keen to offer any, especially not those associated with politics.

Women in public roles always attract comment and criticism focused on the way they look. This was particularly unfortunate for Margaret now because she was just becoming menopausal. 'I was a late starter and an early finisher. I never had the hot flushes. I just got fat,' she says. It seemed particularly unfair at a time when the fashion was fitted dresses that were belted around the waist. Whenever she could she wore jackets over the dresses and she embraced the caftan as demonstrated by Zara Holt, but even that was sometimes the subject of jibes.

On 5 December Gough called on the Governor-General, Sir Paul Hasluck, to accept a commission to form a government. At 2 pm he issued a statement announcing the fact that as it would be at least another week before the counting of votes could be completed, and therefore it would not be possible or proper for the federal parliamentary party to meet before 18 December, His Excellency had agreed that he and Lance Barnard would in the interim form a two-man government. Accordingly at 3.15 that afternoon Gough was sworn in as Prime Minister and Minister responsible for twelve other portfolios, with Barnard responsible for fourteen other portfolios.

When they returned to Parliament House they set in train the end of conscription, the remittance of jail sentences and fines against national service objectors and plans to enable national servicemen in the army in Vietnam to be discharged. Gough also announced the first step towards the recognition of China. At the end of his first press conference as Prime Minister he said:

> The change of government provides a new opportunity for us to reassess a whole range of Australian foreign policy and attitudes . . . the general direction of my thinking is towards a more independent Australian stance in international affairs, an Australia which will be less militarily-oriented and not open to suggestions of racism; an Australia which will enjoy a growing standing as a distinctive, tolerant, cooperative and well-regarded nation, not only in the Asian and Pacific region, but in the world at large.

This speech is important because it shows that Gough saw himself and Margaret as Australian emissaries, taking this new image of Australia all over the world. Their many trips overseas were largely spent meeting and greeting leaders from as many countries as they could possibly cram into an itinerary, in order to establish the 'new' Australia that Gough hoped to create and establish. Prime Minister Menzies had travelled a lot too, but mostly to Britain to see the Queen and watch the cricket, as he saw Australia still very much tied to the mother country.

Gough wanted not to eliminate those ties, but to expand them throughout the world. This was his vision as a leader, formed in the days when his father, returning from the United Nations as Australia's representative, would discuss them with his son.

He had been waiting twenty years to implement these policies and, already an impatient man, he took the nation's breath away when in the first four days of the two-man government, it excluded Australia from competition with all racially selected sporting teams, abolished both the sales tax on contraceptives and the wine tax (perhaps Margaret had influenced him here?), introduced new benefits for the armed forces (based on his own experience as a returned serviceman), discontinued mining leases on Aboriginal reserves in the Northern Territory and applied for the equal-pay case to be opened.

The following week the pace quickened (if that was possible) and twenty-eight more announcements were made, including the establishment of an interim Schools Commission, a judicial enquiry into Aboriginal land rights, to be conducted by Mr Justice Woodward, the appointment of Elizabeth Evatt as the first female president of the Conciliation and Arbitration Commission and the withdrawal of the last Australian troops from Vietnam.

Some Australians were shocked, others exhilarated at the speed of the radical changes that were sweeping the country. *The Sydney Morning Herald* introduced a special panel on its front page listing 'What the Government Did Today'. Margaret worried that Gough had been planning these policies for so long that he would forget that to most Australians who had become attuned to the steady foxtrot of conservatism, he was rock 'n' roll.

Rupert Murdoch hosted a dinner in Sydney to celebrate their victory. Sir John Kerr, then Chief Justice of New South Wales, attended with his first wife, Peg. Murdoch invited Katherine Graham, the publisher of the *Washington Post*, to the dinner, but neither of them knew how difficult it had been for Menadue to get Gough there. His initial reaction to the invitation had been, 'Comrade, I am not a national exhibit.' Everyone, however, enjoyed the evening.

The term 'comrade', which Gough regularly used with members of the Labor Party, began, Margaret says, as an ironic form of address. If some people viewed him as a flag-waving communist then it was his private joke to use the term that communists used. It was an example of his love of self-mockery. Unfortunately, some people took him literally, both outside and inside the Labor Party, and never really understood his use of irony. You certainly never heard Gough using the term 'mate', which seems to have become de rigeur for all politicians, and many Australian men.

Similarly, Gough changed the formal address of 'Ladies and gentlemen', to the plainer 'Men and women of Australia'. His use of language was his point of difference, both within and outside the ALP, and he chose his words and his phrases very carefully.

Margaret and Gough both love to tease and joke with familiar sayings and family codes. Margaret says, 'There was a joke within the family centred around calling each other "love". I'd say, "What are you doing now, love?" And Gough would reply, "Just going to watch the news, love." Suddenly it dawned on us that people might think that was the way we really addressed each other. We didn't stop it, we just made it clear that it was jesting. We're so pretentious we often speak to each other in French. Every night when Gough comes home he shouts, "J'arrive!" It's very childish really. I think we've reached our second childhood. But we don't care what people think, it amuses us.'

Even though it's over thirty years ago now, Margaret still remembers her elation at that time. 'I felt good. It was nice to finally have that good feeling. Of course I felt proud of him, I wouldn't have been with him if I hadn't. I also thought he deserved to be prime minister – he had the looks, the talent and he had worked hard for it. I kept saying to him, "Isn't it exciting?" He just seemed to take it all in his stride. I wasn't fearful at the prospect of being the wife of the PM, and my mother was thrilled to bits.'

THE LODGE

Margaret remembers well her first walk with Gough around the perimeter of the garden of the Lodge. 'There were all these policemen standing behind trees saying, "Good evening, Ma'am." I got the giggles and said to Gough, "I can't believe this," and he replied, "Well, you'd better believe it – this is our life now."'

Just days after the ALP victory Margaret received an offer from the national magazine *Woman's Day* to write a weekly column about her comings and goings, much as Eleanor Roosevelt had done in her daily newspaper column 'My Day'. She leapt at it. From the time she had left school and had refused Packer's offer to be a socialite reporter, she had wanted to write. She felt she had a talent there that hadn't been utilised. For many years she had jotted down her impressions and descriptions of various happenings and events, and she saw this as a chance not just to become a published diarist, but as a means of sharing her experiences with people, particularly women, who would never otherwise get the opportunity to have them.

She adopted a chatty intimate style, which is very close to her own conversational voice. For the first time in our history we could all read about the everyday life of the wife of a prime minister. It is very much a record of domestic happenings, which were in fact what most of her life consisted of, apart from formal dinners and cocktail parties and the interesting people she met, some of which she included. She made no apologies for writing about the domestic aspects of her life – she thought that even though they had been largely ignored or trivialised as mere 'women's work' they were not to be denigrated or dismissed.

So, when the Whitlams moved into the Lodge, she had no hesitation in describing their bedroom.

15th December 1972

Our bedroom is a bit of a mixture. We've taken the one I believe the Gortons had, mainly because one of the bathrooms attached has a proper shower recess – Gough's adamant about the necessity for that.

We've replaced the twin beds (with ends!) with the double bed from the McMahon and Holt-favoured suite, but we've stuck with the bedcover there. It's all pink and yellow flowers, which somehow don't go with the beige butterfly wallpaper in our room. There's a little balcony off the room and a dressing room.

Tonight the PM (how great) and I had a walk after dinner; it was cool, leafy and lovely after the heat of the day.

A few days after their move Margaret's secretary told her that Germaine Greer wanted to interview her. Margaret accepted immediately. She was curious to meet and make her own assessment of the celebrated and controversial author of *The Female Eunuch*, a book that had become an immediate international bestseller when it had been published in 1970.

Although Margaret never embraced the label of feminist – at least not the version propagated by the 1970s media – she does describe herself as a 'fellow traveller', by which she means that she agrees with the substance of their beliefs, if not the manner in which they say it. 'I thought the women's movement was terrific in that people became more aware of women's needs, women's lack of facilities, lack of opportunity and lack of means . . . I am a feminist in so far as I don't want to be trodden on and I don't want to be used as somebody's handbag. I am not an accessory. I'm not an active feminist – I was probably too lazy to stride out and sing songs and make demands. Actually, if I'm honest, I don't know whether I was too lazy or too shy.'

Margaret remembers Greer as charming and very attractive. 'Her hair wasn't wild, more carefully careless. She was very droll. And for some reason – must have been because of my size – she seemed almost in awe of me. She's tall, too, about five foot ten. I was impressed with her as a woman and thought she was much better than her reputation. She was much more polished than I expected and I enjoyed our conversation very much.'

She told her readers on 29 December:

> [Germaine] came to the Lodge a few days after I did. She entered quietly and softly, bearing gifts. A gloxinia in a pot – for me. The erudite, formidable and lovely Germaine Greer was sentimental enough to believe that she could not darken another's door for the first time without bearing gifts. I was enchanted. You would be, too, if you knew Germaine as she is off-camera, off-microphone, off tape-recorder. She is feminine, shy and nervous – yes, nervous. She wore a navy blue midi dress of simple design – long sleeves, tied neckline.
>
> I want you to know that Germaine is a great girl whom few people would recognise. She is romantic, she is pretty, she has a desire to be a mother (which she is, by proxy, to her housekeeper's child) but she has the uncertainty, the

selfishness, that so many clever people have but don't own up to.

Germaine, we would like you to return to Australia to live. We need people like you and we have far more to offer than you know.

The Greer interview was published in *The National Times* on 25 December 1972. It introduced Margaret Whitlam as 'one of the most outspoken and forthright women ever to move into the Lodge'.

The conversation, which had lasted nearly two hours, ranged over a variety of topics. Margaret was all for wages for wives, although she confessed she hadn't even owned a chequebook until 1970. 'Gough just gave me a certain amount for housekeeping and I made do. There were times when it didn't do and we had spaghetti with every remnant of meat in the house put into a tasty sauce at the end of the week, and this happened quite frequently.'

On the subject of abortion she said, 'It certainly shouldn't be a criminal offence for a woman to decide what she's going to do with her own body. There should be a situation where you could simply let it be known that you were having an abortion instead of having a baby. I have seen too many awful results from illegal abortions.'

Greer asked whether she would stop saying such things if Gough told her such views were embarrassing to him. Margaret replied, 'They are my personal and private views. I'm not in a position to make political pronouncements. I'm not a member of Parliament. I'm a private person and I'm entitled to private views.'

In typically provocative fashion Greer slips in a question about whether Margaret has ever been in a situation where she was so bored she thought about picking out a man she found attractive and falling in love with him. Margaret said, 'That's always true. With ladies over fifty there's always somebody who looks interesting.' (She still admits to being 'a mental adulteress'.)

Greer clearly liked Margaret because Claudia Wright, a Melbourne journalist friend of Greer's, quickly wrote to Margaret requesting an interview of her own, and reported that Germaine had told her that she thought Margaret was 'the best political wife in the world at this moment'. Margaret would laugh off such compliments, but be secretly chuffed.

In her interview in *The Sydney Morning Herald* Wright reflected on the difference between Margaret and her predecessors: 'Dame Pattie [Menzies] said little. Zara [Holt] said a lot but achieved little. Bettina [Gorton] was intellectually bright but evasive and Sonia [McMahon] was uninvolved. Margaret Whitlam is the first female resident of the Lodge since Enid Lyons who'll go in with guns blazing.'

Margaret even described her husband as 'a very groovy chap, very alive' and confessed that he had showed his appreciation for her election efforts by 'whispering sweet nothings or sweet somethings in the middle of the night'. And finally she said she had 'not seen or heard from any Liberal wife since the election'.

The reaction of the press to Margaret was very positive. They seemed to be tripping over each other to find new ways of praising her. *The Daily Telegraph* headlined her as 'HOSTESS TO THE NATION' and its opening paragraph said that the new Prime Minister had 'made his best leap forward when he married Margaret Elaine Dovey on April 22, 1942, for in dinkum Aussie language, Meg Whitlam is a "bottler"'. It went on to describe her as 'witty, intelligent and not afraid to speak her mind'.

The Age described her as 'a beaut bird'. *The Sydney Morning Herald*'s 'Look' section even went back to one of her old neighbours in Vaucluse. Mrs Magda Challen, a Hungarian whom Margaret had befriended there 'in the days when foreigners were reffos' said, 'I saw her nearly every day for four years and she was always bright and cheerful and I never had the slightest argument with her. You can't put on a show for that long.' Mrs Challen was genuinely not able to think of one fault in her old friend and neighbour.

Margaret said her faults were that she was 'loud, had a terrible temper and sulked'. As for her appearance, she said she wasn't so inhibited about her height as she used to be, but she would like to be without her double chin. When the journalist assured her that they were part of the Margaret Whitlam that everyone had come to know, she quipped, 'Perhaps I should wear them grandly like "jowls".'

In a press conference at Canberra's Carousel Restaurant, which ran twenty minutes over its ninety-minute schedule, she spoke frankly on topics ranging from equal pay for women (she was in favour), women's rights (in favour), drugs (she thought marijuana should be legalised), abortion (legalised) and marriage (not necessary unless you intend to have children). Never before in the history of Australian politics had the wife of a prime minister allowed herself to be questioned in this manner on social issues, and the press were gobsmacked at her open and forthright answers, instead of the usual evasions and 'you'll have to ask my husband' answers.

However, once this honeymoon period in the Lodge was over, the lack of an established role as the wife of the Prime Minister soon became apparent to Margaret. There was no specific set of duties, no unspoken rules, no prescriptions of any kind. She found herself sitting around a lot, permanently 'on call' to stand in for her husband, to attend functions, to open fêtes and to pour coffee and tea for those who dropped by the Lodge to see him. She knew that her diary would be full of official lunches and dinners, but she didn't expect to have every day frittered away with seemingly no means of living a life of her own. And then there was her role of unpaid housekeeper for the Lodge.

Her column of 11 January says:

> An incredible amount of time seems to be spent in just organising. One would think that a household sporting at all times a cook, a butler and three housemaids would give me lots of spare time. Not so. Basically our routine is this: each day I try to talk with Pat [the cook] about what is happening food-wise during the next few days: how many people are coming to eat, their preferences for food and so on. She then makes out the orders and the butler telephone-orders the grog, some of which he picks up and some of which is delivered. Accounts are paid monthly after a double check by the butler, the cook and me. For any official entertaining – that is, entertaining a state premier, members of the cabinet and diplomats – we're supposed to claim on the Prime Minister's department. So far, though, I've paid no bills nor claimed any deductions. We had Don Dunstan [Premier of South Australia] to lunch today – how does one claim for one lunch? Aside from all this, Pat and Ron keep highly detailed account books regarding shopping and menu-making. We try not to serve the same meals to guests making return visits – all a bit of a change from the old roast leg of lamb routine at our house. This is what we still miss. Haven't had a leg of lamb for ages. Haven't had stewed apple and junket – or tomato and onion pie. Still, soon I'll have my chance when our roster system gets working and I'll have the cooking to do here at weekends. I'm really looking forward to it.

Although she had announced that she had no interest in refurbishing the Lodge, she set an immediate goal of getting air-conditioning for the enormously hot kitchen. She had observed that Pat, their perfect cook, was forced to work under shocking conditions and couldn't think why the previous wives had done nothing about it. Nor could she resist replacing Zara's 'shocking pink linoleum' in the kitchen with black and white tiles. She also worked out how to extend the cramped dining room and the polished mahogany table only seating twelve, which was smaller than her own in Cabramatta, which often seated sixteen.

She dispensed with the butler, who got on her nerves by staring at them whenever he brought in their breakfast in the mornings (she always thought he was trying to see what she was wearing in bed, which she said was often nothing). Apart from his early morning perving he was caught taking a sip from everyone's drink before he served them from the silver tray, so she simply said to the bureaucrat in charge of hiring and firing, 'I'm going away for some weeks soon and I don't want to see him here when I return.'

She was beginning to long for her old life. Unfortunately, just as there were no job specifications for the role, so too there were no conditions for resignation.

By 13 January she wrote from Cabramatta: 'This is my life and I must make the most of it: one of the best bits at present is coming back to the old hearth and home. Last night was fabulous – cooking a meal easily in my own kitchen and watching the telly afterwards. There's nothing wrong with suburbia. In fact, I'm envying the life I've left.'

People were always asking her, 'How do you see your role as the wife of the Prime Minister?' Margaret's characteristically droll but honest reply was, 'I'm still finding it.' The problem was the role had no salary, no pre-requisites and no set requirements. Basically she just had to make of it what she could. No one had actually stipulated that she was required to organise and be hostess at so many dinners, lunches and banquets; that she was required to facilitate so many morning and afternoon teas; that she must change her clothes five times a day; and that for the remainder of her time she must make herself available for whatever task eventuated. She was a woman who in her thirty years of marriage had run her own life as a single mother while Gough was away at the war; as a single mother while he was being a barrister and door-knocking his constituents day and night; and then as a single mother when he was in Canberra as a politician.

Now, here she was, her husband having reached the pinnacle of his career, sitting around like a tame poodle, all dressed up with nowhere to go, waiting to be told what to do. Or forced to skulk alone in the little sitting room watching television, eating her dinner off a tray. And she had to share her bedroom with a never-ending pile of red dispatch boxes, which Gough worked on in the early morning and late at night.

So, with her no-nonsense, practical approach to problems, she first of all demanded to know at least a week in advance what was expected of her and then she made a scheduled program for herself. 'It's all very well sitting on your thumbs doing nothing for a week, but you don't want to do it for three months.'

She said to Gough and those who organised his life, 'I'm not going to be available on Tuesdays in Canberra, that's my golf day. Let me know in advance if you're going to have these men's dinners, or working dinners, so I can go out and see some friends instead of being forced to have dinner alone.'

Determined not to be relegated to sitting around waiting to be needed, like, as she once described it, 'an aged princess in a tower',

Margaret became involved in tasks she thought were worthwhile, as well as taking herself off to the theatre and films in the evening – on her own, if necessary. There were limits to how far she could just be content to be an appendage to her husband and his job. She had quickly discovered that she had to stand up for herself or she would find herself leading a 'nursery life', doing what she was told and not complaining. Being seen but not heard. And that was not her style.

There were some bright spots in the early weeks, however, like the phone call from British journalist David Frost wanting to set up a satellite interview with her. Margaret loves the word 'diverting', which she uses to describe any conversation or event that takes her out of her everyday mundane experiences. She says of David Frost, 'We had a most diverting conversation. He is a marvellous man to flirt with by telephone. The dialogue was absolutely full of double meanings – in the nicest possible way.'

One often catches more than a glimmer of the young woman captured in her first secret journal, who yearns for a Noël Coward life, full of witty, charming men to flirt with her in the most 'couth' manner.

In the interview with Frost there was indeed a lot of flirting on both sides, but a serious moment came when he asked her whether after the endless interviews, commentaries and analyses of her husband, there was still something that she thought the press hadn't realised about him. For the first time Margaret revealed his innate shyness.

'They still don't realise what a good man he is. The press all over the world are so anxious to see him as a viper-tongued, belligerent, unkind man, but he's not. He's really fairly soft and kind. I think it's because he's shy. I only say people are shy if I know they are, and I know he is – basically, he's a shy man.'

For two-thirds of her married life she had attended the opening of Parliament, but this was the first time she'd been alone in the public and media eye, or 'in the hot seat', as she described it. 'I'm told I pleased most people by wearing a bright green and white dress and a small white pillbox hat (which I've had for ages but it goes with almost everything) and keeping my gloves on.'

On their arrival in the Lodge, Margaret also organised a party for the wives of members and senators to meet each other. Rather than the usual sitting or standing around with cups of tea and cakes, Margaret, loving a bit of activity, organised tennis, which she played shouting out, 'For God's sake, Margaret, get the ball inside the court', swimming, in which she was the first to get her gear off and dive in – she said hers was the most drab one-piece of all the swimsuits but at least it encouraged the others to join her – and croquet, which Betty Gorton demonstrated how to play.

Everyone had a very jolly time engaged in these activities, instead of being forced to stand around being decorative and making polite but banal conversation. Margaret had been forced to endure too many of those so-called 'garden parties' and had always sworn that if given the chance she would do it differently.

The Whitlams' entertaining whenever possible was casual and relaxed, as was their style. She and Gough had always been vastly amused by the pretentiousness of some of the dignitaries who had entertained them in the past – at times they could not even look at each other for fear of bursting into laughter.

By the time Margaret and Gough arrived in London in April 1973 on their first official visit in their new capacity, she was enjoying herself. The daffodils were out, the London parks and gardens that she so admired were in full bloom and she was about to celebrate her thirty-first wedding anniversary.

'Ask me an outrageous question and I'll give you an outrageous answer,' was her opening line to the British media. And she meant it.

'One helluva beaut Sheila' was the judgement of *The Sunday Mail* columnist, who continued, 'The Aussies have obviously got themselves a great big bloody beaut of a first lady in the former Miss "Doddles" Dovey, the 6' 2" tall ex-breaststroke champion.' (The nickname 'Doddles' was in fact wrong. Her school nickname was Dobbles Dovey – it didn't stand for anything and was just a bit of schoolgirl silliness.)

The Sun compared her outspoken views to the slit skirts of her predecessor and *The Times* opined that she 'had broken the rule of the League of Prime Minister's Wives, which puts caution before spontaneity'.

When British journalists asked her if she was worried that her chatty diary in *Woman's Day* would make her seem folksy, Margaret quipped, 'Better to be seen as folksy than not seen at all.'

On 21 April Margaret's diary came from Windsor Castle, England. In her homely, chatty style she described the inside of the Queen's favourite castle. The readers looked over her shoulder while she took them through the rooms. No detail was spared.

> The sitting room, in which I chatted with Miss Morrison while the PM was whisked off to his talks with Her Majesty, has two pale, gold-covered armchairs around a small fireplace at one end and a red brocade-covered Madame Récamier-type sofa at the other end. There are three writing tables – and a large one centred between the windows – along the wall a longish buffet laden with decanters and mineral water.

On a little side table are fruit and plates. The walls are papered in striped fuchsia – it sounds strange but it looks fabulous – and the long curtains are white with a green band trim and tie, and there are gold tulip ends to the curtain rods. The small chairs also have red upholstery and the room is bright with lamps and flowers. White blossoms mix beautifully with orchids, and there is a large bowl of bright tulips on top of the large desk.

Everything is beautifully warm – so much so that at night it was necessary for me to remove the pink silk comforter and one of the cream blankets from my downy bed. Everything is so temptingly arranged at Windsor Castle that I had a second bath within four hours. I had bathed at the Berkeley Hotel before leaving London, but I was unable to resist the nicely drawn bath in my pink-and-white papered bathroom before dinner at 8.30 pm.

So, there is the new PM's wife, having daydreamed as the young Margaret Dovey of visiting famous people and romantic places, soaking herself in the bathtub in Windsor Castle, looking up at framed lithographs of flowers and about to have dinner with the Queen of England. It sure beat shelling the peas on the train from Central to Cronulla.

Protocol at the palace was pre-dinner drinks in a little sitting room with vast portraits and a French carpet at about 7 pm, before they all changed for dinner. Prince Philip met her, then in came the Queen Mother in a lovely blue printed silk dress with an aqua cardigan draped over her shoulders, and finally the Queen and Gough joined them.

Her Majesty looked marvellous in a deep cherry-red wool dress pinned with a superb sapphire brooch. She looked prettier than I ever remember – certainly younger than the 47 years she is today. Her Majesty sipped a tomato juice. Prince Philip had a gin and tonic. Princess Margaret then joined us wearing an unusual blue knitted dress with her hair swept up in what I believe is a French Roll. Lord Snowdon appeared soon after looking, as the Princess said, 'as though he'd just come from the stables'. His jeans and denim jacket did look rather operational.

About 7.40 we went up to change, withdrawing curtseys being required. On the tick at 8.30 we reassembled for another drink – this time sherry for Her Majesty. The Queen Mother arrived in a lovely white and gold dress. She really is a pretty, feminine person of enormous warmth. Next, Princess Margaret in a deep red velvet pinafore, long-sleeved evening sweater; the skirt was flared. Every bit a princess. Then the Queen wearing aqua lace re-embroidered in silver and gold, gold slippers, diamonds at her throat and pendant diamond earrings. Her Majesty's hair was more bouffant than I can ever recall it, and a little shorter I think. Rather chic.

The dining room was very grand – red and gold mainly with a vast ceiling. The dinner service was pale green, pale gold and white (Sèvres) given to Her Majesty and Prince Philip as a wedding present by President de Gaulle. Prince Philip admits to being very fond of it and having no intention of it being added to the official Royal Collection. He intends giving it to one of the royal children. Three courses only at dinner. Sensible, beautiful and delicious.

First, fresh salmon, boiled potatoes and cucumbers in sour cream; then turkey with what seemed a million vegetables. The sweet was pineapple bombe with spun sugar – right up our Prime Minister's alley. White wine and/or red. There was coffee and port at the table before we left the room.

TOP The 1960s: there was always a ball to attend, or two, or three …

LEFT In Cornwall, England, escaping on a motoring holiday with Nick, 1967

TOP Margaret's Greek gods – Gough, Stephen and Nick – posing beneath the statues on the Acropolis, 1968

MIDDLE Woman to woman: with Golda Meir, 1970

BOTTOM A formal reception in Canberra with Gough and Tony, 1964

'A stitch in time . . .': Margaret would take her knitting to party meetings

'Let's get this show on the road': in the Whitlams' back garden after Labor's election victory, 1972

TOP Cutting the victory cake with Tony, Catherine and Nick's portrait looking on

RIGHT A kiss and a giggle

'Come on in, girls': Margaret with Kris Klugman at a different kind of a garden party at the Lodge, 1972

'We want Gough': some of the Prime Minister's fans

TOP Nick and Judy Frye's engagement in London, 1973
BOTTOM Autumn at the Lodge

A family reunion at Heathrow in London with Nick, Catherine and Tony, 1973

Entertaining Prince Philip, 1973

Gough and Margaret visit Pope Paul VI in the Vatican, 1973

Gough with his first grandchild, Alexander – Stephen and Sheena's son – 1973. *Back row*: Tony, Catherine, Nick, Sheena, Stephen

An official photograph in the Lodge

RIGHT Taking in the view from Kirribilli House with Queen Elizabeth, 1973

MIDDLE At the opening of the Sydney Opera House with house guest Imelda Marcos

BOTTOM Tea in China, 1973

RIGHT Walking tall on the Great Wall

MIDDLE Entertaining the wives in the gardens of the Lodge

BOTTOM Margaret and Gough with the Governor-General, Sir John Kerr (middle)

Newspix

Newspix

TOP 'Arise Dame Edna': the only imperial honour Gough ever awarded, 1974

MIDDLE A meal with Germaine Greer and Susan Ryan after a day at the International Women's Year conference in Mexico, 1975

LEFT 'Perchance to dream …'

TOP Fun in Paris at the embassy, 1985

MIDDLE Nick and Judy's children, Alice (nine years old), Edward (five) and Peter (four), 1986

BOTTOM The life of the party: Margaret as tour leader on an International Study Tour in Vienna, 1995

Newspix

TOP LEFT 'Love is a many splendoured thing': at the Temple of Love in Lima, Peru, 1996

TOP RIGHT Side by side in Greece, 2000

LEFT Sixty-four years and still going: at the wedding of SA Premier Mike Rann and Sasha Carruozzo, 2006

LEFT Lunch with the grandparents ... Stephen with his two children, Helen and Alexander

MIDDLE Margaret's babies, then ...

BOTTOM ... and now. Tony, Stephen, Nick and Catherine, 2005

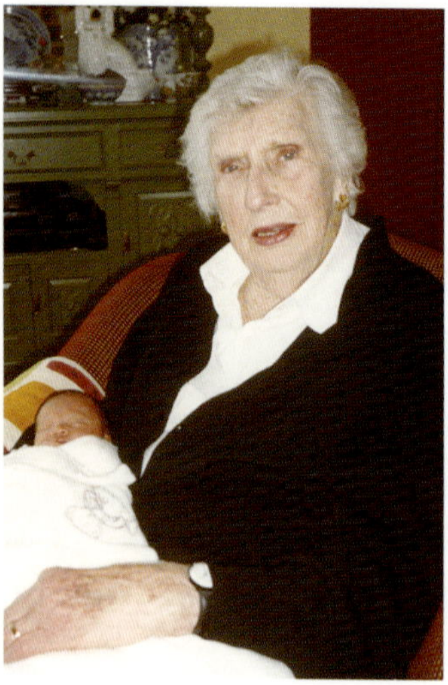 

The newest generation: Margaret with her first great-granddaughter, three-week-old Isabella – Nick's first grandchild; and (*right*) her first great-grandson, three-month-old Oscar – Stephen's first grandchild, 2005

When Margaret returned home she recounted a bit more about what had undoubtedly been the highlight of her tour.

> You can't imagine how relaxed and human the Royal Family are. When the Queen is away from photographers and pressmen she is so amusing and also easily amused. We've all heard about Princess Margaret's talents as an actress or mimic, but I was enchanted by several take-offs Her Majesty permitted herself – mostly gentle send-ups of people around her – even her own Mama. (Yes, she calls the Queen Mother either Mama or Mummy. The late Queen Mary was referred to always as Granny.) You would have loved the sight of the sisters sitting side by side on the deep-piled, cream sheepskin rug we gave Her Majesty for her birthday. They looked like 'the Little Princesses' on either one's teenage birthday.

That was what every Australian could read and enjoy in *Woman's Day*. When it was published, however, there was a surge of letters to the editor from people who believed that Margaret had broken protocol by divulging to ordinary Australians the intimate details of the royal family. They just didn't think it was 'proper'.

Margaret was unrepentant about what she had written, and went on to write about dinner in the wood-panelled, candle-lit dining room of No. 10 Downing Street, and later of their private audience with the Pope. Nothing and no one was going to stop her. She believed in what she was doing.

'I came to represent all the ungainly people, the too-tall ones, the too-fat ones and the house-bound, as I had been, who'd never go to China or Buckingham Palace, and they all went through me,' she said in *The National Times* in 1985.

Apart from once again exposing her view of herself as someone, like many others, whose appearance made her feel apart from the so-called norm, this statement also revealed her identification with those women who never thought they would get a chance to experience such things, except in their dreams. In her deeply felt democratic spirit, she wanted them to ride on her shoulders and enjoy such things with her.

The general response to her visit to Britain by the local Australian press was very positive. Leigh Bottrell wrote from London in *The Telegraph*:

> You actually hear English women saying they would like to meet Mrs Whitlam. Considering the average time an Englishwoman takes to admit that she might like to meet even a new neighbour, the Australian Prime Minister's wife has gone over big in Britain. Meg, who rules the saloon bar of my local pub, actually confided, 'Mrs Whitlam is the nicest woman we've had to see us since Mrs Roosevelt. Almost as nice as the Queen Mother.'

The Sunday Telegraph of 29 April 1973 even did a vox-pop of what Sydney women thought of Margaret. Mrs Bonnie Cameron, manager of a dry cleaners, said, 'She's terrific. She's got everything a woman in that position should have, plus a lot more. I find her terribly refreshing.'

Mrs Carol Foster, a dancer, said, 'She's down-to-earth and sensible. She's got the courage of her convictions and you get the idea that her convictions are pretty hard to shake.'

Mrs Maria Tyra, a housewife, said, 'I think women have needed someone like her for a long time. She has this marvellous common-sense and an ability to put things straightforwardly and effectively.'

Mrs Maureen Ash, a delivery contractor, said, 'She's marvellous.

She's a real woman. There's nothing frilly about her but I'm sure she likes nice things, just like any woman. But you get the feeling that she'd be the first to say there are many more important things to worry about. She's concerned with the real issues of living.'

Miss Marina Willcock, a student, was, however, expecting something a bit more radical. 'It's all turned out to be a bit dull. I don't like her diaries, all about dreary curtains and the deadly humbug of marriage.'

And what was Gough's reaction to her diaries? According to Margaret his attitude was, 'What's the old bag been up to now?'

Back in Australia Margaret continued her endless rounds of 'openings' and 'closings' by her husband's side. When she had married him that's what she knew she was taking on and her attitude was, 'I went along with him, urging him and helping him . . . why moan about it? I didn't find it strange, to me that's what marriage was all about.'

Even though she now knew a lot more about politics, Gough still never discussed his important political decisions with her. There was no sense in which she was an extension of government, nor even an influence on him. People did, of course, try to get at him through her, and she would often pass on a petition or a letter or a document to him that she had been sent, but that was the extent of her political influence.

When they married in 1942 it was accepted that she would make the domestic and familial decisions and he would make the work decisions. Whether he had been a barrister, the head of BHP or the prime minister would have made no difference to their arrangements.

At the end of Margaret's twelfth month as 'the Lady at the Lodge' journalist Lee Patterson spent several weeks on the Australian First Lady's trail and wrote an extended feature article for *POL* magazine, which was accompanied by a lurid caricature of Margaret, complete with fishnet stockings, lace suspenders and tassels attached to her nipples, leaping out of a birthday cake on which burnt one candle.

In the article Margaret explained, 'He is like an oyster now when he is planning something new. I am not received well if I try to comment on his turf. I am more on the outside than I was when he was in Opposition. He can be a vain, irritating man, but I can be irritating too. I am untidy. I talk too much and I interrupt. But if he does something that I think is wrong, I tell him so. That is the privilege of a wife of my vintage.'

She also said that she had become used to Gough being referred to as the prime minister, whereas in the first few months whenever she heard it she would laugh, dig him in the ribs and say, 'That's you!'

As for her public utterances, she had no intention of ceasing to make them. 'I say what I think when I want. I am not a mouthpiece for my husband, or for the ALP, and it's very frustrating for me when people assume that I am.'

Patterson commented, 'If nothing else, Margaret Whitlam has shattered the porcelain image of the PM's wife as some sort of beloved, untouchable and inviolate lady of the flowers who appears and rubs a few platitudes together at fêtes before ascending again to the big house on the hill.'

He had observed Margaret's 'openings' and 'closings', and at the opening of the Australian Regional Conference of International Toastmistresses he witnessed first-hand Margaret giving the person who introduced her as speaking about the role of women in Australia an unexpected roasting rather than a toasting.

> Margaret Whitlam stood up to her full 6 foot 2 inches, in itself an awe-inspiring and impressing statement, and said, 'There

was no mention of me speaking about the role of women when I was invited here, so I am not going to. If you want guest speakers, ask them to speak and give them a subject. I was first asked to open this conference officially and then I received a note of thanks when I accepted, but nothing else. You therefore can't blame me for wondering what it is I am supposed to do.'

There is nothing outrageous about refusing to give an off-the-cuff speech on a topic that the organisers have never mentioned to you before. Margaret is a stickler for doing things properly. If you ask her to do something and she agrees to do it, then you must stick to your original contract. She always prepares in advance for whatever she agrees to do – even if she is going to an opera or a concert she will play the music beforehand just to set herself in the groove. This is a result of her upbringing, her parents, her schooling and her understanding of what constitutes proper behaviour.

This is why so many of what Patterson described as 'diamond, pomp and circumstance-encrusted Liberal ladies', still reeling after being deprived of the divine right to rule, regarded her as a sort of Australian class traitor. 'After all, she is the daughter of a respected lawyer, she did go to a "good" school and what does she go and do but get herself involved with the Bolshevist Whitlam and live out there in Cabramatta amongst the iridescent garden gnomes, Hill's Hoists and fibro villas. I mean, one does take a jet if one is going anywhere further west than Grace Bros, doesn't one?'

Although this is meant to be satirical, it is true that the Liberals accused the Whitlams of being class traitors. There had been the comments at Menzies' 'seduction dinner', and Margaret recalls a similar exchange at an official dinner in Canberra. Liberals and Labor Party members were seated together and she sat next to

Billy Snedden, who eventually replaced McMahon as the Liberal Party leader. They were all having a very jolly time when a Liberal sitting opposite her asked, 'God, Margaret, what's a nice girl like you doing in the Labor Party?'

Margaret replied, 'I belong to the party that cares about people, and I don't see any of you lot doing much of that.' And that, as they say, was the end of that conversation.

When Gough was first elected Margaret was very upset by a letter that he received from a close friend of theirs, who said that Gough was a traitor to his class but that Margaret would always be welcome as an old school friend of his wife's. Gough and Margaret had lived among these kinds of people, had been to school with them, studied at university with them; they had even been to some of their weddings. Now Gough and Margaret were genuinely flummoxed and appalled to find that they were seen as a couple who had jumped the barriers and taken up with the uncouth, rough unionists and the sweaty workers. There were many who held these views and certainly there were members of the Liberal Party who never forgave them for going over to the other team; who never viewed the Whitlam government as legitimate. Gough and Margaret were not only called class traitors, they were also regarded as usurpers of what the Liberals, after more than two decades in government, believed was theirs by birth and right. From the moment the Whitlams moved into the Lodge many pledged to do whatever it took to eject them as soon as possible.

In 1973 Margaret promoted a series on Australia's wildlife for the Paul Hamlyn publishing group, donating her fee to the Australian Conservation Foundation. People nonetheless complained in the media that she was being paid. In her diary she wrote, 'What am I to do? Stay in a cage – wide open to view, of course – and say nothing? That's not on, but if I can do some good I'll certainly try. I'm trying.'

In May it was her mother's eightieth birthday, which Margaret celebrated with her by taking her to lunch, after which Mary went to see the Kirov Ballet with a friend and Margaret returned to Canberra. Margaret admired the way her mother had carved out a full life for herself. The 'old girl', as she had called her affectionately for the past twenty-five years, had organised a program for herself so she was rarely bored or lonely. She never complained if she didn't see her daughter for a month and she simply got on with her bridge, her radio-listening, her handiwork and her visits to the theatre.

Margaret and Gough were like the proverbial Darby and Joan now, as Tony was working as a lawyer in New York, Nick as a banker in London, Stephen as a foreign affairs officer in Geneva, and Catherine was living in a student shared house near the University of New South Wales, where she was studying arts. On the weekends when they were able to spend some time at Kirribilli House on the harbour in Sydney, Margaret would sit on the wide verandah catching up on her correspondence or her accounts and was always amused to hear echoing across the water the words from a loudspeaker on one of the tourist ferries announcing, 'This is where the Whitlam family live.'

October was exciting because there was a royal visit from the Queen and Prince Philip. Margaret boldly decided to have a lunch for them outside in the garden of the Lodge in keeping with her own style of informal formality. Fortunately, the day was fine and her menu was a great success: fresh asparagus (from the Lodge garden), followed by trout with almonds, savoury rice and a mixed green salad. Cheese was served in the French tradition before the sweet, which was gingered pears. The only blot on the Lodge's reputation as far as Margaret was concerned was that there was no hollandaise sauce for the asparagus. Prince Philip had to ask for it.

The reason for the royal visit was the opening of the Sydney Opera House, complete with music and fireworks. It was a huge success, apart from the wind, which would have blown away Premier Sir Robert Askin's chair when he stood up to make his speech, but for the quick-thinking of the Queen and Prince Philip, who grabbed hold of it and held it down. Apart from entertaining the royals, Margaret also had Imelda Marcos as a house guest. Gough had asked her to stay with them. By the time it was all over Margaret admitted in her diary to being tired. Very tired.

Nevertheless, three days later she and Gough were in Tokyo, where she lunched at the Imperial Palace. Although she thought it was rather forbidding from the outside – grey granite surrounded by a moat – she wrote that inside it was 'elegant and beautiful . . . with its space and glass and wood and deep-pile carpets of pastel-hue perfection'.

A series of banquets, lunches and visits to more palaces followed, including an evening of entertainment with geishas. In all the photographs Margaret and Gough look like giants compared to the tiny Japanese. Margaret wished she had been able to have her photos taken without her shoes, which she removed in restaurants. 'One feels such an ox in the presence of these finely built people.'

Early November found them in China where, apart from Gough's excitement at finally meeting Chairman Mao, Margaret conquered one part of the Great Wall and saw the Ming tombs, which house the thirteen emperors of the Ming dynasty from the fourteenth to the seventeenth centuries. She had also been looking forward to visiting the Forbidden City and was not disappointed.

On 30 November Margaret and Catherine flew to London to celebrate Nick's wedding to twenty-nine-year-old Englishwoman Judy Frye. Gough had met Judy the year before, but political duties prevented him from being present at the wedding. His brother Tony, who was working in London, was his best man. They were married in London's Chelsea register office and Judy's parents threw a huge black-tie dinner-dance the following night in a marquee adjoining their large Dulwich house. There were more than two hundred guests, including Rupert Murdoch, recalls Nick in his memoir. Margaret's diary records a 'splendid occasion'.

Nineteen seventy-three was also the year that Gough approved the purchase of Jackson Pollock's painting *Blue Poles*. There was outrage around the nation that the Australian government would agree to spend A$1,130,500 on an American painting. Gough and Margaret's response was to reproduce it on the front of their Christmas card. Now it is worth more than US$100 million and is the most viewed painting in the National Gallery.

When he was Prime Minister, John Gorton had proposed the establishment of an Australian film and television school, which was abandoned when Billy McMahon succeeded him. Now Gough resurrected the idea and asked Gorton to be present when he opened the school. One of its first funded films was *Barry McKenzie Holds his Own*, starring Barry Humphries. Gough and Margaret agreed to be in the film and take on the role of greeting Edna Everage and her nephew Bazza when they arrived at Mascot Airport. Documentary footage of this event shows Margaret and Gough awaiting Edna's arrival and Margaret whispering something into Gough's ear. What was not in the original script were Gough's words of greeting when Edna curtsied to them. He said, taking her hand, 'Arise, Dame Edna.' This is still part of the film and it was the only imperial honour he ever awarded. Dame Edna is now, of course, the best-known and most celebrated Australian dame in the world, even if she is a man in drag.

In January 1974 John Menadue organised another dinner for Whitlam and Murdoch in New York, but when Gough saw David Frost by chance in the foyer of the Plaza Hotel he decided to have dinner with him instead and cancelled Murdoch. Menadue was beside himself. One of Gough's staff managed to get them together for breakfast at Murdoch's apartment two days later but Gough did not go with good grace. He still didn't feel it was necessary to share his thoughts with Rupert Murdoch, despite Murdoch's extensive media power.

At the same time Margaret agreed to become the first woman member on the board of the Commonwealth Hostels, but when it became known that she had accepted a payment of $1950 for doing so, again there was a media outcry. 'AN IMPRUDENT APPOINTMENT' announced *The Age*; 'DROP IT MEG' suggested the Melbourne *Herald*. Margaret refused to bow to her critics and responded to accusations of 'jobs for the girls' by reminding them that she was a trained social worker and that having 'subjugated' herself for an entire year she was very pleased to be doing something constructive for a change.

The government's popularity rating in the opinion polls had declined and even though Gough was considered to be an excellent Minister for Foreign Affairs, he was persuaded by his advisors and a big by-election setback in the seat of Parramatta the previous September that he should hand over the portfolio in order to concentrate on solving the problem of why Labor's stocks had slumped so badly, so soon.

An analysis of their problems revealed that raising interest rates to counter rising inflation before the by-election hadn't helped and that the electorate felt bewildered. 'They're going too quickly, too soon' was the general response, echoing Margaret's concern two years earlier.

In a confidential letter to the Prime Minister, a group of caucus members said that ministers had failed to explain the philosophy behind all their policy initiatives and that since Gough's personal standing and opinion-poll ratings were high, he should become the major salesman for all the policies, preferably through more frequent television appearances. They also said they regretted the fact that they had to communicate with him by letter as he was always too busy to see them.

It was true that because they had been so long out of government many of his ministers were failing to perform well and Gough was spending more and more of his time trying to make up for their failings.

Immediately after losing the 1972 election, the Opposition leader in the Senate, Reg Withers, made it clear that the election of the ALP was, in his words, 'a temporary aberration'. The details leading up to the blocking of the supply bills are well documented in Gough's book *The Truth of the Matter*: 'These bills are always passed in the autumn session to cover expenditure during the months of July to November pending the passage of the budget bills, which are usually introduced in August.'

In response to the blocking of supply by the Senate, Gough advised Governor-General Hasluck on 10 April to dissolve both houses in order to have an election in mid May for the whole Parliament, and not just the half-Senate.

On Anzac Day, 25 April, *The Daily Telegraph* ran a feature on 'the most exclusive girls in the country – the Prime Minister's daughters-in-law.' The article opened with the news that Pip Colman had married Tony Whitlam the previous weekend in a 'surprise Darling Point ceremony'. Pip had been a teacher before she began modelling and *The Telegraph* predicted that she would find the world of politics 'a far cry from the ultra glamorous jet-setting life she leads as a model on the international fashion scene'.

Margaret and Gough, however happy they might have been with their son's wedding to Pip, had another election to fight less than eighteen months after the previous one. The following are extracts from Margaret's private journal:

> Sydney
> Tuesday 30th April 1974
> We're off – last night spelled the beginning. Bands and birds and the best beliefs all mingled to produce an atmosphere as exciting as we've come to expect. E.G. and I drove out to Blacktown at an early hour to collect ourselves, so to speak. I was horrified at the Blacktown Inn to find our rooms at the back (for easy access and privacy) had no television or radio and I had no newspaper or book and two hours to fill.
>
> E.G. and G.F. [Graham Freudenberg, Gough's speech-writer] had The Speech to work on. A radio was soon found so we had the news and then a newspaper arrived so I had a crossword with which to amuse myself.

As this is her personal journal, written for her own record, there is no attempt at gloss or spin. Being the devoted wife of a prime minister during an election campaign second time around is not glamorous.

Now airborne en route to Melbourne. No one talking much, especially not to me. This is likely to be the tenor of the tour. Expecting it I've brought along an enormous bag of work to do – my sort of work. Letters to answer, photos to sort, knitting. Blow everyone. I'll be here when they do want me.

After Melbourne and Tasmania they arrived in Adelaide.

A lot of my time in the past few days has been spent in the bathroom. Many times I wonder why I came along as my opinions are never heard. If I utter someone pulls a face and if I don't I'm stared at accusingly. [This someone is clearly Gough.] It's all a bit of a bore and not nearly the fun we had last time.

The bathroom bit is necessary since there's always someone else in our room when I'm about to dress or undress. Sometimes three or four people.

We left Hobart this morning at 6.30 am – a hellish time with everyone tired from yesterday. As usual my car companion – life partner, call him what you will – uttered not one word on the way to the airport – except to ask the driver to change the radio station.

I'm getting so the word wouldn't even have to be kind to be welcome. What a sad saga this has become. I wish everyone would smarten up and be friendly.

Later. Not likely.

E.G. tripped over something, a briefcase I think, and proceeded to take out his rage on the nearest door. When I demurred I was called a silly old bag. 'Well, you're older,' I said, and inferred sillier. 'But I don't look it,' he said, and added, 'Viperish woman.'

WELL!

Perth was rather pleasant. My part was large enough and very interesting – the child-care centre at Garden City and an aged person's retirement village. Good night at the Savoy Plaza Hotel with much support by Yugoslavs and Italians as well as expected Labor people.

Adelaide Park Royal Motel
Friday 3rd May
Somebody's got to make the coffee! Let it be me. Now I know my role in this campaign. Keeping the coffee coming in motel rooms and ironing the Shirt of the Day. Good Girl.

Did two radio interviews today with Pat Hudson and Andy Thorpe at 5AD. Both will be heard early next week and may be of some help.

Adelaide
Saturday 4th May
Bomb scare at last night's meeting in Norwood Town Hall. Rousing welcome and splendid hearing particularly through the television part. Then I began to wonder what was going on with Barry Brown and Reg Bishop conferring and much movement at the side. Finally Reg came up on stage and whispered to Don and gave me a card which read 'Security. Leave soon without panic' and asked me to give it to Gough when he finished speaking. Five minutes later he did, I did and we did. A bit scary and a bit abrupt as an ending to a successful meeting. As we left the hall I could hear Reg saying, 'Thank you ladies and gentlemen, that ends the meeting,' and we drove away swiftly instead of meeting people and attending the mayor's prepared reception.

Before going out this morning I solved a problem. I asked

E.G. if he would tell me why he wanted me along on the campaign. 'Because you're an asset,' he said. Well, out of his mouth that's a real compliment. 'And,' he added, 'for company.' So there.

In plane at Melbourne ready for Brisbane
Thursday 9th May
The mood has changed. Tempers have improved and morale is high. Enthusiasm at meetings is beyond belief, attendances have created records – the performance of E.G.W. is masterly. No doubt he carries the burden and the team but how well he wears.

The Australian on 10 May reported on the huge crowds that the Prime Minister had attracted: 'On Monday night in the Liberal seat of Bennelong he drew more than 3,500 people. The next night he attracted a huge crowd of more than 10,000 in the heartland of the very marginal seat of Cook. The next night Mr Whitlam got one of his biggest ovations ever from a crowd approaching 4,000 in the outer Melbourne seat of La Trobe.'

John Menadue, who was still working as general manager of News Ltd in Australia for Murdoch, explains that, 'As the economy ran into difficulties in 1974 Whitlam and Murdoch gradually parted ways. In the 1974 election, Murdoch played it down the middle in *The Australian* editorial pages, one senior journalist writing, "Why I will vote Liberal" and the other, "Why I will vote Labor."'

The election was held on 18 May. On 25 May *The Daily Telegraph* ran an article headed 'The Women at the Top', with photos of Mrs Whitlam and Mrs Snedden, focusing on the tension of the two wives while waiting for the last votes to come in. How had Mrs Whitlam and Mrs Snedden survived the gruelling days of waiting?

> The usually outgoing Mrs Whitlam disappeared from public view this week. The lady who walked tall and confident throughout the campaign, stood in pressing crowds, patiently answered hecklers, fronted the press without a qualm, has vanished under a brolly of no comment. Questioned whether she could continue to be as outspoken as in the past she answered, 'If people ask me questions, I'll answer them.' For the lady-in-opposition, Mrs Snedden, the campaign was more difficult. Reserved, suffering from the flu and not used to the press, she answered questions carefully with a tape recorder going.

The article concluded that no two leading women could be more different in personality than Mrs Whitlam and Mrs Snedden. Mrs Whitlam was warm and witty, Mrs Snedden was decidedly frosty.

The result of the 1974 general election was agonisingly close: each party had won twenty-nine Senate seats and there were two independents, so Gough had failed in his attempt to control the Senate. His assessment of the result was that although Labor had won, the double dissolution had really settled nothing. In his book *The Truth of the Matter* he writes, 'Mr Snedden caused some hilarity at the time by his post-election statement that he had not lost the election but merely failed to get enough seats; with hindsight, the statement can be seen as the first attempt to deny the validity of the verdict of 18 May and to deny the legitimacy of the re-elected government.'

The joint sitting of both houses on 6 August 1974 passed the six bills that had been previously rejected and it was the first sitting of Parliament ever to be televised.

It was also the first sitting convened by the new Governor-General, Sir John Kerr. Gough details in his book the many reasons behind his decision to choose Kerr for the vice-regal position and when it was announced the media also welcomed the appointment.

The Age editorialised, 'The Whitlam government has made, by any standards, an excellent choice.'

The Sydney Morning Herald was equally complimentary: 'Mr Whitlam deserves credit for the appointment of an eminent and eminently suitable Australian.'

Gough never discussed his choice of John Kerr with Margaret. She did, however, overhear him discussing the terms and conditions of the appointment with someone he called John on the telephone, whom she wrongly assumed was Mr Justice John Moore, the President of the Australian Conciliation and Arbitration Commission. Margaret was shocked when she realised that it was in fact John Kerr whom Gough had appointed.

> I always thought Kerr was a bit weak. His voice was very tinny. A good-looking man with a high-pitched voice is very suss. I know that PMs are not supposed to tell anyone until it's all official and I didn't ask because I'd assumed it was another John. When I realised who it was I said to Gough, 'Oh dear, you could have done better than that,' and he responded, 'Oh no, he'll be good. He was Chief Justice of New South Wales so he'll know all the duties.'

The day after Kerr was sworn in, Margaret and Gough had lunch with Kerr and his wife, Peg, at Yarralumla. Not only had Whitlam and Kerr known each other well as colleagues over the years but Margaret and Peg had trained together as social workers and remained loyal friends for over thirty-two years. Peg's health had been poor for some time, and not long after that lunch she was admitted to hospital, where she died on 9 September.

Margaret thought:

> Because [Peg] had recently had a stroke [Kerr] took the job because he knew there would be servants and he wouldn't have to look after her if she became really crook, and there would also be someone to look after him. He admitted this. He was purely thinking of himself and that only increased my dislike of him. He was always so pompous and his wife Peg was so unpompous. When she died I was very sad. Of course, then he married wife number two, who had been girlfriend number one for years and years.

Margaret had no time to ponder on the poor choice of her husband for governor-general as she was off with her secretary, Barbara Stuart, to Japan to launch a new container ship for the Australian National Line in Kobe. On 9 August she stood in the early morning sunshine surrounded by crowds of shipworkers and their families and pronounced the words, 'I name this ship the *Australian Emblem*. May God bless her and all who sail with her.' And then with her little axe she cut the cord that released the bottle of champagne that baptised the ship and launched it, surrounded by birds, streamers and balloons. Unfortunately, on the same day Richard Nixon resigned as President of the United States of America, which rather swamped Margaret's launch in the media.

When she returned to Sydney at 6 am the following Tuesday she was tired after her ten-hour flight, but inevitably the press were waiting for her. Margaret, always willing to answer any questions, refused Barbara's advice to say 'No comment' and stopped to talk to them, 'out of politeness'. After all the questions concerning Japan they asked her about inflation there. She said that it was indeed a problem in Japan. Then she added, 'But I think you people do not help with all the hoo ha you go on with. Australia is in a much better position than the rest of the world.'

All hell broke loose, with headlines appearing the following day such as, 'PM'S WIFE THINKS INFLATION A LOT OF HOO HA'.

On Wednesday 14 August Margaret told journalist Claudia Wright that she regarded these reporters as lacking in talent because they had not accurately reported what she had said. But when she attended a lunch at Green Valley Community Centre in Sydney's west, where she was to be guest speaker, three housewives were outside with placards that read, 'INFLATION DOESN'T MATTER? NOR DO WE?', 'MRS WHITLAM, YOU CAN AFFORD TO IGNORE INFLATION – GREEN VALLEY CANNOT' and 'MRS WHITLAM COULDN'T CARE LESS'.

She swept past them with no comment and when she stood up to give her speech she again reiterated that she had been misquoted and her words taken out of context. 'Please don't believe a word you read in the newspapers. The press is an ass.' She even went so far as to say she was beginning to understand Frank Sinatra. (On a recent visit he had called the local Australian press 'parasites, bums and hookers'.)

Margaret added her own descriptions and accused them of being 'vultures, praying mantises, uninvited guests and intruders'. Margaret is a Scorpio and her ability to sting with her words when she was stung was certainly in evidence that day.

About one hundred and fifty housewives laughed and clapped as she turned to the bank of reporters and television cameras and said, 'You wouldn't be here today unless you hoped I'd put my other foot in it. I don't suppose the gentlemen of the press would even know where Green Valley is, or how the other half lives.'

She went on to point out that it wasn't very far across the creek to Albert Street, Cabramatta, where she used to live. When she was asked whether the federal government understood how fed up everyone was about inflation, she said her husband was 'sick at heart' about the whole situation. 'And I am sick about the entire situation,' she added.

The next day the newpapers reported exactly what she had said, especially her comment that the press were 'vultures'. *The Australian* put it on the front page. There were also letters to the editor from members of the Australian Journalists Association, of which she too was a member, complaining about her remarks concerning journalists and calling her comments 'red-neck'. One female member of the AJA demanded she apologise, resign her union membership and stick to social work. As far as the press were concerned, Margaret's honeymoon was over.

On 24 August *The Australian*, together with all the other major media outlets in the nation, announced that Margaret Whitlam, wife of the Prime Minister, was to present her own one-hour television show titled *With Margaret Whitlam*, to be made by David Frost's company, Paradine Productions. The first program was to be recorded in Melbourne on 30 August and was scheduled to go to air early in September.

Margaret was very excited about the prospect of having her own television show. 'Television is just about being interested in people, wanting to know about them and wanting the world to know more about them.'

Her first show went to air on Sunday 5 September and her first discussion topic was pornography, which Margaret declared disingenuously was 'on everybody's lips'. Her opening-night guests were David Frost and Leonard Bernstein, who was in Australia to conduct a series of concerts. She was more of a hostess than an interviewer. 'It's not a show, it's a conversation-piece,' she explained to Bernstein when he got a bit carried away about being 'invited to deflower your virgin series'.

The television critics were not kind, quoting David Frost as gushing all over her – 'She's so good, so lovely, so DIVINE' – and complaining that she talked over the top of Bernstein. Headlines such as 'ALL SO MUCH HOO-HA' were predictable.

Margaret, however, was generally pleased with the show and says she tried to disregard the critics. 'I suspect that most bad criticisms were written by people who didn't see a whole program. Anyway, that's what I like to think. It makes for a happier way to deal with it.'

There were some good responses, though, like the one from *The Age*, which said that, 'In her debut as a talk-hour compère she was so amusingly erudite that I won't be surprised if her show outlives the Labor regime that, indirectly, spawned it.' Words such as warmth, wit, irony and wry insight followed.

The Australian's television critic described her as 'cool, comfortable, very much in control, and curious about each of her guests in turn'.

Margaret admitted in her *Woman's Day* diary that she had 'fallen in love' with Leonard Bernstein. After she had taped the interview Bernstein said he was going on to Victorian Premier Dick Hamer's cocktail party and purred in his New York accent, 'Margaret, you will come with me.' She demurred, but in the end she couldn't resist his charms and Hamer seemed amazed but pleased to see her when she arrived on Bernstein's arm. Margaret recalls:

> Lenny was absolutely gorgeous. In the taxi cab he was rabbiting on and asking me about music. He was touchy but not feely. I

confessed that as far as music was concerned I liked it to float over me. He said 'Oh no, Margaret, it's got to be more than floating,' and he went into this long dissertation. I just loved to hear him talk.

We had a great time together at the cocktail party and he wanted to go on to dinner but I thought it was time to get back to the ranch. I told Gough all about it, of course. I boasted. He didn't seem at all worried.

Who knows – if I'd had the time and the situation I might have had an affair with Lenny, he was a fascinating man. There were possibilities to be tempted by from time to time, but I didn't have the means to do anything about them. When I was about forty, one chap did say to me, 'I really fancy you.' I was a bit stunned. I didn't fancy him, but I never really fancied anyone enough, or had a situation occur when I wanted to break the rules.

Breaking the rules inspired the next media outburst, too. The media were incensed that the wife of the Prime Minister was being paid commercial rates to host a television program. They claimed that with the $400 a week from her television program, $250 for her diary, and the salary from her directorship of the Commonwealth Hostels, she was 'Australia's highest female earner', and that her weekly income was only a few hundred dollars short of her husband's weekly wage.

The Sunday Mail ran insulting headlines like 'Big, Big Purse for Big Marg'. Other columns had headlines like 'Margaret – Shut Up', or aired opinions like, 'Gough Whitlam need have no worry about his financial future. His missus, the voluble hoo-ha political madam, Margaret, will look after him. Mrs Whitlam is guilty of blatant "cashing in" on her husband's good fortune.'

The Sunday Observer claimed that it would cause acute embarrassment to her husband and the Labor Party if Margaret kept the money she was paid for the television show – this journalist claimed that she was being paid $1000 a week for thirteen programs.

Margaret's secretary put out a press release assuring everyone that all her television earnings would be donated to charity, but then in a letter to the editor under the title of 'Maggie's Working Too Hard' a reader claimed she had too many jobs and was taking a living away from 'professional television ladies'.

And then there was the utterly predictable argument, from Mike Gibson in *The Daily Telegraph*, that it simply wasn't 'proper' or 'dignified' for the wife of the Prime Minister to do such work: 'I may be old-fashioned but I believe that the office of Prime Minister of Australia, and everyone and everything connected with it, should still have a certain dignity about it. I don't want to be represented by the compère of a late, late, TV show or someone who writes a housewives' gazette in a women's magazine.'

Margaret ignored the comments and continued to love doing her program and during the series interviewed an Antarctic explorer, a racing driver, a pop music composer, a photographer, a US ambassador and others. Unfortunately, the second series was moved to a later, less popular, time and finally was not renewed.

Meanwhile *The Sunday Telegraph* was reporting that Australia's inflation rate of 14.4 per cent placed it fourth after Japan (25.2), Italy (18.9) and Britain (17.7): 'Leading nations, including America, West Germany and Canada, all averaged much lower inflation rates than Australia, despite being hit by the increase in oil prices.'

On 26 September the editorial in *The News* in Adelaide launched an attack on the Prime Minister's frequent trips away, 'With the economy at a most crucial stage, the Prime Minister is packing his bags for North America. He could hardly have chosen a worse time to be away – with massive unemployment looming, the effects of the budget and devaluation still to be tested and with wage indexation in the balance. Later this year Mr Whitlam will be away again – on a tour of Europe.'

In the same month John Menadue left Rupert Murdoch and returned to work for Gough Whitlam as the Head of the Department of Prime Minister and Cabinet. He started the job believing that most of the cards that had been stacked against the Whitlam government had already been dealt. The first card, wrote Menadue, was the 'external economic shock caused by the US budget and trading deficits to pay for the war in Vietnam. This was followed by the 1973 Arab oil embargo and a 70 per cent increase in OPEC oil prices.'

He believed the second card was the refusal of the conservatives to accept that the Labor Party had beaten them twice and continued to threaten them from the Senate. The third card was the disunity and inexperience of Whitlam's twenty-seven-man cabinet.

Gough was also concerned about the loyalty of the Treasury and its advice, and the fact that senior bureaucrats within it who had worked for the conservatives for the past twenty-three years were unsympathetic to the Whitlam government.

It was with these problems simmering that Gough and Margaret took off for another overseas trip on 15 December. In thirty days they were to visit thirteen countries, including Sri Lanka, Belgium and the United Kingdom. On 24 December an entry in Margaret's private journal is headed DARWIN – CYCLONE TRACY.

Cyclone Tracy had hit Darwin on Christmas Day and despite the newspapers depicting the Whitlams surveying the ruins of the Mediterranean when they should have been surveying the ruins of Darwin, they were in fact listening to Christmas carols in King's College, Cambridge.

On Christmas Day John Menadue travelled to Darwin with Jim Cairns, the acting Prime Minister. Both of them were shocked at the devastation of the city. Menadue saw galvanised roofing sheets wrapped around telegraph poles like crumpled silver foil. Whitlam spoke to them by phone about whether he should return. The unanimous advice was that he should indeed come home urgently.

Margaret agreed with them and thought she should accompany him. She wrote in her diary, 'My first impulse was to fly home with my husband but I was told by him that my duty lay with the maintenance of the program long planned.'

Graham Freudenberg remembers that she argued her case very forcefully and that she and Gough 'had words' over it. Margaret's instincts, both politically and personally, told her that they should be in Darwin together with the victims of the disaster. The social worker in her cried out to help these people however she could, and because of her work on the board of the Commonwealth Hostels, she realised the necessity of giving them shelter and food, and a sense of security.

As a student of history Gough should have remembered the strength that King George VI and the Queen Mother gave those whose homes had been destroyed by bombs in World War II when they joined them in surveying the rubble. Margaret and Gough should have followed their example in cyclone-stricken Darwin.

Gough flew back to Australia on Boxing Day, but despite Margaret's passionate argument that she should accompany him, he refused to change his mind and was adamant that she fulfil their schedule as planned. Gough hates to cancel fixed plans or to let people down and he knew that Margaret would deputise for him extremely well. But he was also determined to resume his trip when he had dealt with the disaster.

Margaret did as she was told and flew on to Sicily and Malta.

But if both of them had cancelled their trip immediately, flown home and moved among the shattered people of Darwin comforting them in their darkest hour, there would have been none of the hostile response that awaited Gough at the airport in Darwin when he finally arrived on 28 December by RAAF plane from Perth.

He was shaken by the depth of the hostility, which slapped him hard in the face. He told Brigadier Alan Stretton, who was in charge of restoration and was being frustrated by federal ministers who were making their own decisions in their portfolio areas, 'They give me the shits as well. Do what you have to do. If you have any problems give me a ring and I will fix it.'

After doing what he could in Darwin, Gough returned to Kirribilli House for cabinet meetings. Menadue tried to argue him out of resuming his overseas trip. But he was adamant. Menadue continued to press his argument in a relentless fashion and eventually Gough looked him in the eye and said, 'Comrade, if I am going to put up with the fuckwits in the Labor Party I have got to have my trips.'

No doubt that was true and he did need to re-energise and re-invigorate himself, but the timing was bad politically. The resumption of his trip to meet up with Margaret in Crete did not sit well with the people of Australia and gave much cheer to his enemies, on both sides of the House. Once again Margaret's instincts had been right and once again they had been ignored.

INTERNATIONAL WOMEN'S YEAR

Some of Gough Whitlam's first actions after assuming office were to remove the luxury tax from contraceptives, introduce paid maternity leave for Commonwealth public servants and bring in a benefit to support mothers. These were initiatives which to Gough came under the umbrella of basic human rights and were areas in which women had been ignored or discriminated against, simply because of their gender.

Gough was well aware that the burgeoning women's liberation movement sweeping and reshaping the world had taken off like a bushfire in Australia, which from the time of its founding had been a very male-dominated society. The title of Anne Summer's book *Damned Whores and God's Police* illustrated all too accurately how Australian women were viewed.

In 1973 Gough had appointed Elizabeth Reid, a philosophy tutor at the ANU and a member of the Women's Electoral Lobby, as Women's Advisor to the Prime Minister. This was the first position and appointment of its kind, not only in Australia but in the world. Reid's job was to advise the Prime Minister directly on women's issues and Gough saw it as a logical step in helping to establish equal rights and equal opportunity for the women of Australia. Rumours swirled among the media that Reid and Gough were having an affair, and she was immediately branded with the condescending title 'Whitlam's Supergirl'.

The media were ready to pounce on her every utterance. They did not have to wait long. Headlines sprung up such as, 'PM's Supergirl Calls for Legalisation of Pot' and 'Supergirl in New Shock', which referred to the attempt by a Country Party MP to table an article written by Reid some years before in the ANU student newspaper, in which she told women to refuse to be sex objects and to try masturbation instead.

It is hard now to recall how shocking such statements were, not just to politicians but to the nation. The media's response was to trivialise and patronise what they termed the 'women's lib shriekers' and to make as many references as they could to what was wobbling under their T-shirts. To their chagrin and blatant hostility, 1975 was declared International Women's Year by the United Nations.

In 1974 Margaret had accepted an invitation from the Prime Minister to be chair of the Australian National Advisory Committee for International Women's Year. She wrote, 'I will be happy to accept the offer and look forward to being of service to you and our country in yet another role.' However, Margaret and Gough were both overseas on the first day of IWY, when the newspapers once again shouted their predictable headlines, referring to the annual grant money that would be allocated to women's projects. On 1 January *The Age* bellowed, '$2 Million for the Sheilas: Surprisingly It's Not a Joke'.

Reid had asked Sir John Kerr, the new Governor-General, to launch IWY. That night on television they both contributed to what Reid called 'a conversation on the issues'. Kerr was not convinced of the need for such a year as he believed that the majority of women was perfectly happy with their traditional role.

The Daily Telegraph captured their exchange of views with the headline 'Sir John & Libber in TV Clash'. Sir John, while not a convert to Reid's views, was certainly interested in her. In *The Truth of the Matter* Gough describes a balmy evening on 28 December 1974 when Reid and Patti Warn, his media secretary, had been sitting in the drawing room at Kirribilli House waiting for the Prime Minister to return from Darwin when they suddenly saw Kerr tapping on the French windows. Once they had settled him down with a glass of scotch he explained his presence by saying that he had been walking alone in the gardens of Admiralty House when he saw the lights on. He had come over to see if he could do anything to help Gough on his return.

When the two women received a message that Gough would not reach Sydney until 11 pm they decided to go to a party being held at Patti's nearby flat. They issued a 'light-hearted' invitation for Kerr to join them. He refused, but lamented his restrictive life and his loneliness after the death of his wife. Not long after they had settled in at the party there was a buzz on the intercom. It was Kerr, who announced that he and his aide had decided to join them.

Sir John made further attempts to be in Elizabeth Reid's company with dinners, lunches and visits, which culminated in a marriage proposal. His main argument to her was, 'Why work for the second most important man in Australia when you could be married to the most important?' Needless to say, she wasn't convinced that was a sound basis for marriage and avoided having any further formal, and certainly informal, contact with the silver-haired head of state.

Margaret's regular column in *Woman's Day* continued to reflect her daily life. February found her in Terrigal at the ALP Federal

Conference, spending as much time as she could swimming in the pool. Photos of her diving prowess appeared in the daily papers.

Nevertheless, she was also forthright in her column about her feelings on IWY, her contribution to the National Advisory Committee and her assessment of a woman's role as a wife, with particular reference to her increasing disenchantment with her own role. She wrote, 'Two days of indolence convince me even more than ever that it is necessary for a woman of my age to have a full-time occupation. No matter how you look at it, the role of a wife is not, at fifty-five, all-consuming.'

She continued with a call to women to take control of their own lives:

> I would say to all women, do what you want to do, particularly if it will be of help to others. It's no use waiting for your husband to allocate some little task. Looking after his physical needs helps him a lot, but fulfils in no way your own need to contribute.
>
> This year I shall apply myself even more assiduously to the jobs I've taken on, and also make more time for artistic relaxation. No one can work out a program for me that will suit me as well as the one I work out myself.

In her March column, she admits that she 'is not a complete subscriber to women's lib, not liking the aggressiveness and shrillness that often goes with the movement', however, she thinks 'the general argument is hard to fault. Women have had a raw deal.'

Even though Margaret had formally accepted her husband's invitation to join the Australian National Advisory Committee for IWY, Elizabeth Reid reveals that Margaret seemed at first, not quite sure whether this was, as she would say, 'her cup of tea'.

At the first meeting of the committee she attended Reid observed that she continued to knit throughout the discussion and had positioned her chair so that it was drawn back and sideways to the table. However, her reluctance to join in the discussion didn't last long and Reid says that she 'very soon became an active member of the committee and respected in her own right'.

April saw Margaret in Darwin with her secretary, Barbara, quietly visiting the victims of Cyclone Tracy and praising their resilience and their determination to 'get on with it'. She found the journey rewarding and thought often about the young women she had met, who were bringing up their children in caravans; of their isolation and yet their calm and their optimism. She looked forward to being part of the planning of the new Darwin.

June brought the Commonwealth Heads of Government Meeting (CHOGM) in Jamaica and she was happy to join the wives of the other heads of government and their advisors in a mini-conference to discuss the role of women in society. Wives from Jamaica, Britain, Canada, Nigeria, Guyana and Western Samoa spoke and Margaret represented Australia. She welcomed any opportunity to share ideas and experiences about their roles.

In June there was also the big IWY conference in Mexico, where Margaret was the chair of the Australian delegation, which consisted of three official delegates.

'MUM'S THE WORD AS THE BIG YAK-YAK BEGINS' sniped *The Daily Telegraph*. For the previous year she and the delegates had been meeting with various groups to discuss the document that they would present at the conference. Margaret thought the women's libbers probably considered her to be 'a bit wet' – not militant enough – but nonetheless she quickly became an established member of the team, and she was respected by all the women who worked with her. Reid noticed that she never asserted herself as the wife of the Prime Minister, and involved herself with great humility and grace in all aspects of the conference.

Attending made her very aware of the appalling situation of women in third-world countries and she was deeply moved by their personal stories. However, it was not all depressing. She met up with Germaine Greer and had lunch with Gloria Steinem, who she thought was very glamorous and charming, with a wonderful sense of humour. She remembers that they ate a Mexican delicacy called turkey with chocolate sauce, which is named for its colour because it is very dark gravy.

Susan Ryan, at that stage a candidate for the Senate, was on the delegation, but not as a nominated candidate. She thought Margaret was 'a beacon of commonsense' within the conference, which generated a lot of noise, excitement and controversy because many of the women involved in it were so inexperienced. Ryan says that when there was bad press there would be 'lots of bursting into tears and heightened emotion and non-coping behaviour' and that Margaret would always settle everyone down.

Even though Margaret didn't instantly embrace the women's movement, Ryan felt that she was an involved and acute observer. 'I don't think her temperament is political. She's not one to put herself in the front line or take on a fight. She's more the person who calms the conflict, the sane voice.'

Ryan was impressed by her lack of vanity and her basic humility. 'When we were swanning around Mexico City going to presidential receptions, she was so dignified yet relaxed. Anyone could come up to her and have a talk and people were thrilled to meet her. Even Germaine was a bit in awe of her.'

While being warm and relaxed with everyone, Ryan noticed that she was no pushover either. 'She would often make sharp observations about people whom she didn't think were doing the right thing.' Ryan was even more impressed that after a big celebration on their last night, when they'd all drunk a large number of marguerítas, Margaret still behaved impeccably. The next morning when they had to catch their plane home they were all feeling a little the worse for wear. Margaret had visited the markets and done a lot of shopping during her stay, including purchasing a big, heavy chess set, which she was carrying home as hand luggage. They had to change planes in Dallas and queue for a long time, and Margaret's arms were straining with the weight of her chess set, but she didn't complain other than to comment that fewer drinks the night before might have added to her strength.

Then the clerk who was rebooking them onto the plane came up to Margaret and asked her if she would like to come to the front of the queue.' She replied immediately, 'No, I'll wait my turn.' Even Ryan said that under the circumstances she would have been tempted to think, 'Oh, goody,' and accept the offer, but Margaret's reaction was consistent, in that she never sought or accepted advantages that weren't available to all, and she never, ever 'put on side'.

This refusal to accept special privileges was not just good politics on Margaret's behalf, nor was it just good manners from her upbringing. She has a genuine sense of what's fair and she would have considered that to jump a queue because you are the wife of the Prime Minister is simply not fair.

Not that being the wife of an increasingly controversial and unpopular leader was always a source of advantage.

In July Margaret received a letter from Joan Reeder, the editor of *Woman's Day*, informing her of the decision to drop her column. Reeder wrote, 'You may think that this decision is somehow mixed up with the present problems of the government and/or with the fact that we have recently been sold back to Fairfax. But neither of these things is so. The fact is, Margaret, that we think the column has run its course.'

Margaret accepted this decision with the stoic calm that had become her standard reaction to rejection. She did not argue, or retaliate, or seek to punish with whatever power her position afforded her, as some wives of past prime ministers might have done. This was simply not her style. It would take a much bigger rejection than that from a women's magazine editor to bring out the sting in her Scorpio tail.

In August the Women and Politics Conference was held in Canberra, and was described by the media as 'organised anarchy'. Hundreds of women from community groups from all over the nation were there, excited and energised by the fact that this was a government who had allocated money that could be used for one of their causes.

The media were not all that interested in the speakers, or the discussions, but became apoplectic at the opening cocktail party held in King's Hall at Old Parliament House. 'A drunken display of exhibitionism which under normal circumstances would have required police intervention,' trumpeted *The Daily Telegraph*.

The newspapers couldn't agree, however, in their various reports on whether it was spray-paint or lipstick that spelled out 'LESBIANS ARE LOVELY' in the women's toilets. They also described a 'disgusting display of vandalism in Parliament House', which was, in fact, some bras draped over the statues. Nor were journalists amused at the large number of women who turned up in men's suits, sending up the specified dress code of 'lounge suit'.

Incensed by the misrepresentation and the hysterical beat-ups of the press reports, several hundred women marched on the offices of *The Canberra Times* to protest and demand a right of reply. In August 2005, thirty years later, many of those same women again gathered in King's Hall at Old Parliament House for cocktails and a dinner. It was a very tame and dignified gathering compared to 1975 – more like Anzac Day for the feminists. Gough and Margaret sat at the head table enjoying the food and the festivities and a large number of people came to pay court and thank them for their contribution to their lives. Margaret was unfazed by the attention, but she did say she was pretty chuffed when Gough turned to her later and said, 'Well I think you certainly brushed up better than a lot of those women, Margaret.'

The media were intent on attacking the women's libbers and the Prime Minister's 'supergirl', but the budget of 1975, produced by the new Treasurer, Bill Hayden, who had replaced Jim Cairns, was more to their liking.

Bill Hayden and his wife, Dallas, both remember the Whitlams being extremely kind to them when Bill first entered Parliament. When the Whitlam children were small the family had visited the Haydens on the Gold Coast and Margaret took all three children for a swim on her back. Bill also remembers being summoned to the Lodge for lunch, where Gough said to him at the door, 'Margaret will be here. She does tend to burble on a bit. Just let her go and then we'll have our talk.'

Hayden, in fact, viewed Margaret as 'self-possessed, articulate and good-humoured, with clear views on a range of subjects'. He especially admired the way she never allowed herself to be overwhelmed by the atmosphere of Parliament House. He says, 'Gough never intimidated her. Nor did he try. Margaret always reminded me of Eleanor Roosevelt, in that she was tall and competent. In different circumstances Margaret, too, could have chaired UN conferences.'

However, unlike Eleanor's husband, Hayden said, 'Gough was always well-behaved and there were definitely no dalliances.

His only indulgence was an occasional cigar and a small glass of cognac if he'd had a good run in the House.'

Many years later, when Hayden was Governor-General, he invited the Whitlams to a function at Yarralumla where Gough had been invited to speak. 'It was one of his bad nights and he went on and on and on. Eventually, Margaret said audibly, "Will somebody tell that man to shut up and sit down?" When no one did as she had suggested, she started banging her walking stick on the floor until eventually Gough sat down.'

Meanwhile, in 1975 Hayden's budget was quickly followed by another press uproar – this time with Deputy Prime Minister Jim Cairns at its centre. A letter signed by Cairns was produced, which authorised George Harris, the President of the Carlton Football Club and a friend of Shadow Treasurer Phil Lynch, to undertake the raising of loans while he was overseas.

Cairns initially claimed that he had no knowledge of signing the letter but Whitlam finally forced him to resign. At the time Cairns had been preoccupied with a woman called Junie Morosi, his new principal private secretary, with whom he had sworn he was not having an affair (it took a new century for him to tell the truth), but for whom he did confess to a journalist he felt 'a kind of love'. The tabloids went berserk over the phrase.

Gough had largely ignored Cairns's personal indiscretions, believing that his personal life was his business, but Margaret was convinced that the twice-married ex-air-hostess had indeed come to dominate not only the Treasurer's days, but also his nights. While men swooned before her exotic looks and her palpable sexuality, Margaret thought Cairns was making a complete fool of himself, his wife, Gwen, and the government. She suggested to Gough that he should have a talk to him, but Gough continued to toss off the rumours as tabloid hysteria. In truth, he was too shy to tackle people on personal matters. His confidence and extroverted performances in Parliament were the antithesis of his skills in personal relationships. Like many actors, he was comfortable on the stage in front of an audience, but he found it very difficult to confront people on a one-to-one basis. His method was to avoid them, or delegate someone else to talk to them or explode into a temper tantrum to which there was no response. In all these instances the kind of intimacy needed to navigate personal discussions was avoided.

In September 1975 John Menadue, as head of the Department of Prime Minister and Cabinet, told Gough he thought that the Women's Affairs unit would be more secure inside the department than in Whitlam's private office. When Elizabeth Reid was informed of this decision she was furious, seeing it as a devious move to make her a public servant and therefore shut her up. (Menadue still denies this was his motive.)

Seeking a final meeting with Whitlam in late September she was intending to submit her resignation if he persisted with this course of action. She also wanted to inform him, privately, that Kerr had personally told her and Clifton Pugh, who was painting Kerr's official portrait, that he was going to dismiss Whitlam and force an election to be called. According to Reid, Kerr was given to monologues about himself and his importance.

The meeting between Reid and Whitlam took place in his office. They were there alone, and Gough would have hated the emotional tenor of her conversation. She talked, he didn't. She paced the room with tears running down her face as she tried to explain to him why she thought moving her to the Department of Prime Minister and Cabinet was the wrong decision, that the women voters would not be pleased and that if he persisted with it she would resign. Reid says he was totally unresponsive to anything she said. Nor were her revelations about Kerr's intention to dismiss him commented upon.

'It was as if I hadn't spoken,' she said. 'I was standing there in his office and I was in tears . . . he was probably as embarrassed as I was.'

Gough claims not to remember her conversation with him about Kerr's intentions, and perhaps even at the time it didn't really sink in because he was so uncomfortable about Reid's display of emotion. To have a crying woman telling him something he did not believe about the man he had appointed as Governor-General was simply not to be taken seriously. She was upset, she was angry with his decision and he would have just wished she would shut up and leave the office so he could get on with his work.

Reid said, 'I walked away feeling that I was the wrong messenger, that in Gough's head I was this woman who was his advisor on women, so how could I possibly have something as grounded and shattering as that to say to him?' She left his office, never to return.

Gough certainly never repeated what Reid claims she had told him about Kerr to either Menadue, or to Margaret. When asked why she hadn't talked to Margaret about what Kerr had told her, Reid said, 'I didn't work that way. He was my boss and I worked to him. I talked to Margaret about International Women's Year.'

If Gough took in her information at all, he clearly dismissed it immediately. Even if Margaret had known what Kerr intended, there is no guarantee that Gough would have taken any more notice of her in this matter than he did of Reid. He was always firmly convinced that Kerr would never take action against the government.

He no doubt thought he had far more pressing problems on his agenda than such hearsay or speculation. As a result of the dramatic rise in the price of oil in 1973, newly rich Middle Eastern countries began lending what were called 'petro-dollars'. Rex Connor, Minister for Minerals and Energy, was keen to secure a Middle East loan to fulfil his dreams to build a major gas pipeline grid in Australia, linking all the gas fields to consumers, petro-chemical plants, uranium mines, railway electrification and coal exporters. He said he needed the money to 'buy back the farm'.

Neither Connor nor his head of department, Sir Lennox Hewitt, trusted the Treasury or its officials, so they set about getting the money through other agencies. In October 1974 Connor had been introduced to a Pakistani money-broker based in London called Tirath Khemlani, who claimed he could raise the loans from the Middle East.

In December 1974 the Executive Council signed a minute that authorised Connor 'to borrow for temporary purposes four billion US dollars and to determine the terms and conditions for borrowing'.

The general view, as Menadue states it, was, 'If the Snowy scheme could be built under the defence power of the constitution, why couldn't loans be raised for major energy projects?'

The Treasury, needless to say, was firmly opposed to the raising of loans outside its approval and control, and daily leaks to the media became powerful weapons in the destabilisation of the government. The Melbourne *Sun News-Pictorial* ran a story on Khemlani with a photo of him sleeping on a stretcher in a London basement. No one really knew where he had come from and who he represented, and such pictures contributed to the idea that he was a rather shady character. His name continued to exert a sour and suspicious odour, and on 20 May 1975 Whitlam ordered Connor to cease all loans negotiations with Khemlani.

But Connor refused to let go of his vision of Australia developing its own energy resources and behind the Prime Minister's back he continued to make unauthorised contact with Khemlani and other possible lenders. Night after night he slept in his office, waiting for a message of confirmation from the teleprinter. It never came. Khemlani seemed to have disappeared into the ether, but the damage had been done.

It soon became clear that Connor had deceived the Prime Minister and he therefore had to resign. Malcolm Fraser, who had replaced Snedden as the Opposition leader in March, used his resignation as proof that the government was on the nose, and on 15 October 1975, because of what he called 'extraordinary and reprehensible circumstances', he announced that the Opposition would defer the supply bills in the Senate. The Senate voted 29–28 to defer the budget.

The following day the trade unions threatened massive retaliation against the Opposition over the blocking of the supply bills. In Murdoch's *Australian* on 17 October, Paul Kelly reported that, 'Opposition members claimed that if Mr Whitlam continued to stay in office without seeking a general election, the Governor-General had the power to dismiss him as Prime Minister and commission new ministers.'

Margaret read these articles with increasing alarm and constantly asked Gough if 'everything was all right'. He assured her that she had no cause to worry and she believed him. She had seen him weathering many political crises and challenges in the course of his career as a politician and he had always been successful in solving them. She had no reason to doubt that his confidence in his ability to deal with the tactics of the Opposition was well founded.

Nevertheless, she made a point of sitting in the visitors' gallery during parliamentary sessions to witness for herself his success in carrying a motion on the floor of the House of Representatives expressing confidence in the government and condemning the Opposition for their deferral of the budget in the Senate.

Both her morale and that of the government were lifted when Whitlam delivered a rousing, fighting speech pledging that the Senate's rejection of the budget would be taken to the people in the half-Senate election that he was planning. She was also encouraged by the words of Liberal Senator Steele Hall, who believed that the Senate, the Liberal Party and the Liberal leader, Mr Fraser, had sown the seeds of their own destruction, and that the Opposition parties would crack in the Senate within the next few weeks. On 18 October the headline in *The Australian* said 'GOVERNOR-GENERAL WILL ACT SOON, SAYS FRASER'. Meanwhile, there were violent demonstrations against the Opposition's blocking of the supply bills in Hobart and Brisbane.

On 21 October Fraser had his first meeting with the Governor-General and the next day he announced, 'The Opposition will abide by any decision reached by the Governor-General.' In Paul Kelly's book *November 1975* he writes, 'From the time that Fraser left the meeting [on 21 October] he never wavered in his belief that Kerr would intervene, finally, on the Opposition's behalf if Whitlam refused to call a general election.'

While hindsight is always a great source of wisdom, it is clear that Fraser had discerned Kerr's insecurity regarding his position, or Kerr had actually spoken to him about his fear of being dismissed if Whitlam sensed he did not have Kerr's full support. Whitlam, however, never believed that Kerr would betray him or deceive him in terms of his support.

But he did know now that, unlike 1974 when he had called an

early election, the public mood had changed, and that if he was forced to an election in late 1975 he would lose.

In the South Australian election in July 1975, Premier Don Dunstan, in consultation with Whitlam, had disowned his association with the government in order to get across the line. He survived. Just. In Queensland under Joh Bjelke-Petersen the Whitlam government was very unpopular. When Gough had been invited to meet the teams at a rugby match in Brisbane he had been booed from the football ground. With his characteristic self-mocking sense of humour he had turned to Ron McAuliffe, a Labor senator and a popular president of the Queensland rugby league, and said, 'Don't you ever bring me here again if you are as unpopular as this.'

Even Margaret's mother, usually so jolly and bubbly, had rung her to say, 'Darling, couldn't Gough just do something that would make him popular with the people?' Margaret reassured her that he was doing what was right and that he would win through in the end. And when she herself sought such assurances from him, he showed no signs of doubt that the path he had chosen was correct and proper.

Deferral of supply would not have been possible if the established convention of replacing outgoing senators with members from the same party had not been broken by the conservative premiers in New South Wales and Queensland. Labor lost two senators as a result of this flouting of convention.

Gough felt that the conservatives refused to accept that in 1972 and 1974 they had been defeated fairly, that they never accepted the Whitlam government as legitimate. Between 1973 and 1975 ninety-three bills were rejected in the Senate, which was more than the sixty-eight bills rejected in the first seventy-three years of Federation. Whitlam, however, stood firm against the deferral by the Senate on the grounds of obstruction and on the convention that governments are made and unmade in the House of Representatives and not in the Senate.

Malcolm Fraser backed Reg Withers, the Leader of the Opposition in the Senate, in his belief that the best tactic was to defer the bills and force the government to either run out of money, or agree to an election.

Whitlam considered that it was inappropriate to involve the Queen or the palace in the dispute and that it should be resolved politically within Australia. When it was suggested to him that the Queen's representative in Australia, namely the Governor-General, should be invited by him to address the Senate, or perhaps both Houses of Parliament, urging the Senate to pass the supply bills, Whitlam rejected it on the grounds that it wasn't correct to involve the Governor-General in political disputes.

Gough was a stickler for proper procedure and correct behaviour, not only because of his legal training, but also because of his upbringing, and the values and codes instilled in him by his father regarding good leadership. Besides, Menadue claims that he had recorded proof that the Governor-General had assured him, as well as his close friend and confidant Jim McClelland and Attorney-General Kep Enderby – together with many others – that the government could rely on his support. Even Catherine Whitlam remembers Sir John at Kirribilli House supporting the government's position.

There were, however, several factors that Gough had clearly not considered. There were signs, which others saw, that he either failed to see or was not receptive to recognising – because he simply would not believe it – that Kerr would not necessarily act on Whitlam's own terms in these matters, in other words according to 'proper procedure'.

Firstly, Kerr's recent marriage to his second wife, Nancy, had changed him. Sir John had become particularly sensitive to Whitlam's public utterances that he would do whatever the Prime Minister ordered him to do. He was a vain and weak man who, without the solidity and security of his first wife, began to doubt how he was viewed. Gough certainly never bothered to massage his ego, or to reassure him of the security of his position, nor did he attempt to reassure his second wife that she would continue to reside in Admiralty House, which seemed to be very important to her.

In fact, on 16 October at a dinner at Government House for the Malaysian Prime Minister, Gough joked 'It could be a race between me getting to the Queen to get you dismissed and you terminating my commission as Prime Minister.'

Such a joke was not amusing to someone already feeling insecure, and the fact that Gough made it publicly was also embarrassing to a man becoming obsessed with his status.

Margaret, however, was very much aware of Kerr's weaknesses. In particular, she noted his insistence, and that of his new wife, on pomp and ceremony, which only reinforced her view that he had not been one of her husband's best appointments.

Margaret says that Nancy was at pains to demonstrate her own status and sophistication. Gough still refers to her as 'fancy Nancy' because he claims that apart from being Kerr's mistress, she had been engaged by the Department of Foreign Affairs to look after French officials at the School of Public Administration and South Pacific Commission from French Polynesia, Tahiti and New Caledonia.

One of her more obvious pretensions was her insistence on having the dinner menus for Government House printed entirely in French. At one formal dinner Gough pointed out a mistake in the menu to her in his usual blunt, school-teacherly manner in front of the other guests. He said, 'Nancy, I'm surprised. You've made a mistake in your French.'

She bridled and responded, 'Oh Prime Minister, you can't mean that.'

But Gough laboured the point, which was not appreciated by either her or her husband. Margaret said to him later when they were alone, 'That was not a clever thing to do and won't stand you in good stead. She doesn't like being corrected. You could have done that more diplomatically.'

Gough dismissed her comments, but Margaret was very attuned to other people's reactions and she knew that it was foolish to embarrass those who were vain or pretentious, even if you were right in your assertions. Such public humiliations are rarely forgiven.

Increasingly Kerr let it be known that he was not the Prime Minister's puppet, and yet he was clearly afraid of being dismissed if he didn't do what the Prime Minister ordered.

On 6 November the political pressure was at boiling point and Fraser visited the Governor-General once more. According to Paul Kelly, Fraser said, 'I told the Governor-General that if Australia did not get an election, the Opposition would have no choice but to be highly critical of him. We would have to say that he had failed his duty . . . to the nation.'

Fraser clearly knew that by threatening Kerr with repercussions when the Liberals were in government (as all the polls predicted would happen were there an election) he was escalating the Governor-General's insecurity. Fraser knew that the stand-off had gone on too long and that if Kerr didn't act soon there would be no time to hold a general election before Christmas. Fraser had already telephoned the Commonwealth Electoral Commissioner in order to ascertain the last date on which such an election need to be announced. He was told that it would have to be 11 November, or early the following week.

On the evening of 10 November Margaret and Gough were in Melbourne, as Gough was the speaker at the Lord Mayor's banquet. Malcolm Fraser and his shadow treasurer, Phillip Lynch, were also guests at the banquet and the Prime Minister generously offered them a ride back to Canberra on his VIP aircraft. Thus Gough and Margaret spent their last night together as the PM and the PM's wife with Malcolm Fraser sitting behind them. After they landed in Canberra Margaret continued on in the plane to Sydney. Menadue met Gough at the airport with some papers to sign and actually heard Lynch ask Fraser, 'Do you think he knows?' The words at the time meant nothing to him.

DISMISSALS

On the morning of 11 November Gough awoke to a beautiful Canberra day – clear white light and pale blue sky. He normally enjoyed walking around the gardens of the Lodge in the stringent eucalyptus-scented air of the early morning, but today he was preoccupied with what he hoped to achieve. By the time the hush of evening had settled around the Lodge, he hoped to have secured a half-Senate election and broken the deadlock in the Senate.

Margaret, too, had a meeting on her mind when she walked out onto the verandah at Kirribilli House to look at what she considered to be the most beautiful harbour in the world – and she had certainly seen most of them. It was the last board meeting of the year for the Commonwealth Hostels Association, and as a director she had invited the board to the house for drinks and lunch. The harbour was at its sparkling best and the sky was already Reckitt's blue. She remembered how they used to rinse all their white clothes in Reckitt's – thank God she didn't have to do it now. She thought to herself how easy it would be to spend all day just sitting out there soaking up the sun and the beauty, but she knew she had better get cracking.

At 9.30 am the Prime Minister and his ministers Frank Crean and Fred Daly met with Fraser and his shadow ministers Phillip Lynch and Doug Anthony in Parliament House to try to find a possible solution to the impasse between the two parties. Neither Fraser nor Whitlam would move an inch. Fraser held out for an election for the House of Representatives, and Whitlam told him that he was going to see the Governor-General that very morning to request a half-Senate election. His intention by doing so was to rid himself of the renegade replacement senators from New South Wales and Queensland, and for the first time include the elected senators from the ACT and the Northern Territory.

Fraser and Lynch returned to Fraser's office and decided that the best approach to the Liberal–Country Party meeting arranged for 10.30 am was to have no discussion but simply to ask them to trust in the judgement of the leadership.

On the other side of the building Whitlam was on the phone to the Governor-General, informing him that he would be calling at Government House with a document to formally request a half-Senate election. Kerr made no comment, hung up the phone and promptly went off to a remembrance service at the war memorial for Armistice Day.

Whitlam went straight to the ALP caucus meeting, where he reported on his discussion with the Opposition leaders and his communication with the Governor-General. From there he went into the chamber of the House of Representatives to deal with the censure motion that Fraser was bringing on. The debate followed the familiar lines of argument that had been pursued on both sides for the past four weeks. Fraser attacked Whitlam over the loans affair, the resignation of Connor, the sacking of Cairns and his attempt to govern without supply. 'To try to govern without appropriation of money by Parliament is the first significant step on the path to an Australian dictatorship,' asserted Fraser.

Whitlam's response was that it was the Senate that was behaving unconstitutionally. 'The Leader of the Opposition is seeking to reduce the powers of the House of Representatives in a way never before attempted in Australia.'

In Government House Kerr's official secretary, David Smith, had phoned Fraser's private secretary and suggested that Fraser leave Parliament House ten minutes after Whitlam as Kerr wished to see him.

The Prime Minister was delayed and Fraser arrived early. Smith took him to a nearby room to wait. Fraser's car had been parked around the other side of Government House. Whitlam had no knowledge he was there when at 1 pm his car pulled up at the front door and he was ushered into the Governor-General's study.

Even though Whitlam knew from *The Vice-Regal News* that the Chief Justice, Sir Garfield Barwick, had called on Kerr the day before at Kerr's request and against the wishes of his prime minister, he did not know what advice Barwick had given the Governor-General. He was about to find out.

They were in Kerr's study – just the two of them, face to face. Kerr asked Whitlam if he was prepared to recommend a general election. Whitlam said he was not and before he could present his document requesting a half-Senate election Kerr handed him his own document of dismissal, saying that in that case he had no alternative but to dismiss him. He added that the letter of dismissal was supported by the Chief Justice. Gough said to him, 'But I thought I had advised you that you should not seek his advice.'

Kerr replied, 'Oh well, we all have to live with these things.'

To say that Whitlam was shocked would be a monumental understatement. Never, despite all the warnings from other people that Kerr was not to be trusted, did he imagine that Kerr would take the action he did. Whitlam didn't argue, he didn't refuse the document, he did not buy any time. He simply took the piece of paper, they shook hands and he walked out.

Fraser then walked in, eager to accept the conditions offered to him as the newly appointed caretaker prime minister.

In the dining room at Kirribilli House Margaret and her board members were finishing their drinks when she was told there was an urgent call from Canberra. It was Robert Millar, Gough's driver. He said, 'The boss asked me to ring you to tell you that he's been sacked.'

Margaret asked, 'What do you mean?'

'He told me to tell you that he can't ring you at the moment, but he's been sacked. That's all I know. He said he'll ring you later.'

Margaret put the phone down and returned to the dining room table. The word 'sacked' boomed in her ears. 'Sacked' – surely not. How? Why? When? She knew she would have to put the questions out of her mind for now and wait for Gough to ring.

'Anything wrong, Margaret?' asked one of her colleagues, concerned by her worried expression. She forced herself to give a jolly laugh. 'No, of course not. Now, let's have this delicious food.'

Thirty minutes later she heard the phone ring again. It was Gough.

'He's sacked me.'

'Who's sacked you?'

'Kerr.'

'Don't be ridiculous. He can't sack you, you're the elected prime minister.'

'I walked into his office, he asked me whether I was going to agree to an election of the House of Reps. I refused. He said, "In that case I have no alternative but to withdraw your commission," and he handed me a sheet of paper.'

Margaret said, 'How ridiculous, why didn't you just tear it up?'

'Because, Margaret, it was a legal document.'

'So what? You should have torn it up. There were only two of you there. Or you should have slapped his face and told him to pull himself together.'

She meant it.

Gough said he had to go, there were people he had to see, he would ring again.

She put the phone down and was aware of a strange sinking sensation in her stomach, as if a stone had landed there, lying heavy and waiting – what for? Probably another stone.

She composed her expression into a calm smile and returned to the table. That was the story of her life – preparing a smiling face.

The word 'sacked' flashed on and off like a neon light inside her brain. He couldn't have been 'sacked'. He had been elected – twice. It couldn't be right. He'd fix it, surely he could fix it. He always had in the past. Sacked? It couldn't be right.

It was still a dazzlingly beautiful day on the harbour, which stretched before them as they ate their lunch. Margaret smiled and chatted and nodded and when they had finished their coffee she returned with them to finish the meeting in North Sydney.

She found it hard to concentrate. Why hadn't he called again to tell her what was happening? What was she meant to do? Sacked? What did it all mean?

One of her fellow board members, sensing from the phone calls and her worried expression that something was wrong, eventually said to her, 'Why don't you buzz off home, Margaret? We'll finish the meeting. Don't worry about it.'

At 1.45 pm John Menadue was eating a sandwich in his office at West Block, waiting for a call from Whitlam to confirm that the

Governor-General had agreed to a half-Senate election. Instead, the phone rang with a call from David Smith. 'I am ringing to inform you that the Governor-General, Sir John Kerr, has dismissed the Whitlam government, and Malcolm Fraser has been commissioned to form a government.'

In a stunned state Menadue rang the heads of the Treasury and the Public Service Board to tell them what he had just been told. No sooner had he hung up than Whitlam's driver called to say that Whitlam wanted to see him urgently at the Lodge.

Gough was sitting in the sunroom eating a steak for lunch when Menadue entered. Gough's apparently calm demeanor at this time is absolutely inexplicable to many people, Bill Hayden included.

'How could he just sit there, eating a steak?' he has wondered. 'Why wasn't he trying to get a plan organised? I know he is a trencherman at the dinner table but you would think that under such circumstances he would be too churned up to eat.'

Gough's explanation is that he had asked the staff to prepare him a steak for when he returned from Government House and as they had he therefore felt he should eat it. Another explanation is that his mother had always cooked delicious food for her children, especially her beloved son. Whenever he was upset she cooked him something special. In a state of extreme shock, it would therefore seem only natural for him to attempt to calm down and think while eating.

'The bastard's done a Game on me!' he shouted at Menadue.

He was referring to the 1932 dismissal of the Lang government by Governor Sir Philip Game – ironically the one political incident that Margaret remembers her parents discussing.

Suddenly the Lodge erupted into total chaos and confusion as Fred Daly, Frank Crean, John Mant and Graham Freudenberg burst into the sunroom. Confusion and shock on their faces, they discussed what was to be done. The former Prime Minister began to draft resolutions for the afternoon sitting of the House of Representatives. What they had all forgotten in the heat of the revelations was to tell Ken Wriedt, the ALP leader in the Senate, what had happened.

By the time Margaret arrived back at Kirribilli House her doctor, John Hammett, had heard the news in an ABC bulletin and was waiting for her. 'I thought you might be suffering from shock so I called around, just to see if you needed anything.' Margaret was very touched by his thoughtfulness and did admit to feeling rather stunned, but not in need of medication.

She did, however, pour herself a bloody mary while they sat together in the living room waiting for the phone to ring. Gough finally rang to see how she was and explain what was happening.

'I'd better come down straight away,' Margaret said.

'No,' replied Gough, 'you stay where you are. I'm driving to Sydney tomorrow anyway.' His voice, so firm and assured, had its usual deep resonance, and she thought it best not to argue, even though she desperately wanted to be with him.

While the rest of the nation, whatever their politics, shared a sense of complete shock and disbelief, and still remembers where they were when they heard the news, Margaret sat by the phone hoping desperately that Gough would ring again to tell her he had fixed the problem and that everything was back to normal.

Nick and his English wife Judy had only returned from the United Kingdom to live in Sydney five days before. Nick heard the news in a taxi on his way back from lunch to their barely furnished house in Woollahra in Sydney's eastern suburbs. At first what he heard did not greatly alarm him because the news report had said that a vote of no-confidence in Fraser was being put to the House of Representatives. He says he thought to himself, 'Dad will be back in power before the day is out.'

In the meantime Margaret had received another call from Gough's driver to tell her about the intended vote of no-confidence and she, too, took heart from the news.

The afternoon sitting of the Senate began with some Labor ministers, including Wriedt, unaware that Whitlam had been dismissed and that they were no longer ministers. By the time they knew what had happened, the Appropriation Bills that three of them had brought forward had been passed.

At 2.24 pm the Senate of the twenty-ninth Parliament of Australia adjourned, never to meet again.

Meanwhile, across at King's Hall in the House of Representatives, Whitlam was moving his motion of no-confidence in the new Prime Minister, which was carried sixty-four votes to fifty-four. The Speaker announced his intentions to convey the House's message to the Governor-General and he suspended the sitting until 5.30 pm.

Crowds – angry, emotional crowds – began to swell outside Parliament House. A communal chant of 'We want Gough' echoed through the halls.

By 4.45 pm David Smith was standing in front of them on the steps of Parliament House. He read a proclamation from Sir John Kerr saying he was dissolving both Houses amid the hostile roaring of the assembled masses.

Whitlam, who had been standing behind Smith while he read the proclamation, took over the microphone and there was ear-splitting cheering and whistling. Towering over them at the top of the steps, he was at his most intense and charismatic. He boomed, 'Ladies and gentlemen,' and the crowd became silent. He paused, a dramatic pause, and said, his eyes glinting with revenge, 'Well may we say "God save the Queen", because nothing will save the Governor-General.' This was followed by a characteristic upward tilt of his head.

The applause was thunderous and those words were burnt into the memory of Australians everywhere on 11 November 1975.

He continued, 'The proclamation which you have just heard read by the Governor-General's official secretary was countersigned "Malcolm Fraser", who will undoubtedly go down in Australian history from Remembrance Day 1975 as Kerr's cur.' The screams and hysterical cheering were deafening.

Furthermore, as a dedicated historian he couldn't resist instructing them, 'I'm the first prime minister to be sacked since George III sacked Lord North.' He then urged everyone present to 'maintain their rage and enthusiasm' for the next four and a half weeks.

The Speaker, Gordon Scholes, had tried unsuccessfully to see the Governor-General before this proclamation was delivered but Kerr had refused to see him. It was now too late. The deed was done.

When Margaret received a call from Gough to tell her that the Governor-General had refused to see the Speaker, but that it had been agreed they would stay on in the Lodge until after the election, her response was, 'Well, I'm leaving Kirribilli House before midnight. It's not proper that I stay here. I'll go to the flat.'

Gough agreed that was probably a good idea as Kirribilli House was technically a government house and he was no longer the head of the government. Jo and Rita, the two women on the staff who looked after them at Kirribilli, had already been to the flat, lined the drawers with kitchen paper and generally helped them settle in with a few necessary items. Gough and Margaret had always thought of their flat in Darling Point as a special hideaway where they could occasionally stay, just the two of them, when they had no official engagements that necessitated staying at Kirribilli. They had assumed it might eventually be a nice place to retire, but had always thought that would be many years ahead.

Now, suddenly, Margaret realised it was their only home. At least, until the election result. She began to feel panic rising in her throat and, determined not to let it get a grip, she rang Nick and Judy. Tony was working overseas, she would have to contact him later. Before they arrived Catherine appeared on the doorstep looking as wide-eyed and shocked as her mother felt. 'Are you okay, Mum?' she said, giving Margaret a long, hard hug.

'Yes, darling, I'm fine, but I'll need your help moving some of our personal stuff from here to the flat. Dad thinks it's best. The girls here have offered to help.'

Stephen was between postings and working in his office at the Department of Foreign Affairs when his wife, Sheena, rang to tell him what had happened to his father. He decided not to ring or attempt to see his father on the eleventh as he knew he would be far too busy, but he rang his mother to confirm that she was with family. The next day he saw his father twice, as much as anything to reassure Margaret that Gough was coping with the shock.

On the night of the eleventh the family gathered at Kirribilli House for the last time and Jo and Rita insisted on cooking a wonderful dinner for them. Nick opened some bottles of French wine that had been there since Billy McMahon's residence. Margaret set the tone: no questions. No going over things again and again. No speculations. No anger. They would wait for their father to ring, eat well, drink up and be optimistic about what lay ahead. If it was at all possible to make the most of this situation into which they had been catapulted, Margaret was determined to achieve it.

After dinner they continued to help Margaret move her personal things into the flat and she slept alone, fitfully. The next morning Margaret and her daughter-in-law Judy went into the city, early, to buy a television set because, like the rest of the nation, Margaret wanted to see events unfolding in Canberra hour by hour. Everywhere they shopped people kept stopping them and saying, 'Good on you,' and 'Keep fighting,' and 'Don't give up.'

Margaret smiled and thanked them for their support, but she still felt as if she was in a daze and couldn't quite believe what was happening. When they returned, carrying the television, the journalists were waiting outside the apartment building in Darling Point. She talked to them all in her usual straightforward fashion and even did a television interview on the balcony.

Though she was still a little confused about how the dismissal had happened and the exact constitutional conventions that had been broken, she was very angry at the manner in which it had come about. Those people in the Opposition who had treated them like class traitors and always assumed that they had the right to rule because they were 'the crème de la crème' of society, had, she said, behaved dishonourably and disgracefully. She had thought they were all at least gentlemen and that they would have played the game by the rules. Clearly, she had misjudged them.

For that pompous Kerr to have never spoken to Gough about his insecurities, for Fraser to have plotted a coup behind the back of the elected prime minister was, in her eyes, behaviour that was sly, deceitful, indecent and dishonourable.

Gough did not sleep one wink on the night of the eleventh. He paced around the room, distracted. The only time he appeared calm was when he was sitting at his desk recording what had happened. It was as if doing so would somehow make the day's events more real and less like a nightmare out of which he couldn't seem to wake. Later, on 15 November, he told journalist Kerry O'Brien that he had never had a bigger shock in his life.

On the night of 12 November Gough again did not sleep at all. It was difficult for Margaret that they were apart because she wanted to be with him and understand what was happening. 'He had all his cabinet around him, and his staff. They were doing what they had to do. At least, I suppose they were. The whole thing was totally chaotic as far as I was concerned.'

It was two days after the dismissal before Margaret saw her husband. She was very pleased to see him, but by that time he was fully into election mode and totally focused on how to convince the voters of Australia to maintain their rage and return his government to power. Nevertheless, that night when they were alone in the dark, she took him in her arms and held him close.

In the days and weeks that followed there was no time for bitterness, recriminations or 'what ifs' – the only thing that mattered was winning the election on 13 December. There was not a moment to waste. When they set off on the road again, the crowds of support were bigger than they could ever have imagined. Emotions ran to fever pitch when Gough appeared on stage.

Margaret usually sat in the front row, her hearing nearly deafened by the crowd's constant rhythmical chanting of, 'We want Gough.'

For the third time in three years she found herself walking behind her husband as he strode down the aisles of meeting halls, surrounded by thousands of supporters screaming and cheering. She smiled and waved and did her best to keep his spirits high between these emotional public outbursts of affection and support.

Every night when they went to bed together in different cities and towns across the nation, their confidence grew because of the huge crowds, the wild enthusiasm and the generous donations of money for the ongoing campaign. They truly believed they were going to win and that Kerr's decision to sack Gough would eventually be to their advantage.

It had always angered Margaret that the election win of the ALP in 1972 had been regarded almost as indecent by conservatives. They had been stunned to think that the Australian public would consider the Labor Party to be fit and proper to be in power and they had clearly been determined to get rid of it by fair means or foul.

She regarded John Kerr and Malcolm Fraser with absolute scorn: scorn for what they had done, and scorn for the manner in which they had done it. She simply couldn't understand it. She couldn't forgive them and she doubted that she'd ever forgive them. 'I was very, very angry and surprised that those conservative people could act so much against the proper conventions and everything they always said they held dear.'

If she had been described as Gough's secret weapon in 1972 and 1974, then she now became 'Gough's open missile'. She played a very prominent part in the campaign and spoke at rallies, meetings and with groups. She did everything she was asked to do and more.

She told *The Age*, 'The whole business got my dander up so much I was ready for anything. I travelled the length and breadth of the country with him, usually walking a few feet behind him, and everywhere we went we were greeted with hordes of on-side, loving, articulate, supportive people and we thought, Everything's going well, we'll win this election.'

Whitlam's main targets were Kerr, Fraser and the Senate, while Fraser focused on the government's economic failings, increasing unemployment, rising inflation and the necessity to get the private sector moving.

Whitlam was a flamboyant, colourful speaker, while Fraser was wooden, flat and factual. But despite the huge responsive crowds Gough was drawing in, the opinion polls continued to put the Liberal and Country Party coalition ahead. Still, the Whitlams never let up. If Gough had any doubts about being returned as prime minister on Saturday 13 December, he never allowed them to show, either publicly or privately.

On 11 December a rally in a Melbourne playing field drew a crowd of 20,000 supporters. Margaret observed how, their faces upturned, they hung on her husband's every word. Everywhere they went he was lionised, deified. When he declared, 'This election will decide whether parliamentary democracy will survive in Australia,' the applause was ear-splitting. In Sydney the next day another magnificent reception from the crowd kept their hopes up and their spirits high.

On 13 December 1975 Margaret and Gough voted at their local polling booth and, cocooned in the ongoing adulation of their supporters, flew back to Canberra and the security of the Lodge to await the election results.

It was clear by 8.30 pm from the tally-room results that the Labor party had lost, and by 10 pm they had to face the devastation of that loss. It was catastrophic for the ALP. There was a swing against them of 8.3 per cent in urban seats and 5.2 per cent in rural electorates. The coalition achieved 53.1 per cent and the ALP 42.8 per cent of the total Australian vote.

It was only when it was clear that they not only had no hope of winning, but that this was a devastating defeat, that Margaret took herself off, quietly and discreetly, to the butler's pantry. Graham Freudenberg noticed her leave the room and followed her. And there, out of sight, among the canned tomatoes and jars of jam, she leant on her friend's shoulder and finally let the tears flow. She sobbed long and hard. She sobbed for her husband, for the party, for all the people who had worked so tirelessly for them, and she sobbed for the loss of a dream: a dream that they would be vindicated and be returned, triumphant, into the Lodge, to fulfil their vision for the country.

At 11 pm Gough Whitlam arrived at the tally room with a dry-eyed, composed Margaret by his side, together with several members of staff. As he entered, the familiar chant of 'We want Gough' rang through the room, but when he raised his hands and the chant died down it was clear from his voice that he was totally deflated by the loss. Dignified, quiet and controlled, he conceded defeat, congratulated his opponents and expressed his heartbreak at losing so many of the ALP's younger, promising politicians. He thanked everyone who had worked so hard in the recent weeks.

The journalists lined up in front of him asked if he would stay on as leader.

'Let me think about that,' he replied.

And then the toughest question of all to face: 'Why did Labor lose?'

Gough drew in a deep breath and said in a voice already resigned to sorrow, 'It is the fate of any government at a time of recession, and especially a reformist government, which ours was.'

With that he turned away from the media and with Margaret, tall and straight, as ever by his side, they left the tally room and disappeared into the darkness of the moonless Canberra night.

Margaret was as devastated as Gough with the result. She had really believed that the Australian people had wanted them to stay on in the Lodge. But they had both been wrong and those who had turned up to the rallies to support them were just the true believers. They had been preaching to the converted. It was over.

Once they had packed up their personal possessions from the Lodge and deposited them either in a new government flat in Canberra, or their flat in Darling Point, they tried to get on with their lives. Gough was duly elected the Leader of the Opposition and whenever he railed privately against Kerr, Fraser and the Murdoch press, who had backed Fraser in the election, Margaret's response to him was always, 'It's done. There's no use in crying over spilt milk. We have to move on.'

Early in 1976 Richard Butler entered the Whitlam's lives. He was based in Singapore as a member of the diplomatic service and when Gough had arrived there for the funeral of the Malaysian Prime Minister, Butler was assigned as the charge d'affaires to look after him. They spent three days together, visiting various dignitaries, and Butler found Gough to be a very impressive man in every sense. So impressed was he that when the position of principal private secretary to the Leader of the Opposition came up, Butler spoke to Bob Hawke about taking it. Hawke told him, 'Don't be such an idiot. Gough's finished. Don't go near him.' However,

Butler was determined to try and help put Gough back into power because he believed that what had happened in Australia was wrong. He took the job.

On the first day in his new position he met Margaret, who often popped into the office. The two of them hit it off immediately. Butler said that they had shared cultural interests, a similar sense of humour and were both devoted to Gough. But more importantly, he was able to witness first-hand how her strength and her steely resolve were essential to her husband's well-being.

Butler found Gough to be 'a towering man intellectually, morally and temperamentally'. In his view the only other man that he has met in his entire political and diplomatic career that had that same aura around him is William Jefferson Clinton. Both are men of great intellect and fabulous erudition, but both are personally flawed. In Butler's view, Gough's flaw is his temperament.

He believes that Gough's pig-headedness did him much harm on 11 November because rather than seeking to defeat the motion of denial of supply in the Senate, he barred himself in his office and wrote the speech that he would give in the House. In other words, he was more concerned with the historical quality of his speech than getting to Ken Wriedt, the leader in the Senate, to tell him to refuse to pass the supply bill. Butler says he knows there were people knocking on Gough's door shouting, 'Stop writing the speech and turn your attention to what's happening.' He admits that it is easy now to be wise after the event, but he still believes that Gough's temperament often prevented him from making the right decision. Nevertheless, he has never regretted choosing to work for him, and says that Gough was everything he had hoped he would be.

Still, in early 1976 Butler observed him to be a 'divided soul' and in a 'terrible state'. Part of him was focused on gritting his teeth, clenching his fists and fighting on, while the other half was a man who seemed to have been smashed with a sledgehammer.

Butler says it was Margaret who looked after Gough, who on a daily basis sustained him and whose total and unconditional love eventually healed him. Butler says, 'I had a really schizophrenic time with him. At one moment he would be barking orders at me and I'd say, "It's on your desk," and he'd say, "Don't talk to me like that," and I'd say, "It's on your desk." And then on other occasions he'd come and sit in my office, his large frame slumped in a chair, and I could feel his burden, of his just needing to be helped.'

Butler is adamant that it was Margaret, above all others, who was responsible for getting him through this time. 'Where he was rocky, she was stable. Where he would lose his grip on things temperamentally, she would remain equable. Where he would feel clearly that people hated him, she would love him more. She was absolutely superb.'

Butler says that while Gough taught him a lot in the political sphere, it was Margaret from whom he learnt about the human sphere. 'She kept the faith. She kept the faith of their marriage, she kept the faith of their love, she kept the faith of Labor.'

Butler observed the many times that Gough would speak to Margaret in very abusive terms. 'Sometimes he would forget that I was in the room and he would turn on her and give her a tongue-lashing that was quite wrong.'

And how would Margaret respond?

'She would just say, "Oh, shut up, you silly old goat! Go and have a shower and cool off."'

Gough's bearing and his confident, opinionated character caused a lot of people to admire and love him, but it also caused an even larger number of people to find him offensively arrogant.

Margaret, Butler believes, is exactly the opposite. People admire her because even while she occupied a position of stature and authority, she always maintained incredible humility. In Margaret he saw not the phoney self-effacement of many women who had held that position, but genuine humility.

Butler says, 'She stood up there next to him and said to the world, "I support my husband and I am loyal to him," but she never projected any sense of her own self-importance or vanity. She was personally humble, but free of that bullshit self-effacement that so many Australians have, which is the obverse of tall-poppyism.'

He remembers that often when he and Gough and Margaret drove away from a venue or a meeting and engaged in a post-mortem discussion, Gough and Butler would give their usual critical assessment of someone and Margaret would often respond with something like, 'Yes, but he was very interesting, wasn't he? And he was charming, too.'

She has a genuine fairness and curiosity about people, together with a charitable view of the failings of ordinary human beings, observes Butler. Nevertheless, if she thinks someone is behaving badly, she will tell them so.

There's nothing like a public humiliation, or a loss of some kind, to sort out who your real friends are. After the dismissal, Nick and Judy were ignored or snubbed by many of their neighbours, and were blackballed from joining a small swimming club at Bondi Beach, the Rose Bay Surf Club, to which other members of the family belonged. Catherine's reaction was to threaten to resign in protest, but her mother renewed her daughter's membership and her own, explaining to her that you never let your enemies think they have destroyed you.

You can, however, let them know that you know how they have behaved.

The first time Margaret met one of the known perpetrators of the blackballing she said to her, 'Don't expect me to talk to you because I know all about your part in blackballing Nick and Judy.'

She said the woman was shocked, but Margaret is determined to remain a member of that club until the day she dies. Now that their enemies have left the club and Catherine swims frequently at Bondi she, too, is pleased her mother took the action she did and refused to let them be hounded out.

Margaret is ferocious in defence of her children. She once told reporters, 'I have developed a vicious tongue and I no longer hesitate to use it.'

What Margaret considers to be 'vicious', however, is pretty mild by current standards. Everyday road rage would garner you more vicious abuse than Margaret could ever muster.

After the dismissal the teachers at her grandson Alexander's nursery school cheered in front of him. Margaret found that very distasteful. Apart from anything else she considers that it's not a proper way to behave in front of a little boy, especially as Alexander's parents had always made a special effort never to have political discussions in front of him. Although, clearly, like most children, he had absorbed much more than they had realised – his response on seeing Fraser's face on the television after the elections was, 'I knew that nasty man wanted to live in Grandpa's house.'

Whatever she thought of Fraser, Margaret always liked his wife, Tamie, and when Tamie gave her party for the political wives at her new home, the Lodge, and asked Margaret to attend, she accepted with warmth and civility. In fact, on the day she moved into the Lodge, Tamie said she was very touched to find a letter of good wishes from Margaret, who would have thought it extremely rude not to have left such a note, despite the conflict between their husbands. Margaret thought Tamie probably didn't know how the dismissal had happened any more than Margaret did. Wives of prime ministers are often the last to know anything.

When a television film titled *The Dismissal* was made of this period in Australian history, the celebrated actress Ruth Cracknell played the part of Margaret Whitlam. The next time Ruth saw Margaret she said to her, 'It wasn't much fun. All I seemed to be doing was standing around in the background.' Margaret responded, 'Welcome to my life.'

As soon as Gough was voted out, vicious rumours about the Whitlams' marriage started to spread through Sydney's smart eastern suburbs, especially among those who had always believed the Whitlams never should have been in the Lodge in the first place. Margaret's brother, Bill, a barrister by now, who lived in the eastern suburbs, rang her up to tell her that he had been to three separate 1975 Christmas parties where he'd been told Margaret and Gough were getting a divorce. Many of the rumours were more lurid and usually featured Gough bashing Margaret, or her stabbing him.

When Gough was in hospital having an operation on a hernia Catherine remembers being told many times about another rumour concerning the reason that he was there. 'Mum was supposed to have shot him in the bum because she had found him with his Qantas steward lover.' The rumour-mongers would stop at nothing.

At the beginning of 1976 Margaret toyed with the idea of writing a book about her husband – the private man as only she had known him. Hand-written pages torn from a journal, dated 26 March 1976, reveal her motivation.

> This seems a good day to begin. For, once again, I was shocked and hurt by the attitudes of an outsider. Outsider? Unbeliever? Enemy? Now I wonder why I was so polite to the over-dressed, ridiculous woman who came up to the official table after lunch and said something like, 'I didn't appreciate being jostled on the stairs by your demonstrators.' My demonstrators? What was she talking about?
>
> Well, there was a small gathering of people outside the Hilton as we came to the opening of the American centennial celebrations and some of them did wave that excellent Eureka flag – but *my* demonstrators? Who does she think she is? What does she know of me? Or mine? It's obviously time to speak up – to let them know of the gentleman I married – to react.
>
> I'm sick of hearing how he beats me – how we're divorcing, how much money we've stashed away in foreign countries, how many ruins we've visited or caused. Oh, what rot it all is, but at the same time how offensive and how hurtful that people should believe it.
>
> Wasn't it enough for the G-G to ruin our lives? Is there to be no end to speculation and jubilation?
>
> The man that I married is, as he was, a gentle man. Two words or one, take your pick. Both apply.
>
> . . .
>
> Next week the old man and I will have been married thirty-four years. We shudder at the headlines commissioned by enemies. We thought we'd never have to but glow in the knowledge of our steadfastness.
>
> My God, they're talking about the man I married.

I won't have it. Who do these people think they are? Is this Australia?

Where am I? In the flat that we (emphasis on the 'we') bought over a year ago as a weekender. Put that in your pipe and smoke it, as the coarser kids used to say at school. Officialdom was okay most of the time but Gough and I yearned for a part of our town where we could disappear, where he could read in the sun and I could cook and potter, all without surveillance.

Well, it was all made possible in the second week of November 1975. What I mean is the flat was furnished adequately and the occasion was afforded inappropriately. It was never our intention to live in the Cabramatta house again. It is too large for our now dispersed family situation. And no brickbats to Cabramatta. Some of my best years were spent there. I enjoy very much returning there. When we lived in that much maligned suburb our children were part of the scene and I like to think contributed to it.

I was part of the extracurricular routine – in that over seventeen years I must have participated in everything from school canteens, Red Cross activities to political policy meetings. That was a time many Australians shared with me as the wife of the PM. I had entrée everywhere and it indeed exceeded every expectation ever dreamed about with regard to the role of wife of the PM.

Well, now it's stopped. Someone else has that job. Good luck to her, and luck is needed. More than ever I want you now to know the man that I married, the sometime PM . . .

I have to tell you that [Gough] is a perfectionist. Nothing is started if it has no prospect of completion, and preferably successful completion.

When we were first married he, Edward Gough Whitlam, was in the reserve of the RAAF. I could never really understand why his parents chose not to call him Edward. My brother Bill has always called him Eddie instead of Gough. To me it's a very unchristian name but it does have a lot of meaning to the family whose antecedents served under General Hugh Gough in India.

I have resented the last six months because of the vicious lies and rumours that have been circulated and mostly because of the victimisation of a good man.

I know. I married him.

I have not regretted it.

Thirty-four years is a long time. During this time I have hoarded, treasured, saved much memorabilia – call these love letters if you will, but look at them, think about them. Could this man be the danger certain interests are conjuring up? It's not on, mate.

Here is a dedicated, honest man. People with the upbringing of EGW are excused selfishness, arrogance, greedy incompetence and lack of charisma if they belong to the Liberal Party, that most conservative group. Can't we have a bit too?

Well, anyway, you can have a look at some of his letters, mainly to me. I like them, I treasure them, I now share them with you.

Clearly, this was intended as a preface to a collection of Gough's war-time letters to Margaret, which she intended to edit and have published. Regrettably, not only did she never write the book, she eventually destroyed many of Gough's most personal letters. When asked why, she shrugs her shoulders and says, 'I don't really remember now. Probably because in the end they were no one else's business.'

Her only comment after re-reading these faded notebook pages scribbled in her own handwriting is, 'Oh dear, I really had my dander up didn't I?' But the fact that a normally even-tempered, calm woman like Margaret allowed herself to express these emotions of distress and hurt is a testament to their depth at the time.

In the end, Margaret had the desire, but not an urgent drive to allocate the time to write such a book. Like her journal of 1941, started but never continued, the practicalities of everyday life intervened. And she buried the emotions. Nor did she really wish to make herself vulnerable by exposing her wounds. Although she was hurt and distressed by the rumours, she was determined to ignore them and get their lives back into a routine. She didn't miss living in the Lodge – she enjoyed the freedom of having a flat in Canberra and one in Sydney, and being able to see more of her friends. She knew that the hurt and rejection she and Gough both felt now would take its own time to heal. Meanwhile, they had lives to live and shared interests and friends to begin to enjoy.

Margaret started taking classes in modern Greek at the ANU and the University of New South Wales. Her lectures in Sydney were at the law school in Phillip Street on Mondays from 6 to 8 pm, after which she and Gough would catch the 9 pm plane to Canberra, then return to Sydney again on Fridays. Sometimes she would have just done the grocery shopping and when she went through airport security she'd slap a large parcel of meat on the table for scrutiny. The security staff would joke with her, 'Got the meat today, Mrs Whitlam?' This is the real Margaret – no airs and graces – wife of the former prime minister, cracking jokes about carrying the chops and the roast as she boards a plane.

She was constantly on the move. She had two small cars, one in Sydney and one in Canberra, and she buzzed around in both, visiting friends and fulfilling obligations in each city.

Gough was back to his usual routine and Margaret commented to the media that there wasn't much difference between being prime minister to being leader of the Opposition 'except you didn't seem to get so many brickbats as the leader of the Opposition. And I certainly don't miss living at the Lodge.'

She had lost none of her zest for living, or her ability to cause a stir. In November 1976 in *The Age* she attacked commercial talk-back radio broadcasters as being 'dyed-in-the-wool Liberals' who daily urged suburban housewives to support the conservatives. She in turn urged women listeners to free themselves from the 'mental thraldom' of their 'pernicious influence', which she believed had, together with an inherent snobbery, helped bring down the ALP the previous year.

Nineteen seventy-seven was a crucial date for the Whitlams: the election for which they believed they should have been allowed to remain in power was due at the end of the year. To be rejected by the Australian public after they had experienced two years of coalition rule and the lacklustre leadership of Malcolm Fraser would, Margaret thought, be the worst dismissal of all.

The acerbic London *Daily Express* journalist Jean Rook arrived in Sydney prior to another visit from the Queen in March 1977, and on 23 February *The Sun* published her profile of Margaret.

The article began, 'Mrs Gough Whitlam is a huge, sweeping woman. A land mass in herself. She's 6' 2" with a face like a cross between Boadicea and a Roman emperor.' And as if that was not insulting enough, she compared Margaret's long, athletic swimmer's legs to a kangaroo's.

Why would Rook begin on such a bitchy note? It seems she was extremely upset with Margaret for describing in her *Woman's Day* diary the details of her visit to Buckingham Palace, including the colour of the eiderdowns, the pictures on the bedroom walls and who drank what. Why would Rook be so offended by that? Well, it was just not proper for a mere colonial, even if she is married to the Prime Minister of a former colony, to reveal such intimate royal details to the lowly hoi polloi.

Rook asked Margaret how she intended to deal with the presence of the Governor-General at the upcoming royal gatherings. Margaret told her the truth. 'I shall treat him as if he didn't exist. The situation is totally obscene. The man is dishonourable and rude. When I think of the times we were in his company just before he did what he did to Gough and how he said nothing right up to the last moment, I'm disgusted. The man did a total about-face. I regard him as the most dishonourable person I have ever met.'

Even the snippy Rook was impressed, not just with her candour, but with the fact that Margaret had driven herself to Rook's Sydney hotel and had no objections to being interviewed in her hotel bedroom. She is astonished that Margaret 'even fed her own parking meter'. (What did she think? That she would have a lady-in-waiting stuffing coins into the meter at regular intervals?)

And if Rook had had any lingering doubts about Margaret's attitude to rank, Margaret soon put her right. 'I can't stand affectation,' she pronounced. 'I am happy to be back to shopping for my own brussel sprouts in supermarkets, without a bodyguard.'

'And what do you think of those who consider themselves to be the Australian establishment?' asked Rook.

Margaret gave her a blast with both barrels. 'The Australian establishment is illegitimate and offensive. I just loathe watching aggressive, possessive Australians scrambling for imperial honours.'

As for her notorious diary in *Woman's Day*, Margaret assured Rook that, 'It certainly didn't worry the Queen – I've met her since, and she seemed quite amused by all the fuss it caused.'

Hoping to stir up some headlines regarding the Whitlams' marriage, no doubt hearing the rumours of their pending divorce, Rook asked if her husband knew what she was saying about Sir John Kerr.

'He never minds me,' said Margaret. 'His attitude has always been, "What has the old bag been saying now?" I don't mirror my husband's views. It's so absurd, just because you're a politician's wife, to sit around like a dummy saying nothing, or echoing him. You might as well give up living.'

Rook asked her how she felt about Mrs Fraser.

'I shall speak to her – why not? It's not her fault. Lord knows, I'm not jealous of her. She's got a terrible job. I loved being the PM's wife but, my God, it's hard work.'

Finally, Rook wanted to know how gladly Margaret would bow to the Queen. Sections of the English press, it seems, are always obsessed with how far the colonials are prepared to subject themselves to rituals of obeisance to the British throne. Margaret soon set her straight. 'The Queen is a darling. I shall sweep into my full curtsey. Actually, I do it very well. And, anyway, it's good exercise.'

Before Margaret left she gave Rook a traditional Aussie serve regarding her previous articles about her. 'I read every word you wrote about my "snooping" diary on the Queen. I found your reaction rather critical and strange. I'll be interested to read what you make of me now that we've actually met.'

As she had no doubt intended when she agreed to the interview, Margaret left Rook in no doubt that she was not about to be put down, trivialised or intimidated by anyone. The events of 1975 had sharpened her protective instincts and, in an ironic twist, developed her confidence in tackling all forms of criticism. She no longer took people at face value, particularly journalists, and even Rook, who was known as 'the First Lady of Fleet Street', was left in no doubt that Margaret wasn't about to be bullied. In fact, she even admitted that Margaret had conducted her own interview and that she had said very little.

Nothing, it seemed, was going to shake Margaret or her world, after what she had already been through. However, in September of that year, she was, as it turned out, shaken again.

She and Gough were in Tianjin in China on an official visit. After an evening banquet with the local mayor they retired to their hotel bedroom and before going to sleep discussed the possibility of squeezing in a visit to a nearby cathedral the next morning.

Just before 4 am Margaret woke up to a strange feeling that the wall behind the bed had disappeared and that somebody was trying to hit her on the head with a hammer. She described the noise as 'absolutely deplorable'. Because it had been so hot Gough had dragged a big floor-standing fan into their bedroom to cool the air. The fan was at the foot of the bed. As the walls shook there was suddenly a dreadful sound of what seemed to be thunder from outside. The curtains blew out and Margaret thought for a minute they were going to be sucked into the night. The fan fell down.

Gough said, 'I think it's an earthquake.' They quickly decided that they had better get dressed because he was obviously right and it wasn't stopping.

Suddenly people in the corridor were shouting, 'Come on, come on! You must get out, there'll be another one.' Margaret was sitting on the side of the bed with one leg off it and she said to Gough, 'Turn off the electricity because something will blow up if you don't.' While he was doing so the dressing table crashed down onto her leg, gashing it. She put her hand down and felt blood and stickiness, and thought 'That's the end of that, I won't have a lower left leg.'

Gough raced into the bathroom, grabbed a towel, wet it, wrapped it around her injured leg, and scrabbled around looking for their clothes. He'd just dropped his clothes beside his bed, so now he pulled them on again. Margaret had washed her underwear and left it in the bathroom, but she found a pair of slacks and a shirt nearby and pulled those on. Even though she couldn't find her shoes, she found Gough's under the crashed dressing table. Outside their room the shouting was even louder, 'Come on, come out, we must go, we must go!'

Margaret said, 'I'm not going without my shoes.' Fortunately she found her sneakers and shoved them on her feet. She pushed everything she could find into her dillybag, Gough picked up his attaché case and out they walked, down the stairs with one Chinese member of staff to help each of them, and a torch to light their path.

They were on the seventh storey, and beside the lifts there was a great crack in the floor about three feet wide. The Chinese ordered them to 'jump over'. They did as they were told and then scrambled down the stairs in the dark. Everybody was calling out, 'Are you all right?' and Margaret was replying 'Fine, thanks very much,' feeling as though every moment was going to be her last. At each floor they had to jump over the crack, which diminished until the ground floor, where it was barely visible.

The hotel had been built specially to withstand earthquakes and indeed it had done so. They were about 20 kilometres from the epicentre of the quake. After Gough and Margaret had spent a couple of hours sitting in the gutter just across the road from the hotel, waiting, the locals somehow managed to gather everyone together in buses and cars and take them to an athletics ground out in the open where no buildings could fall on them.

Margaret says, 'By this time I was dying for a pee. I could see an outside loo nearby and I joined the queue, hanging on desperately until my turn arrived. No sooner had I shut, but not locked, the door than a large male barged his way in, "at the ready". I thought I was going to be raped but in due course everyone was comforted.'

From the athletics ground they were transported to the Tianjin Club, where first aid was being administered. Margaret was persuaded to see a medical officer, who wanted to stitch her leg. But she said she didn't think it was necessary because she was scared of letting him do it. So he gave her a tetanus injection and then just bound it up.

The next day, a Nicholson cartoon depicting the incident was published in the Australian press. It showed Margaret and Gough in bed together, with Gough asking, 'Did the earth move for you, Margaret?'

Letters to the editor complained that it was disrespectful to the Whitlams. Gough, however, ordered a copy of the cartoon immediately. Even though the earthquake was very frightening at the time, Margaret admits that the cartoon still makes her chuckle.

Richard Whitington, Gough's secretary, insisted on being the person in their party to return to the damaged hotel in order to retrieve the Whitlams' personal belongings, among which were – most importantly for Margaret – her knickers. The Chinese hotel staff had bundled everything up and when Richard returned with the parcel, all bundled together were Gough's official papers, the bowl of fruit from the sitting room and Margaret's knickers.

As the 1977 election drew closer Margaret was interviewed again, this time by *The Sun* as part of a series they were running called 'Meet the Wife'. Journalist Michael Wilkinson opened with the lines, 'Margaret Whitlam is probably remembered as the most colourful, controversial wife of an Australian prime minister. In spite of her husband Gough being ousted from office nearly two years ago and Meg making only occasional headlines since, she has lost none of her way with words.'

Note Wilkinson's familiarity in calling her Meg. Only her eldest son has ever called her Meg.

Margaret described her usual program of activities for him. 'Tonight I'm going to Yass to talk to two hundred and fifty women at a dinner. Next week I'm opening a seminar of New South Wales welfare workers and the week after that I'm speaking to the Friends of the Australian Opera.'

She admitted that it had taken her a while to realise that people had sometimes used her while she was in the Lodge. 'All sweetness and light to your face, but behind your back they are saying, "Oh, we had to ask them."'

She did admit to being cynical 'these days' and 'more of wake-up to people'. Refusing to admit that she had any regrets about her outspokenness, she claimed she only answered the questions that were put to her, and she did emphasise that some of her answers had been taken out of context.

When asked to comment on the performance of her husband's government, honest as always, she replied, 'The problem was they went at it like a bull at a gate. I think they worked too hard and tried to do too much too soon – but they could see what needed to be done . . . When I think of all those red boxes of government papers always beside the bed. It used to be lights on at 5 am and right into the red boxes.'

Nevertheless, would she like another term at the Lodge? 'I do hope to go back. It would be very nice as a vindication.'

In saying this Margaret was not being as honest as usual. The truth was she didn't particularly want to go back to her former position as wife of the Prime Minister, but she wanted the Australian people's confirmation that Gough had been unjustly treated. And this time, if given the chance to undertake the same role, she made it perfectly clear that she would be much more her own person.

Although she desperately hoped for Gough's sake that they would be re-elected, she did notice that this time when she was doing a pre-election walk-through in a mall there would be an occasional 'boo' and people would shout comments at her such as, 'Gough's got to go.' She hated people shouting at her and she could see no useful purpose in just strolling through a shopping mall unless you were going to shop – it always looked so staged. But she would continue to do it if asked.

On 19 November 1977 she celebrated her fifty-eighth birthday on an RAAF jet with cake and champagne supplied by the media. She was, yet again, by her husband's side, on another campaign trail.

The election was held on 10 December. Margaret joined Gough, available family and party workers at Gough's Sydney office in Westfield Towers to await the results. Early in the night she thought they might have a hope of winning but, as more and more results flashed onto the television screen, she felt the previously buoyant mood in the room deflate as fast as an old balloon left over from a party. She made no effort, this time, to jolly everyone along. She knew that it was the end of what had been a very long road. Gough had told her that if he didn't win this time he was going to resign his leadership of the party and sit on the backbench until he knew what the next phase in his life would be.

As usual, he made a moving speech and he remained a dignified figure as he thanked everyone who had worked so hard and been so loyal. He announced that indeed he would be standing down as the ALP leader. All his staff listened with tears coursing down their cheeks. He didn't allow himself that luxury. Neither did Margaret.

Not only had her husband lost the election but her son Tony, who had previously won preselection for Fred Daly's old seat in 1975 and then won the seat of Grayndler, had now, due to a redrawing of the electoral boundaries and the swing against the ALP, lost his chance to continue sitting in the House. Margaret knew that Gough had hoped Tony would be given a chance to show his talents. But it was not to be. The Whitlam years were over.

After the disastrous election of 1977 Margaret's goals were clear – to move on and help Gough to do the same. She rang as many people as she could to tell them the results and to reassure them that they were both fine.

First the Governor-General had dismissed them and now, for the second time, so had the majority of the Australian people. She would accept it, but she didn't personally understand why they had been so firm in their rejection of her husband. He had done so many wonderful things for them in such a short time. Perhaps the pace of change had been too fast, but she knew that apart from being an impatient man, he had been thinking and working on these policies for the past ten years so, of course, they weren't new or threatening to him. What was clear was that the people of Australia did not wish to return to a Labor government.

Now what would the Whitlams do? They were both still relatively young with a great deal to offer. Something would turn up, she thought to herself. It always did. The important thing for both of them was not to get bogged down in the past. But that was easier for her than for Gough – politics was his passion. And he was hurt, deeply hurt, yet again. She would help him get over it, help him accept what had happened, help him get on with their lives. She wouldn't allow any self-pity or wallowing. Not that either of them were prone to those emotions. Thank God for stoicism.

Margaret did not worry about the fact that they would now have to live on less money. She had coped in the past with a lot less than their parliamentary pension. But she felt sorrow for Gough and the way he had been treated. She was still angry at those who had acted as if only they recognised decent values, good manners and all the traditional virtues. In her judgement they had, in fact, shown themselves to be greedy for power, deceitful and shabby.

As far as her own life was concerned, there was a lot about politics she wouldn't miss.

Perhaps she could begin to feel useful again in her own right.

Perhaps she could indulge her love of writing and golf.

Perhaps she could see more of her friends and go to films, theatre and ballet without having to think about the obligations of the next day.

Perhaps she could begin to live a little for herself.

AFTER POLITICS

If the life of Margaret and her husband had been a three-act play, the final stage direction would have read 'EXIT LEFT'. The denouement had happened. The tragedy was complete. No longer centre-stage in the life of the nation, they both needed to find new roles for themselves in the aftermath of what amounted to three dismissals. Unlike Shakespearean tragedies, in which the hero or heroine falls from a great height, gains wisdom and then dies, Margaret and Gough, both wiser and to some extent sadder people, had to face their final defeat, hopefully learn something from it and continue their lives.

She was fifty-eight and he was sixty-one. Both of them were too young to curl up and wait to die, or sell up, move to the country and become recluses. Besides, it was not in either of their natures to give in to what fate or their own actions had determined.

Failures can teach you many things, one of which is where your loyalties lie. Once the Whitlams were no longer at the centre or even on the fringe of power, many remaining courtiers and hangers-on dropped away, their enemies exposed themselves and their true friends and admirers remained constant. Their four children formed a rock-solid circle of support around them, as did Gough's sister, Freda; Margaret's brother, Bill; her sister-in-law, Sue Dovey; and Margaret's mother. Unlike Gough, who had spent the past twenty years or more working to achieve his goal and then losing it – he believed unfairly – Margaret had known the sour taste of defeat earlier in her life. She had tasted fate's cruel indifference, constant – no matter how unfair you judge it to be.

When she had competed in the swimming at the Empire Games and, due to a debilitating throat infection for which there were no drugs powerful enough to cure, had come last in her race, she had learnt that however humiliating the public defeat, however unfair the reasons for it, there is only one way of dealing with it – you have to hold your head up, get back in the water and keep swimming.

She had also been forced to accept that her height, over which she had no control, had prevented her from gaining leading roles in plays in which she would have dearly loved to perform. Instead of walking away or turning her back on the theatre she had learnt to be content with minor roles, or even being the voice off-stage.

Throughout her married life, Gough had always been centre-stage and Margaret's role had always been a supporting one. She was, in her own words, billed as 'Also present, Margaret Whitlam'. Nevertheless she had treated this role seriously, given it her best shot and made the most of it. She was noticed, valued and respected for her efforts. Now she had to find a new position, or re-invent an old one.

In 1978 Gough retired from Parliament and the Whitlams moved into an apartment in University House at the ANU in Canberra because Gough had been invited there as a visiting fellow. While he gave lectures and supervised his postgraduate students, Margaret did one course in literature and another in Greek. Tuesday was her golf day, she joined a bushwalking group and a woman's group that organised visiting lunchtime speakers.

Although Gough went to the staff club occasionally for lunch, he mostly came back to the apartment and if Margaret was not there, he ate the food she had left for him. Pampered by his mother with specially prepared meals, Margaret had continued the tradition. Like many women of her upbringing and generation, she said she found it easier to continue what he was used to than force him to learn to cater to his own culinary needs at this late stage in their marriage.

On weekends they returned from Canberra to their apartment in Darling Point and their life in Sydney. This pattern continued for the next few years.

Margaret says, 'Gough didn't seem to miss politics. He wasn't depressed, he certainly wasn't suicidal. In fact, he had some very good students at ANU. With time to read his beloved reference books and no pressures, he was as happy as Larry. He would have been jolly good as an academic.'

In 1979 they spent a month in the United States at Harvard University when Gough was made a visiting professor of Australian Studies, in the chair that he had established during his prime ministership. Margaret loved her time at Harvard and quickly settled them both in.

One of the people she met while there was the revered writer Eudora Welty, whose books Margaret had read and admired. She remembers, 'She was a funny thing, with a big voice and a little frame. She wasn't retiring or self-effacing, but exuded the kind of confidence that comes from knowing what she was talking about. The students adored her.'

When they returned to Australia, they came back to Sydney full-time and Margaret found herself being invited to join various organisations whose boards believed that she could make a valuable contribution. For once she was being asked to do things as Margaret Whitlam, not as the wife of the Prime Minister, and she liked the feeling. In the jargon of today, such invitations were very 'empowering'.

In 1977 she was appointed as a director of the Sydney Dance Company, on whose board she served until 1982.

From 1978 to 1980 she was President of the ACT Council of Social Services, which she saw as an extension of her profession as a social worker, and in 1978 she was also appointed to the council of Sydney Teachers' College, becoming its president in 1982 when it became the Sydney College of Advanced Education.

'I liked being on these things. Teaching had always intrigued me and I was very interested in knowing about the curriculum and liked having some influence in choosing new staff members,' she says now.

At the end of 1978, her mother died. Mary Dovey, or the Moth, as Margaret's friends had affectionately called her, had been gradually fading, although she was vain about her good looks until the end.

'The last week she was in hospital, in St Vincent's, I rang up to see how she was before I went in to see her. The nurses said, "She must be all right today, she's got the lipstick on already." And this was before I had mine on. Even though she was vain about her appearance, she was quite jolly up until the end.'

Now there was just Willy and Margaret.

In 1979, after one of the Whitlams' regular European trips, Margaret stayed on for a few days in London without Gough. She liked to see friends, go shopping and be free to plan her own days without having to consider his needs. Staying at the Royal Overseas League as usual, she was shopping nearby in Bond Street and was about to cross the road, when her leg simply refused to move. She had felt something strange shift down there the night before when she had turned over in bed, but had thought nothing of it in the morning. Now, no matter how hard she tried, it would not obey her. The only way she could make any progress was to literally lift it up manually and then place it down, as you would with a mannequin's doll.

Seemingly frozen to the spot, she remembered a shop called Swaine Adeney Briggs, in Piccadilly, outfitters for hunting, shooting and fishing gear, and managed to struggle to its doorway.

'Yes, Madam, can I help you?' asked the attendant.

'If you brought me one of your walking sticks you could,' replied Margaret.

And so, with the help of a folding cane purchased on the spot, she managed to get herself onto the plane home. Gough was very surprised, shocked even, to see his wife walking with the aid of a cane when he met her at the airport. Margaret had always matched him stride for stride. This marked a period of change for both of them, because it really signified the beginning of the deterioration of Margaret's mobility. She has had many different types of canes since, but one is always by her side.

Doctors informed her that the pin, which had been implanted so many years ago after her fall in the laundry at Cronulla, had worked its way out of her hip, and now must be removed. After the operation Gough insisted she keep the pin, which was made from the metal alloy vitallium. As it had a hole in the top Margaret decided to get a chain and wear it as a pendant. The pin jewellery, however, never eventuated because in the end she misplaced it. She says, 'I put it in a safe place and it's still there.'

Walking with the aid of a cane didn't stop her agreeing to become the chair of the Opera Conference, a national voice for

Australia's opera companies. She loved the fact that she and Gough were now free to indulge their mutual passion for opera and theatre. They were easy to spot on opening nights and became popularly known as the 'twin icons of the opera'.

In 1980, however, Margaret's hectic pace, the aftermath of the political turmoil the couple had endured and her eagerness to create a new life full of her own professional commitments came to an abrupt halt when she found herself in hospital having suffered what she described as a heart spasm. Since the 1950s she had suffered from arrhythmia of the heart. 'My blood pressure was up and my heart was beating too fast at times. This had happened before and doctors had told me not to worry about it.'

Having had her heart monitored with every conceivable test, she was prescribed medication, and urged to lose weight and to take life a little more slowly. Her response was to accept an assignment from the Australian National Railways to travel thousands of kilometres around the country gathering material for a travel diary to be published in *New Idea*. Her justification was to point out how much more slowly she could take it on train journeys.

Titled 'Margaret Whitlam Makes Tracks across Australia', her columns, written in her usual chatty style, were warm, informative and practical. In her first column she wrote:

> Playing trains is something I've always wanted to do. In my day that was only for the boys. Not any more . . . the bathrooms are extremely workable. The curtain enclosed me totally and yet gave me room to move . . . It would have been quite adventurous and proper to share a table and perhaps a bottle with a stranger. Not that there's a need for that, as wine is also sold in half bottles. The single traveller is well cared for, a good thing to remember.

Nineteen eighty-two found her agreeing to chair the board of governors for the Law Foundation of New South Wales, an organisation that granted scholarships for postgraduate study. For the first time since she had been a social worker at Parramatta Hospital Margaret felt as if she really had a life of her own, separate from that of her husband. No longer a political appendage, the smiling face behind or beside the great man, she revelled in the sense of freedom and autonomy that she was experiencing. Her newly found freedom also allowed her to take time to squeeze in a Musica Viva tour or two.

Claire Nichols, at 103 her most elderly friend, remembers meeting Margaret for the first time in 1982 on an opera tour in Bayreuth.

> She was very easy, charming and friendly. When the tour went on to Salzburg I remember thinking that I couldn't afford to buy a big expensive lunch but I loved her company so I suggested lunch anyway, and as it turned out all she wanted was a sausage and a beer. She's very unpretentious. Even though she's very knowledgeable about music, theatre and books, she never talks down to you.
>
> When we were finishing our tour I said, 'I'm sad now that I won't be able to see you.' She said, 'What's wrong with seeing me when I get back to Sydney?'
>
> So she came to my place for lunches and from then on we travelled together quite a bit. Once, when we were on a bus tour, there was a very disagreeable woman who was always keeping us late. I said to Margaret, 'She's a pain in the neck,' and Margaret's response was, 'Oh, she's basically a nice soul.' It's not that she doesn't see other people's faults, she just thinks there's no point in going on about them.
>
> Another time when she and I and a couple of other woman friends rented a villa in Italy, we shared a room for three weeks

and I couldn't help noticing that Margaret was always in a good mood. When something went wrong, like the day I washed my hair in the shower and flooded not only the bathroom but half the villa, she threw open the door of the bathroom, shouted at me to get out and then burst into laughter when the water surged down the passage.

At long last Margaret was living her own life and was free to be herself and make her own contribution by using her talents and experience in areas other than politics. This was the post-political life she had secretly longed to live, compatible, but separate from that of Gough.

On Australia Day 1983 she was made an Officer in the Order of Australia in recognition of her work in the community, in adult education and the arts. She was delighted to receive it and looked forward to making an even greater contribution in these areas. Life was exactly how she liked it.

Four months later, early one morning in a hotel room in Adelaide, where Gough was centenary professor of law at the university, the phone rang. Gough answered it and Margaret, who was still in bed, could hear him laughing and then saying, 'I'll have to ask Margaret about that. Can I ring you back?'

When he put down the phone he sat on the end of the bed and said, 'That was Hawke. He has offered me the job at UNESCO which Fraser had given to Kerr and which Kerr had to abandon. What do you think?'

Margaret admits now that she suddenly understood the phrase 'my heart sank'. But, she replied, 'Well, it's a bit of an opportunity, isn't it?' She knew she would hate giving up her boards and the life she had created for herself but she thought it would have been 'too mean to Gough' if she had refused to let him accept the offer.

By August they were in the south of France, at Villefranche-sur-Mer, ready for an intensive month-long course in French.

> We had a delightful flat that looked out over the bay and a driver at our disposal. He'd pick us up in the morning, take us to school, then pick us up and I'd do a bit of shopping on the way home and we'd sit out on the balcony with a drink and do our homework. It was lovely.
>
> We'd both only done French at school. My accent improved quite rapidly. Gough's didn't, but it didn't really matter because he always had interpreters.

In Paris the apartment they were allocated in the Australian Embassy on Rue Jean Rey had originally been built for the ambassador, and was now used by the OECD or UNESCO ambassadors. Designed by Australian architect Harry Seidler on land secured by the Australian government after World War II, they were on the seventh floor in the front building above the chancery, with a magnificent view of the Eiffel Tower and the River Seine. They were the envy of local Parisian society, who loved attending parties there. In good weather they entertained on the huge terrace between the dining room and the salon, which was the main entertaining area. Day and night the *bâteaux mouches* and the working barges cut a path through the river. It was a view 'to die for', says Margaret.

She knew she should have been delighted to be living there, although she thought that their private quarters – a very big suite with a huge bedroom, bathroom and dressing room – were furnished more like offices than bedrooms, with desks but no free-standing dressing table. Here she was, as she had dreamt in her youth, actually living in beautiful, sensual, seductive Paris. At first, however, she felt strangely subdued. Depressed, even. She couldn't understand it. Why was she not elated? Why was she not thrilled at the opportunity to live in the most beautiful city in the world? She thought the feeling would pass, that she was just disoriented at the sudden change in their lives. But it didn't go away. It nagged at her like a toothache.

As usual, the media were keen to report on their new life. A feature article in December 1983 in *The Australian Women's Weekly* detailed Margaret's glamorous new life. This time she did not neglect to explain in her candid fashion, her contradictory feelings about her new role.

'Being the wife of someone important isn't very entrancing. It's very difficult to achieve a role of one's own and do all the things expected of a wife. I had quite a career of my own in Australia before I left. I suppose I'll get involved here, eventually, but sometimes I feel I'm *rien*, nothing, a has-been.'

Even while she is voicing words like 'nothing' and 'has-been' Margaret is waging a war against them. Once having spoken the devil, she sets about defeating it.

She would never allow herself to be gloomy in a social situation, she would consider that to be irresponsible and self-indulgent, and over lunch with the *Women's Weekly* journalist she chatted freely about her past experiences with the British royal family. The journalist lapped it up.

> Once, when the Queen and Prince Philip were on an Australian tour, Gough introduced the Queen to Al Grassby [Labor's immigration minister] remarking that Al tended to dress in a somewhat flamboyant manner. Observing Al's colourful tie the Queen remarked, 'Andrew would love a tie

like that,' so Gough arranged that the next morning the tie was delivered to the Queen. Some years later we were having lunch at Buckingham Palace – just the Queen, Philip, Andrew and Edward. The two boys were wearing jackets that were buttoned up very high. Suddenly, in the middle of the first course, Andrew unbuttoned his jacket and revealed Al Grassby's tie. The Queen said, 'I was wondering why you had your jacket buttoned up like that.'

We used to see Philip during our courting days when we went to Romano's. Philip was often on leave during the war at the same time as Gough. He is much more aloof than the Queen. I always had the feeling that I was very much the scullery maid in his presence. But she never gives that impression.

(In 2006 when the Queen and Prince Philip were in Australia for the opening of the Commonwealth Games, Gough and Margaret were invited to Parliament House in Canberra for a state dinner. Margaret was taken aback when as soon as Prince Philip saw her he greeted her very warmly. She says, 'He didn't just shake my hand formally, he took both my hands in his in a very familial and warm gesture. I was quite overcome. I suppose the lesson of that is if you live long enough, you may have to change your impressions of people.')

After lunch, when she and the journalist had settled down for coffee in the private sitting room overlooking the Seine, Margaret's irrepressible sense of humour burst forth.

'The other evening when Gough and I were going out the door we suddenly saw a flasher. I kept looking back at him but Gough kept telling me, "Don't look, Margaret," and then I saw he was looking just as hard as I was.' Chortle, chortle.

When the journalist and the photographer returned to the apartment for an evening reception, they saw Margaret dressed in a new 'glitter' top and elegant black pants made on the Left Bank, standing beside Gough, shaking hands and greeting guests from Commonwealth and European nations.

'Margaret was the ideal hostess, moving from group to group, introducing strangers and keeping a close eye on the caterers who had set out tables of exquisite-looking savouries,' the *Women's Weekly* reporter wrote.

Margaret is not by nature, introspective, but her sense of loss and dissatisfaction with her life in Paris would not go away. So, she finally took the time to confront the reasons for her melancholy, to force herself to deal with it.

She realised that she was depressed because she was once again the wife of the man with the important job. Every day was marked by Gough's official appointments and dinners, many of which she was expected to attend. Yet again, she had to fit her life around his work schedule and play hostess to his commitments. Yet again, she was 'also present'. She desperately missed the autonomy of her life in Sydney, where she felt she had finally carved out her own identity as Margaret Whitlam, not just Mrs Whitlam, appendage to her husband and his career.

Once she had finally admitted to herself what was making her feel 'blue', she set about, as she had during her early days at the Lodge, creating a schedule of her own, with time and regular space allocated to her own interests and pleasures. And having ceased to allow herself to be viewed as a passive extension of her husband's working life, she began to enjoy the many delights of the city.

Once again, she made her time work for her, and for her and Gough as a couple. Without Margaret, Gough would have spent his time outside work staying at home reading, or visiting the galleries. She was the catalyst for their weekend adventures – picnics in the country, informal lunches and dinners with friends.

She began by taking herself off with their cook to do the shopping across the river in Passy, a very old and chic shopping area of Paris. Here, the cook showed her the best places to buy meat, cheese, fruit, vegetables and bread and, as Margaret piled her basket high with all the delicious fresh produce, she began to feel at home. She even persuaded Gough to go to the market with her one Sunday, but it wasn't a great success.

'He didn't want to initiate anything himself. I kept saying, "Would you like to go and have a look at the cheese stalls up there?" and he'd say, "No, no." He's always got to be with me.'

Margaret's job was to inform the cook of their schedule for the week so she could plan their meals accordingly. Apart from the huge public reception and dining rooms, they had their own kitchen in their private quarters, together with a small sitting room, dining room and a big study. There were also two huge bedrooms in the front and two smaller ones at the back, all with big bathrooms. These quarters were beautifully cared for by Mano, a slight Tamil woman, and Ah Ping, a delightful Hong Kong Chinese.

Guests would be asked what they wanted for breakfast and their trays for the morning would be prepared. Margaret would often take the breakfast trays into her friends' bedrooms herself.

On weekends, when the French tend to go to the country for the weekend, they gave the staff time off and Margaret enjoyed cooking at home. On Saturdays she and Gough would go to the theatre or the opera, or sometimes into the country for lunch. Often they loved to just cross the river and walk for miles, exploring the city.

French customs for entertaining amused them: being expected to wait until the last dinner guest arrived and then being given no choice of drink other than a glass or two of champagne before sitting down for dinner. Margaret always found her facility to speak French was best at cocktail parties.

By September 1985, when she wrote her own account of a week in Paris in *Woman's Day*, she was clearly much more at home and in tune with herself and the joys of the city. She began with Wednesday, which was her market day.

> My ploy is to take the Métro from Bir-Hakeim up to La Motte-Picquet and walk back through the sellers to Dupleix, filling my basket as I go, but leaving room on top for bread and papers. There's my favourite cheese lady: as round and jolly as her cheeses. Tomatoes from Morocco, oranges from Algeria, cherries from all over. I love mixing strawberries, raspberries and redcurrants and sprinkling them with blackcurrant syrup, or buying little melons and filling them with raspberries and a spoonful of port. In the evening a small reception in the large chancery with an exhibition of books called 'Aspects of Australian Poetry'.
>
> Thursday usually offers more mundane matters: a visit to the chiropodist, or a shop for more rubber-soled shoes – essential for comfort on cobblestones.
>
> In the afternoon a meeting in the apartment with my conversation group. Seven French women and seven English-speaking women, all wanting to improve in the use of the others' language. We meet for two hours, one hour in English and one in French, while the hostess serves tea and cake.

The night is opera, the Folies Bergères, or the Comédie Française, or just dinner with friends. Friday is not very social as Parisians tend to nip off early to the country or the sea so I make it a girls' lunch, or a window-shopping spree. Saturday and Sunday are for peace and quiet – listening to France Musique, writing letters, or helping with EGW's book, *The Whitlam Government*. Sunday is for sightseeing and music in churches. Monday the shops are shut and it's the best night for television. This summer we are being treated to a very controversial and modern production of Wagner's *Ring Cycle*.

Tuesday most galleries are closed but there are still good ones open like the Carnavalet and Victor Hugo's house in the Marais and the Marmottan and Balzac's house in the 16th arrondissement. Once a month I go to my hairdresser, Laurent, for a hair-cut.

It all sounds too fabulous to be true, but Margaret also wrote that sometimes it was very lonely.

'It's not all go. There were months of loneliness without family, most of whom have now visited, although there was the compensation of a lovely long mid-term leave last Christmas.'

What she didn't tell the readers of *Woman's Day* is that while they were on leave they attended an open-air performance of *The Tales of Hoffman* in Sydney's Domain. Upon their arrival (and it's pretty hard to miss them) the crowd gave them a spontaneous standing ovation. They were both very touched by the warmth of the welcome. In *The National Times* in February 1985, journalist Kristin Williamson observed, 'If there is political royalty in Australia then the emeritus emperor and empress would have to be Gough and Margaret Whitlam.'

Margaret would, of course, snort at any notion of such titles.

Neither did she report on the visit of a young man called Mark Latham, who lived with the Whitlams for a month in 1985 in the Paris embassy to help Gough with research for his book.

Margaret says, 'I found him brash and I had to pull him into line. He seemed over-confident and I thought he needed some of his rough edges smoothed out.' She did her best to support him and teach him the necessary social graces that would be required were he ever to need them, but she was underwhelmed by young Latham, despite the fact that Gough had taken him under his tutelage and had high hopes for his political future.

A more popular visitor from Australia was Kathy Lette. Kathy had known Margaret since she and Catherine Whitlam had worked together on weekends selling books at the Angus & Robertson store on Pitt Street, in Sydney. Catherine was now at university and Kathy was, like most of the other weekend staff – would-be writers, poets and musicians – writing her first novel, *Puberty Blues*. Kathy says that she and Catherine got along well together from the start because, 'She's the grown-up and I'm the juvenile delinquent.' Catherine taught Kathy how to swim and introduced her to Margaret, with whom they both swam and surfed regularly at their Bondi club. Kathy says, 'They were both giants and I'm a bonsai.' Whenever there were jellyfish in the water she would climb onto Margaret's back to protect herself.

She claims Margaret as her role-model. She left school when she was fourteen and it was Margaret who encouraged her to read widely. When Margaret read Kathy's book *Girls' Night Out* she made a point of visiting her to tell her how talented she thought she was and what she considered were the strengths and weaknesses of the book.

'She took me seriously as a writer and was so gracious and constructive. I love the way she treats everyone the same. Whether it's the Queen or the cleaning lady, she treats them as she likes to be treated. She has no tickets on herself.'

Kathy remembers a particular Parisian lunch that demonstrated Margaret's ability to remain totally calm in a moment of crisis.

The setting was a very posh restaurant, Pre Catalan, in the Bois de Bologne. Gough was in the front seat of the embassy car next to Henri, the chauffeur. In the back seat were Catherine, Kathy and Margaret. The car pulled up directly in front of the restaurant, where the maître d' and the head waiter were standing waiting to greet their distinguished guests. Henri got out to open Margaret's door, but she doesn't like to stand on ceremony so she was in the process of getting out of the car herself. This is how Kathy Lette describes what happened next, in her own colourful, inimitable style.

> I don't know whether she'd lost weight, but as she got out the elastic on the waistband of her skirt went and the skirt collapsed to the ground. She was suddenly standing in a puddle of skirt, and she was wearing these huge white step-ins, thigh-length down to the knees.
>
> We all just stood there in a fugue of shock. We couldn't move. We just stood there, open-mouthed. The maître d' and his welcome party weren't collapsing – they were French, they were frozen. They were looking like Stonehenge monuments. We were all staring at Margaret, waiting for her cue, to see what she would do. Out of the restaurant windows French elite are looking out at her, open-mouthed.
>
> I would have gone and jumped off the Seine Bridge. I would have died of embarrassment. But Margaret just looked down and said, 'Oh, hello.' That's exactly what she did, she went, 'Oh, hello.' She turned around and – she must have done this on purpose – with her bottom towards the window, towards the

upper-class French voyeurs, and bending from the waist because she's not good at bending from the knee, she gave them the full view of the Whitlam posterior. Then she picked up the skirt, zipped it up, turned around and said 'Onward.' And onward we all cruised into the restaurant, as if to the château born.

She was not fazed – not a blush, not a raised eyebrow from her. Nothing, just absolute calm. Gough was on the other side of the car oblivious to what had happened, but Catherine and I were in hysterics by then. Once she'd picked the skirt up, we erupted, literally screaming with laughter. We practically had to be hospitalised from hilarity. It was such a sight gag, it was worthy of Monsieur Hulot. And of course the French, being French, did nothing. They just kept their noses so far up in the air we were looking up every nostril. I thought, What a woman. The French are supposed to be suave but she out-suaved them. What a woman.

Just as Margaret had taken an interest in Kathy's early career as a writer, so, too, she tried to teach her French. Kathy freely admits that her French vocabulary consisted of rendez-vous, liaison, lingerie and croissant.

Nevertheless, Margaret did not give up on her, taking her to French plays, saying, 'You might just absorb something by osmosis.'

One night she took her to the Australian embassy cocktail party. 'Très gelée' (very frozen) and 'très jolie' (very pretty) are extremely similar in pronunciation. Kathy spent all night telling the ambassador that his wife was 'très gelée'. When the politician didn't respond, Kathy assumed that she just hadn't spoken it correctly and so she would say it again.

All night I hounded him about how frozen his wife was. When I told Margaret in the car going home, instead of saying to me,

'Kathy, I can never take you out again without a muzzle,' she just went into hysterics. She fell about. For weeks afterwards wherever I was she'd come in and tell me I was looking frozen. She just thought it was the best thing ever. Other people would have been furious with me. She's always looking for the comedic. She has a very robust sense of humour.

The Whitlams' term in Paris was considered a great success and, like every other aspect of Gough's career, much of that success was due to the woman at his side. Margaret is and has always been his rock, his constant companion, his compass. Kathy Lette has observed them at close quarters for many years now, and she is certain that Margaret is his major strength because she is able to put everyone at ease and provide the social lubricant for every occasion.

Like many brilliant men, Gough will tend to monologue you rather than engage with you. Once, I made the mistake of asking him how he got on with his dad and five hours later, via the Han dynasty, he was getting around to answering the question.

Margaret's the one that everyone loves. They respect Gough, but she's the social magnet. And she's more disarming than a United Nations peacekeeping corps. Her family were clearly very urbane and sophisticated. Self-made people who didn't worship their creator.

The other major strength of Margaret's is that she's not judgemental. When I met her I was this knock-about surfie girl who'd left school really young – no sophistication, no culture, no polish, no poise – and she spent time trying to educate me, but never in a condescending way. She's like a girlfriend to me. I totally forget how old she is and one day when we were discussing sex I said to her, 'I can't believe you've only had sex with one man in your life. How would you know whether he was a dud root or not?'

Margaret was laughing at me and Catherine said, 'Do you know how old my mother is, and what generation she's from? Of course she's only had one man in her life.'

I said, 'Well, I hope Gough's not a dud root, Margaret,' and without blinking, she replied, 'Absolutely not, darling.'

Margaret did have, however, what she likes to call, in her own romantic style, 'a secret love affair with Lennie Bernstein'. And it happened while she was living in Paris, a city she views as the most romantic in the world.

One morning while reading the paper she noticed that Bernstein was conducting several concerts with the Israeli Symphony Orchestra at the prestigious concert hall La Salle Pleyel. She immediately bought a ticket and was very excited at the thought of seeing Bernstein again, as she felt they had formed a special bond all those years before, when after she had interviewed him on her television program he had taken her to Premier Hamer's party.

However, the day before the concert she was commanded to attend a diplomatic dinner on the same night. She reluctantly gave the ticket to a friend and boldly wrote a personal note to Mr Bernstein telling him how disappointed she was at being prevented from having another opportunity to see him, and suggesting that he might have time to come to the embassy for a drink before he left Paris. The note was duly delivered to the stage door.

The next morning she received a call from Bernstein's personal assistant to say that he couldn't do that as he had another concert performance and several rehearsals. He invited her to come instead to a rehearsal and he gave a time, place and detailed directions about security, in order for her to be admitted.

Margaret was thrilled and moved around other appointments to ensure she was there at the allotted time. Unfortunately, the security guards at La Salle Pleyel refused to admit her because by the time she arrived the rehearsal was already in progress. Margaret wrote another note and asked for it to be delivered to him. It read, 'I came, I saw, but I was conquered.' And that, she thought, was the end of that.

The next morning an enormous bunch of flowers was delivered to her with a personal note from the man himself. Margaret immediately called to express her thanks, and was put through to the man she called Lennie. He had a dreadful cold and was agonising about the performance. 'Margaret,' he said, 'be not concerned about our inability to talk. We will meet again. And we will embrace.' Margaret confessed that after those words, 'I was his forever.'

Unfortunately, they never did meet again before Bernstein died, but Margaret, the true romantic, has never forgotten how beautifully he behaved towards her.

Finally, in 1986 it was 'au revoir' to Paris and 'g'day' to Sydney.

Near the end of their journey home James Strong, then the CEO of Qantas, met them at Sydney airport. Strong remembers that Gough assailed him and complained that although he and Margaret had travelled side by side all the way from Paris, on their final leg from Sydney to Canberra Qantas couldn't seat them together. Strong assured Gough that he would see what he could do to rectify the problem. As he bid Gough farewell, Margaret pulled him aside and said quietly, 'I wouldn't try too hard, James. Quite frankly, I could do with a break.'

They both quickly slipped back into hectic schedules: they hardly had time to settle into their small Darling Point apartment when they were once again travelling away from home around Australia, fulfilling various duties and commitments. Only a month after their return Margaret told a journalist that she had been to Melbourne alone three times already, and once to Canberra with Gough, who had meanwhile been to Perth and Brisbane.

Gough was now chairman of the board of the National Gallery, a fellow of the Sydney University Senate, and a member of the Constitutional Commission and the Australia–China Council.

Margaret was appointed to a six-member organising committee to review the state government's role in adult education. She was delighted with the appointment because adult education had been so crucial to enriching her own life in Cronulla and Cabramatta. For many months she and the other committee members planned an international conference on the role of government in adult education. John Wellings, head of the New South Wales Board of Adult Education, and Anne Krone (later Wellings), an adult educator, organised the week-long conference, which began at the Opera House, then travelled to Kiama, Canberra, Milton Park in Bowral and back to the Rocks in Sydney for a farewell dinner. It was a huge success.

Margaret was also involved in fund-raising activities for the Australian Opera and was a judge on the National Book Council's Awards. She had an open invitation from several magazines to write articles of her choice, and was enjoying freelance book reviewing for the major newspapers.

Did she miss Paris? was one question all the media asked. It was a trap question because if she admitted that she did she might sound like a superior Europhile who had turned her back on her country; if she said she didn't she was in danger of looking ungrateful for the fact that the government had paid for her and her husband to live in a luxury apartment in one of the most beautiful cities in Europe. So her reply was always, 'I miss its physical beauty, but this really is the best place in the world to live.'

This was not just pleasing pap for the Sunday papers and the women's magazines – Margaret does have a deep love for her own country and a particular pride in her birthplace, which she is never reticent in expressing. Happy to be back in close contact with her four children, her five grandchildren and her old friends, she was also keen to return to playing golf, getting her handicap down and swimming at her beloved Bondi.

However, the rumours that Gough's political enemies had spread about the Whitlams' marriage and its alleged break-up before, during and after the dismissal, surfaced once again when they returned from Paris, particularly in Sydney's eastern suburbs, where they continued to live. These rumours now had a new twist. This time they focused on Gough's friendship with a man called Andrew, forty years his junior.

Andrew's family had migrated from Argentina to Cabramatta and Gough had presented his sister with an academic medal for Spanish at Cabramatta High School. Andrew subsequently met Gough through his parents when he was twenty-two and immediately looked to him as his mentor. When he decided to become an Australian citizen, he asked Gough if he could change his name to Whitlam because he so admired him. Gough was flattered and agreed.

Gough's children, however, were less pleased that this stranger now bore their name. Nor did they like the vicious gossip that swirled around the streets of Double Bay every time Gough called into Andrew's women's fashion shop there for a chat and a coffee, sitting openly at a table on the footpath.

Margaret became sick of the snide remarks and when Gough announced that Andrew was accompanying him overseas because of his decreasing mobility, Tony explained to his father that this would only feed the rumours, giving fuel to his enemies and adding to Margaret's distress. Stephen went instead to help him. (Paul Keating suffered from similar rumours when he was seen dining in Paris with a young, good-looking man. It was Patrick, his son.)

When asked what she would have done if the rumours had been true Margaret says, 'Tell him to pull himself together and not be so stupid.'

Would it have been the end of the marriage? 'Absolutely not,' she replied.

By 1987 Margaret's hip was causing her serious pain. Arthritis had set in soon after the pin had been removed. This meant a hip replacement, one month in St Vincent's Hospital and walking on crutches until it healed. Margaret never complained because it was better than being in pain. And anyway, she loathed people who constantly whined about their health problems.

The Whitlams' time away from Australia had only increased both the media and the public's interest in them and by October 1988 they were back on the front cover of *The Sydney Morning Herald*'s 'Good Weekend' magazine in an article by Craig McGregor entitled 'THE WHITLAM DYNASTY: INSIDE OUR FIRST POLITICAL FAMILY'.

Having brought up her family almost as a single parent due to Gough's absences in Canberra and in his electorate, Margaret was pleased to report that, 'The older they get the more our children like each other . . . and us, which is nice. Tony and Nick are terrific mates, they go to the football together, the third one, Stephen, has always been a bit of a cat who walks alone. Catherine is mates with them all, but if there's going to be any siding she sides with Stephen as they were the two youngest.'

The 1988 report card on the family announced that Tony Whitlam (44, 6 foot 5 inches), had tried to follow his father into politics as an MP from 1975–77, when redistribution forced him into another electorate, which he lost in the massive anti-Labor result of 1977. Two years later he had stood for preselection for his old seat and lost to the New South Wales conservative candidate. He had become a barrister, and was now a QC. He and his solicitor wife, Pip, had no children..

Nick (42, 6 foot 3 inches) was described as a successful businessman, currently partner to Malcolm Turnbull in a small investment bank, and very involved in the Sydney financial and social scene. He and Judy had three children – Alice, 11, Edward, 7, who were adopted, and Peter, 6, who was intellectually handicapped.

Stephen (38, 6 foot 2 inches) was a diplomat with the Department of Foreign Affairs and was divorced from his wife, Sheena. They had two children, Alexander, 17, and Helen, 12.

Catherine (34, 6 foot 2 inches) was a manager in human resources at the New South Wales Water Board, was unmarried and now used the surname Dovey.

The catalyst for Catherine's name change was a decision in 1978 by the Catholic bishop of Bathurst to rescind her first teaching appointment to a local Catholic school purely because of her family name. She had been interviewed and told that she had the job. On Christmas Eve the school wrote to her to withdraw their offer. The bishop was a staunch DLP member and had told the school that he was not prepared to employ a Whitlam.

Catherine was devastated. Margaret was terribly distressed and considered it to be very un-Christian behaviour. Even though Gough was upset over Catherine's decision to change her name, Margaret stood by her right to do so.

Margaret was quite forthright in the article about the fact that apart from her sister-in-law, Freda, a former headmistress of PLC Croydon and a moderator of the Uniting Church, the Whitlam males tended to be more intellectual than the women they married.

'Gough's mother was a very bright woman, but I wouldn't call her an intellectual, whereas his father and Gough I would. I wouldn't call me an intellectual either, although I'm okay.'

This was an honest assessment and not intended to be self-deprecating. Margaret is instinctual rather than analytical. While a woman of a strong and imaginative intellect, she would always prefer to dip in and out of a broad range of areas that interest her, rather than undertaking an in-depth intellectual pursuit of one particular area or aspect.

The article was positive and celebratory of the Whitlam dynasty, emphasising how proud of all their children Margaret and Gough were, and how when they were all together they made a very handsome family portrait – each of them, however, having a distinct personality despite their shared heredity and upbringing.

Margaret turned sixty-nine in November 1988 and Nick and Judy had a special barbecue to celebrate her birthday. Although she was still using a cane to help her walk, if her children thought that this might slow down the pace of her activities they were wrong. She had just agreed to chair the National Council for International Literacy Year. Her own children might have all done well academically, but she wanted those who were less gifted or privileged to be able to overcome their reading difficulties in order to have more opportunities. She knew that reading was basic to a fulfilling life and she was still an avid reader at every available opportunity.

Nor did she neglect her duties to the Labor Party. In February 1989 *The Canberra Times* reported that over two hundred women had paid to have tea and sandwiches and listen to speaker Margaret Whitlam, who was doing her bit to raise money for the five woman on Labor's ticket in the forthcoming election.

The federal member for Canberra, Ros Kelly, told them, 'Mrs Whitlam was a great personal inspiration,' and Rosemary Follett said she was 'not only one of Labor's great women, but one of Australia's greatest-ever women'. Margaret ignored and rebuffed such accolades because she genuinely believed that she had only done what was asked of her. She had never seen herself as a political figure.

'I haven't done much at all – I have just been in the background. A bit more than making the tea, but not much.'

All her life she had been playing supporting, not leading roles, but even if she had been a 'voice-off', she failed to realise that people appreciated what she brought to it. Australia had been starved of female political leaders and although Margaret was never elected, she was always standing there next to her husband, and her presence was a powerful one. If she was asked a question, she always answered it as honestly as she could.

She never took herself too seriously and was happy to be the easygoing, light-hearted foil to Gough's earnestness and determination to be right. She freely admits now that she never bothers to argue with him any more. 'I've found that the best way to punish Gough is to ignore him . . . I don't compete, I just let him rave on.'

Dame Leonie Kramer, however, has been in a constant state of competitive warfare with Gough ever since they first met. They are engaged in an on-going competitive mutual teasing match and she once stated publicly that even in the after-life, whether it be heaven or hell, they will still be discussing with each other who has the better brain of the two.

Even though she is not a close friend of Margaret's she is quite unabashed in praise of her particular qualities, which she has observed casually whenever they have met over the years. She gives Margaret one of the best tributes one human being can give another. 'You just feel better in her company.'

Phillip Adams, journalist and broadcaster, would no doubt disagree with Dame Leonie on many things, but not in her opinion of Margaret Whitlam. He says, 'Everyone, over the years, has always had this respect for Margaret because they know she's a straight-shooter. She's a class act.'

Although he met her when they were both in hospital – he was 'having half my innards removed' and she was having a hip replacement and they were rattling around the hospital corridors with their little stands and bottles – he regrets that he's never been close enough to tell her how much he admires her.

As he says, 'If I went up and gave her a huge hug and said, "Margaret, I think you're great," she'd writhe with embarrassment and say something like, "Steady on!"'

He says whenever he sees Margaret with Gough he is reminded how

> when Roman generals had triumphal entries into the great city, having conquered Gaul, they'd throw up one of those arches and the general would be given a ticker-tape welcome through the cheering crowds. Out of sight, crouched down by his seat, there'd be a slave saying, 'Remember, you are just a mortal.' That was Margaret's role in life. Gough never took her

seriously, but she did a great job of taking the piss out of him for thirty years.

Adams believes that Margaret has been the perfect consort for Gough and that they have been and still are a successful double act.

> When you think of Gough, you think of Margaret. He's lucky to have had Margaret. She brings such warmth. But is Margaret lucky to have had him? She's certainly had an exciting life with him, but what about the constant barrage of phones and people knocking on the door and the open house you'd be almost forced to keep as his wife. You just look at Margaret and you trust her. She has an aura, a radiance about her.

Margaret would snort at this, but he's right. Human interaction reinforces the need we all have to feel connected with each other and Margaret Whitlam is a walking example of this. The word 'charisma' is greatly overused but if it means the ability to draw people to you then Margaret undoubtedly has that aura about her.

TRIPS

The 1990s were to usher in a new phase of Margaret's life and present her with a new role – that of international tour leader.

Early in 1990, at a further education conference in Bangkok, Margaret and John and Anne Wellings cemented a business partnership that was to last throughout the decade. For ten days at this conference Anne shared a room with Margaret. There is no better way to really get to know someone.

Not only was Anne's view confirmed that Margaret was a consistently even-tempered, easygoing person, she also saw the 'good-time' girl that emerged when she was away from Gough and her family responsibilities, and was free to be herself.

Their room, thanks to the bottles of rum that 'the girls' had purchased, became known as the 'rum corps barracks' and was the regular gathering place for conversations and late-night parties for other Australians and friends they had made at the conference.

Anne and John said Margaret was invariably the life of the party and that even though she could drink with the best of them, they never saw her drunk, or even slurring her words. The mornings after the parties she was always bright, apparently without any hangover (or at least none that she was admitting to) and was always eager to enjoy whatever new adventures the day might bring.

The Wellings realised that Margaret would be the perfect person to lead the international study tours that they had decided to launch. When they asked her if she would work with them to help plan and lead the tours, Margaret jumped at the opportunity.

Here she was, aged seventy-one, being offered her dream life, her ideal job. Her social-worker training would be useful in helping people make the most of their trips, and all those years as a politician's wife of learning how to get along with all types of people, how to engage them in conversation, and her genuine interest in their lives and their families, would be put to good use.

Her passion for travel had been fulfilled by accompanying her husband to various parts of the world, but she was very much shackled to his schedule, which included official functions, visits to factories, schools and hospitals, and she was rarely able to see the places she would have chosen. While realising that it was a privilege to be given the opportunity to travel on behalf of her country, an itinerary of, for example, fourteen countries in three weeks, wasn't exactly relaxing.

Now she would be able to plan the itinerary that would give her tour members time to absorb the best that various cities had to offer, with free time allotted simply to wander and explore.

Her interest in opera, music and literature could be satiated by visits to the best companies and artists in the world; her love of good food and wine from every country could be explored by tasting the best of each region.

For Margaret, travelling overseas was also a chance to learn more about the world, its various cultures, the nature of different people and their customs. This new role of tour leader was quite simply made in heaven as far as she was concerned.

Even though she was now in her seventies, this new decade seemed to Margaret to be shaping up as her most exciting yet. In

July 1990 she accompanied Gough to China. One date that stood out was 24 July.

They were in the city of Qingdao and as part of their official duties had been inspecting hospitals. After dinner they returned to their hotel, tired. They collapsed into bed and had just turned out the light when Margaret realised that she needed to go to the toilet. Scrambling out of the bedclothes, she picked up her cane. But somehow it became caught under the bed and she crashed to the floor.

Needless to say, Margaret was in agony. Gough called for help immediately. It came quickly, but the attendants were unable to fit their stretcher into the hotel lift so they had to roll her up in the carpet on which she had landed and carry her down the fire-exit stairs to the waiting ambulance.

They took her to the local hospital where it was discovered she had broken her right wrist and right leg. At first they tried to set her broken wrist without the aid of an anaesthetic. With the assistance of an interpreter and Gough they were soon dissuaded from that course of action. They set the wrist while she was under a full anaesthetic, but when she returned to Sydney it had to be re-set and is still out of alignment to this day.

Her leg was in appalling pain so they gave her medication, but it only succeeded in making her feel dopey. She was then forced to wait another day until they could transport her to Hong Kong. Still unable to fit the stretcher in the lift of the Hong Kong hotel where they had taken her in the meantime, she was carried up to her room inside the same rug and placed on top of the bed on it. If she hadn't been in so much discomfort she might have been able to laugh at these incidents worthy of a Marx Brothers film. However, marooned in a rough carpet on top of a hotel bed in Hong Kong, the wife of the former Prime Minister of Australia found it hard, for once, to see the funny side of her predicament.

Despite the heavy medication, the waiting and the pain continued to be excruciating. Margaret is, nevertheless, a stoic and she endured the night. When they finally transported her onto the plane she was positioned in the very back, curtained off on a stretcher and placed across three seats, next to the toilets. She could hear other passengers queuing for the toilet and saying, 'I wonder who's behind those curtains. Poor thing. Fancy being stranded back here.' Poor thing indeed. Margaret was feeling sorry for herself.

'It was so terrible. All I could do was drink some juice and hope for the best. I had a lovely doctor who was a Pom with the Australian Embassy. He had a daughter in Australia so he was very happy to accompany me home. He sat beside me all the way and kept asking, "Do you want to wee?" or "Do you want some juice?"'

The catheter that had been inserted was too small and had to be removed, which later resulted in a bladder infection. The entire trip was a hellish nightmare, made worse for her by the fact that Gough, who was sitting at the front of the plane, didn't come back to see his wife once in the entire trip home. 'I was really cross about that. He said he was too embarrassed to walk the length of the plane past all the people and he knew there was nothing he could do. I wasn't pleased. I'm still not pleased. That's really the only time in our marriage that he's done anything that's really disappointed me.'

Still, one disappointment in sixty years is not a bad record.

Now, whenever she's sick and Gough has to go interstate, she is happy for him to do so. 'It's better if he goes. I don't encourage him to visit me. He's not good in hospitals. We talk a lot on the phone – I prefer that.'

After what seemed an interminable flight, she was transported from the plane by ambulance to Sydney's St Vincent's Hospital, where she was met by her orthopaedic surgeon, Dr Roarty, her

GP, Dr John Clubb, and the hospital's famous nun, Sister Bernice. Never had she been more pleased to see these three people.

She was finally ready to leave the hospital after a month, with a new pin and plate in her thigh. When Catherine was cleaning out the cupboard in her room, she pulled out what looked like an old piece of hessian.

'What on earth is this, Mum?' she asked.

'It's my magic carpet,' replied Margaret.

While the carpet may have saved her life, nothing, it seemed, could save her much loved brother Willie, who, while she was in St Vincent's, was admitted to the hospice across the road. He was only sixty-six, but had been suffering from oesophageal cancer, having had a tracheotomy two years previously. The day before he died staff managed to take Margaret across the road in a wheelchair to his room. She was very distressed, but moved by the bravery he showed in confronting his death.

She made the decision not to attend his funeral because she thought that by arriving on crutches she would draw too much attention to herself, which would detract from her brother's service. She wept for him alone. She now regrets her decision as she missed out on being part of his friends' and family's farewell.

Margaret was now the only remaining member of the Dovey family.

In 1991 Margaret was finally ready, and eager, to launch herself into her new career as tour leader for the Wellings' international study programs (ISPs). Her first tour was in September and began in France.

'Sitting high in a coach was a different way for me to travel from Charles de Gaulle Airport to downtown Paris. I had made the journey often before but it had usually been in an embassy car. This time I had thirty people who were depending on me to show them something of France . . . There is always a sense of excitement for me in arriving in Paris.'

The first thing Margaret does as soon as she has settled into her hotel in any city or village is go out immediately and explore the neighbourhood and her surroundings.

Between 1991 and 1999 she took eighteen trips to twenty-four countries, and was involved in the planning of a further sixty-nine tours for the Wellings' international study programs. She even wrote a book about these trips, called *My Other World*. It is full of the best places to stay and eat and visit, interspersed with practical tips on how to make the most of your time in whatever city or country you are visiting. She dedicated it to Gough, inscribing it: 'To my dear husband, who still says he taught me everything I know.'

It was her riposte to Gough's dedications to her in his various publications. In his first book, *The Whitlam Government*, he wrote: 'To my best appointment, Margaret Whitlam.' The dedication in *Abiding Interests* reads: 'To my most constant critic, Margaret Whitlam.' And in his book *My Italian Notebook*, it is simply: 'To my prima donna.'

Just as she had described all that she saw, tasted and heard in her columns for *Woman's Day* when she was the Prime Minister's wife, Margaret wrote her book as a means of allowing those who would perhaps never visit these countries to share in her experiences, to be a part of 'her other world'.

What did she do about leaving Gough behind for periods of up to three weeks to fend for himself? Once again, she organised their lives to suit them both. He could, of course, have moved into a hotel or a club, but he said that he preferred to stay at home with his reference books. Margaret cooked enough food and put it all in the freezer, together with instructions for re-heating. She organised 'the kids', as she still calls them, to check up on him and take him to their homes or out for meals on weekends.

Then, when the Wellings were planning a study tour to Eastern Europe, they asked Margaret if it might be possible for Gough to lead the tour with her, as they wanted to make use of his vast knowledge of the region, and of his contacts. Gough happily accepted the offer and so began his involvement with the tours.

On their joint trips the Wellings had an opportunity to observe the Whitlams' relationship daily. John Wellings noticed that Margaret always looked after Gough and made his comfort and needs one of her top priorities. Nevertheless, she would not stand for any nonsense. 'He does have his dark side and can be difficult, but Margaret ticks him off like she would a schoolboy who was misbehaving.'

Gough's knowledge of the history of most parts of the world is encyclopaedic and, as a result, he would often have trouble adhering to the thirty-minute rule for the kind of talk required on the tour. Margaret would take responsibility for alerting him to his time limit. Once, when they were in Thailand, Gough said to John, 'Don't let Margaret sit near me when I'm speaking. She makes those clicking noises with her tongue and it puts me off.'

Barry Jones, former president of the ALP, who also led some of the ISP tours, loves the story that John Wellings told him about another time when Gough had control of the microphone and was droning on and on. John realised that most of the travellers on the bus appeared to be asleep. Margaret offered to go and sit up the front and encourage him to wind up his lecture. After some time passed, Gough was still going so John also snuck down to the front of the bus, only to discover that Margaret, too, had fallen asleep. Gough was talking to a completely comatose audience.

Sometimes Gough led tours without Margaret. John observed that on these occasions, such as one trip to the Black Sea, Gough seemed quite lost. When Margaret isn't with him, he rings her constantly. John remarks, 'He doesn't have Margaret's ease with people and a conversation with him tends to be one-way, in lecture style. He is excellent at conveying information, but has very little small talk. On the other hand, Margaret finds it very easy to relate to everyone, knows how to put them at ease and is not at all intimidating. She has a real talent for turning every occasion into fun.'

When Margaret took a tour on her own she became more of a party person. John says, 'When she was with Gough she toned it down a little.'

Anne noticed her 'girlish enjoyment' of everything and says there was even 'a naughty girl aspect to her', such as having a bloody mary at 11 am. She never saw Margaret happier than eating German sausages and having a beer or clapping her hands in time and getting everyone else to join with her at a Strauss concert.

> She always had time for every single person. Before the tour even started she would know their names, and by the end she'd know the names of their grandchildren. She would weld the group together by constantly taking photos and after the trip she would write an individual handwritten letter to everyone and include photos of them. She didn't see it as a marketing exercise, or as a responsibility. She loved to do it.

Margaret never lets politics influence her in terms of her initial judgement of people and she and Gough made a particular point of treating everyone equally and with respect on each tour, regardless of their political affiliations.

The Wellings observed that on one literary tour led by Margaret Gough spent a lot of time with the wife of a former member of the Country Party simply because she was an interesting person. On a tour to Italy, Gough asked the Wellings if he could join Margaret because of his love of Italy. One man who had signed up to go on the tour was a former Liberal Party candidate, who let them know he wasn't pleased with Gough's presence. However, by the end of the tour they were seen by all the others to be spending a lot of time together – they had developed a mutual respect for each other's intellect.

On another tour to Turkey and Greece Gough paid for his sister, Freda, to join them, and she had a lovely time. The Whitlam siblings do not see a great deal of each other socially, except on occasions like birthdays and Christmas. But in the past few years, because of their advancing age, Gough has made a commitment to ring Freda every Sunday morning at 7, to touch base and talk about what each of them has been doing.

Freda says that their parents brought them up almost as only children rather than brother and sister. Their basic values, however, are very similar, and they are both deeply imbued with their parents' belief that their main duty is to serve the community and to help those less privileged than themselves.

Freda was never close to Margaret, but she greatly admires how much she has contributed to her brother's career.

> He's not really a sociable person, whereas she can talk to anyone, and that has made it a lot easier for him. He's devoted to her, in his own way, and very dependent on her.
>
> Margaret was brought up to be social and she loves going out. Gough goes out if there's a reason. We were brought up to

serve the community first and second to that we would prefer to stay at home and read.

I know she thinks I'm a wowser, and [it's true] I don't drink, but I would rather have a serious discussion than go out. I still help a lot of people with their legal problems, or if an injustice has occurred to them. I teach at the University of the Third Age – Latin and religious studies.

Freda is very forthright and perceptive in her assessment of her sister-in-law.

Margaret's a very sensuous person – she really savours things, like eating a mango or loving the feel of velvet or satin – whereas I love art but I'm not sensuous, except in my love of words. Gough has his romantic moments, but they are when it suits him. Whereas Margaret is on for it any time.

The main difference between Gough and me now is that I live in the present with my students, whereas he tends to live in the past. He's very fortunate to have had such a good wife and mother to his children, who are all devoted to their parents.

Nineteen ninety-three was a particularly busy year for the Whitlams. During their UNESCO years they had made many contacts around the world, and they were now asked to be part of the lobby team selected to help Australia win the 2000 Olympics bid.

In May they had taken an ISP tour to China and Hong Kong and while they were in Beijing they were confronted by huge street banners saying, 'We look forward to the year 2000 and the Olympic Games.' They realised how confident the Chinese were of winning and they passed this information on to the other lobbyists and to John Coates, who was President of the Olympic Committee, when they met them in Geneva in June.

In August they were asked to join Coates and Perry Crosswhite, a member of the bid team, as lobbyists in Africa. They visited thirteen African countries, where they spoke enthusiastically to delegates and their sub-committees. They took with them a portable video of the facilities in Sydney that were already in position, and plans of those that were in preparation. Their aim was to concentrate on the sport that was of prime interest to the area they were visiting, and their strongest card was the fact that they were there in person.

The fact that Margaret had represented Australia in swimming was another reason she tended to be recognised and her energy and enthusiasm for winning the bid was inexhaustible. 'We had a few days in each place, which included Cameroon, Kenya, Mali, the Ivory Coast, Uganda, Swaziland, Zimbabwe and Botswana.'

Margaret remembers the wife of the UNESCO representative from Zimbabwe, who lived on a farm outside Harare, put peanut butter into the mashed pumpkin she served for lunch. (Margaret swears it is delicious.) Margaret found these visits to people in their own homes were always fascinating.

In Swaziland the Australian delegation were taken out to dinner at a smart restaurant by the King of Swaziland and his four wives. As they were leaving she looked over at a group that had been very noisy and noticed that one of the men had put his penis on the table. Not blinking an eye, she muttered to Coates, 'That man we just passed is exposing himself.' He went back to have a look for himself and returned to reveal that the man had actually stood at the table and urinated against it. Gough asked Margaret which man. When Margaret pointed out that it was a journalist, Gough quipped, 'Wouldn't you know it, another press leak.'

In September the delegation assembled in Monte Carlo for the final round of lobbying, and more grand dinners in grand hotels.

> We were staying in the Paris Hotel for five days and in between official activities I put my feet up and went for swims. We were busy chatting up everybody and going out on the lake. On the big announcement night I was sitting next to Dame Joan [Sutherland], who was wearing her yellow T-shirt emblazoned with the word AUSTRALIA. She told me off for not wearing mine. I had it all folded up in my bag and she made me go to the toilet and put it on. It was so exciting when we won by only one vote. And that vote was from Africa.

Immediately Gough and Margaret flew in triumph to London, where they set off on an ISP tour of literary England. It is tiring just reading the itinerary. Margaret calls this decade her years of indulgence, because all her years of being housebound and child-bound in the western suburbs of Sydney were now being balanced by these tours.

Nineteen ninety-four consisted of 'the Great Russian Journey with Gough and Margaret Whitlam' and 'Mostly Music' in Switzerland, Italy and Austria. In 1995 Margaret led two tours, one entitled 'the Heart of France', and another 'Mostly Music' in Switzerland, Italy and Austria later in the year. Whenever she arrived in a different country, no matter how tired she was, her spirits soared. She couldn't wait to get out there, walk the streets and take in the new sights, sounds and smells.

Unfortunately, parts of her body were not keeping up with her spirit. By Christmas she was in St Vincent's Hospital again, having her left knee replaced. Christmas Day was spent in a hospital bed, as various members of her family dropped in with 'treats'.

In May 1996, undeterred, she was back on the road, this time to Italy. Gough accompanied her, then in September they led a tour to Argentina, Peru and Bolivia. That Christmas, however, she found herself in a bed in St Vincent's once more. This time it was for what was called 'a revision' of her hip replacement.

She never likes to dwell on her hospital visits and demands for details are met with a wave of the hand. Her means of dealing with her health problems is always to 'just bat on'.

By May 1997 she and Gough were off again, leading a tour to Spain and Portugal. But the doctors had decreed that the roads in Portugal would be too bumpy for her hip so she reluctantly left the group after the Spain segment.

That September Margaret and Gough took an ISP tour to Germany, after which Margaret continued on to London to stay at the Overseas League and see some friends on her own, in particular Tony's former girlfriend Kate Maclaren, and Kathy Lette. After Kate had broken up with Tony in the 1960s she had moved to swinging London, but she never lost touch. Margaret always sought her out when she was in London and included her in family get-togethers, insisting on her being in one of the endless family photos that she loves to take, wherever she is (much to her children's frustration and annoyance – they all attribute her obsession with photo-taking to her unabashed sentimentality).

Now that Kathy had left Sydney to live in London with her new husband, Geoffrey Robertson, Margaret organised a lunch so that Kate and Kathy could meet. She took them to Bibendum, the smartest restaurant in London at that time, and Kathy arrived with a gift for Margaret.

The discarded wrapping paper revealed an outsized pair of

rubber gloves with frilly cuffs, large bunches of grapes on the wrist and a huge plastic diamond ring on the wedding finger. Margaret immediately put them on and ate her lunch in them. When the chef came out to shake hands with her, Margaret, hooting with laughter, remained gloved. Then Paul Hamlyn, co-owner with Terence Conran of the restaurant, rose from his table and came over to pay his respects, and he too had to shake the rubber gloves and congratulate her on the size of the diamond. It was a hilarious lunch.

Kate remembers that she and Kathy staggered home for a quick nap, but, to their amazement, Margaret headed for the bus stop. She was midway through a systematic exploration of London bus routes and was taking the 328 to its destination at Golders Green, returning in time for the theatre in the West End.

Later that week she took herself off to have dinner at Kate Maclaren's house with Kathy and Geoffrey Robertson. This is how Kathy describes the evening:

> We were treating [Margaret] like a Ming vase because we knew she was fragile after the hip operation. Kate's place was upstairs, so on each landing we'd put a seat and a glass of champagne so she could have a rest. It took her a long time to get up because she'd stop and have the drink. We had a great dinner, then we did the same thing going down, and I drove her back to the Overseas League where she was staying.
>
> Geoff was with me. I said, 'I'll wait in the car. Can you just see Margaret up to the door?' because she's a national treasure. So he helped her up the stairs, and I was watching from the car, and they got to the marble landing at the top and then I saw them both go *whoosh*! The staff had washed the marble floor, but there was no sign up. And they both fell. Geoff chipped

his tooth and fractured his rib. Margaret skidded and fell hard. I got out of the car and rushed up to her, and she was already saying, 'I'm all right.' I told her I was going to get the manager but she told me, 'No, no, don't make a fuss, don't make waves.' She insisted on going up to her room. She kept telling me she was fine and she was still walking. I should have taken her to the hospital. But she was so adamant.

Margaret was not fine. She was embarrassed and in agony.

I staggered to the desk and got my key and said to the fellow, 'What have you done to the steps?' He said, 'The porter washed them,' which didn't seem a very satisfactory response. I realised once I got to the room that I was not fine. I climbed into a nightie, took a couple of painkillers and got into bed. I tossed and turned and I couldn't get comfortable. My knee was very bad. My head hurt where I'd bashed it on the door – I was on the verge of a concussion, as it turned out. Eventually I phoned down and said to the porter, 'Have you got a house doctor?'

He said, 'Well, yes, but he doesn't live in the house. I'll call him if you want.'

'Well, yes, I think I do,' I said. So, anyway, he called the doctor, who called me and asked, 'Do you want me to visit?'

And I said, 'Yes, please.'

'Well, it will be a hundred and seventy pounds. Cash,' he said.

'That's a bit steep,' I said.

'It is one in the morning,' he said.

Fortunately, I'd been to the bank that day and got out enough play money to finish up the holiday. Anyway, he came and he was most solicitous, most concerned. He rang the ambulance and then he rang the emergency department at St Thomas'. They took me to the ambulance in a kind of pusher, like a child's pusher. Of course, here's my knee killing me sitting in this chair, while they negotiate all the stairs to get me out of the club. Then, they took me to the ambulance and stuck me on a stretcher and away we went.

They were very good at the hospital, but they didn't have any doctors on until the morning. They wouldn't give me any painkillers because I'd already taken a couple and, as I say, I was on the verge of concussion. All the X-rays they took proved that I did not have a fracture, and the results of whatever other tests they did apparently looked okay. Eventually, in the morning, I saw the specialists and then they sent me home. At a certain stage they brought breakfast around, which was pretty grizzly. They gave me steel crutches, which were quite helpful. I got back to the club by midday.

Margaret still has the little green message slip which was awaiting her on her return.

ROOM: 28
TO: Mrs Whitlam
FROM: Kathy Lette
MESSAGE: I just rang to see how you are. Geoff's covered in bruises! Can I come and see you tomorrow? Please get lots of rest.
DATE: 28.9.97
TIME: 9.35 am.

Margaret had arranged to meet Jean Frye, the mother of her daughter-in-law Judy, for lunch. She had rung her from the hospital to say she was going to be a little late, and explained why.

Jean said, 'Oh my God, why didn't you tell me? I would have come and got you.'

Margaret reassured her that she was on her way and not to worry.

I'd booked us into a little buttery for lunch and because I was a bit late they'd given the table away. They said I'd have to wait. They probably didn't want me to come in because I looked so terrible. I staggered upstairs with the help of the crutches and the house manager arrived saying, 'Can we send up your lunch?'

Everybody rallied; Jean settled me and rang Kathy and Kate, who quickly came round with food, of course, and to do my packing because I was due home the next day.

I've still got the crutches. They're clearly labelled 'St Thomas' Hospital'. I had two beautiful black eyes. A really good look.

I had a stopover in Bangkok for twelve hours. I booked a hotel room, had a sleep and a meal, and even a couple of hours' sleep on the plane.

When I arrived home Gough was shocked. He said, 'What on earth have you done to yourself?' We were supposed to be going to the opera the next night and he said, 'Who will I take to the opera?'

I said, 'Me,' and I went, heavily covered up with make-up and sunglasses, otherwise the rumour mongers would be at it again.

Kathy Lette thinks that Margaret's insistence on never making a fuss or creating trouble sometimes works against her. It is the only failing she can ever find in her role model. A distinguished international barrister, Geoffrey had offered to sue their insurance company on her behalf for no fee, for failing to alert them to the wet marble floor. Margaret not only refused his offer, she didn't even seek to have her medical costs reimbursed. She says she couldn't stand all the fuss and the messing around.

By May 1998 Margaret was fully recovered, and was back in France, leading a tour about artists' lives and their works. After this she went to Venice to attend Catherine's wedding to Kim Williams, who had previously been married to Kathy Lette. Margaret was pleased that they were all still good friends, and Kim was delighted to become a member of the Whitlam clan, since he had known them all for years.

That September Margaret was due to take an ISP tour to England, Wales and Scotland. She was really looking forward to it, especially as Stephen had booked to come on the trip and they hoped to meet up with some long-lost Scottish relatives.

On the day of her departure, as usual on such occasions she had filled the freezer with food for Gough, packed her bags and checked her to-do list. She was about to sit down and wait for the car to pick her up, when she noticed that the cord to the heater was still plugged in. Thinking it might be dangerous for Gough, she stood up and proceeded to pull out the plug from the wall. Somehow she managed to get the cord tangled around her leg and she tripped, crashing onto the floor and falling on the side of her previously broken hip. This time, however, she fractured her pelvis.

She quickly realised that she had broken something because she couldn't get up. So she slowly dragged herself over to the portable phone, pulled it down off the side table and dialled first her doctor, then her daughter.

By the time Catherine arrived the doctor and the ambulance officers were with Margaret. Catherine came through the door and saw Margaret, by now sitting in a chair, having a quiet weep and feeling very sorry for herself. Catherine, the tough schoolgirl from the western suburbs, burst into tears at the unfairness of it all. How could her mother have had such bad luck?

Margaret was weeping not just because of what she perceived as her own stupidity in fussing over the cord, or her own clumsiness in falling over it, or the fact that because she was so tall she always crashed hard to the ground, or the fact that her bones had become so fragile and brittle with age and osteoporosis; she was weeping because she wouldn't be able to go on the trip that she had planned so carefully and had been so looking forward to, especially because Scotland was where her mother's side of the family still lived.

Even though there was no operation to mend the pelvis – it would just take time – she still had to spend three weeks in St Vincent's, where they had to put her on a frame, with which they hoisted her up to bathe her for the first week. Margaret said she felt like a trapeze artist in a circus. It was another Marx Brothers moment, but again one she couldn't really enjoy.

Stephen ended up replacing his mother as the tour guide. He studied her notes and did his best, together with the Wellings, to make up for her absence. The members of the tour even made her a special photo album so that she could feel she had shared in their experiences.

Stephen also discovered something she had been hiding from the family. Earlier that year Margaret had taken one sixth of a share with the Wellings in a race horse. Justice Dovey had been the vice-chairman of the Australian Jockey Club and Margaret had always enjoyed a little flutter on the horses. She loved going to see the horse and when Stephen was on the tour the Wellings told him about it. 'I don't think Father knows about this,' was his response.

It was Margaret's little secret and, even though the horse was kicked in the barriers and never won a race, Margaret had a lot of fun sharing her secret purchase with the Wellings.

She may have kept her share of the horse to herself but Anne says Margaret has no real private side. 'She is always the same – in public and in private: warm, approachable, fun-loving and interested in you. I have been with her in so many different countries, and on so many different occasions when she has been ill and low, or healthy and high, and she has always been exactly the same person.'

On Mother's Day 1999, after a lunch party with her ISP friends, Margaret arrived home and flopped into her chair. She was feeling strange. The living room seemed to be slowly spinning around her in circles. Gough immediately rang Catherine, who jumped into her car, collected her mother and took her to the emergency department at the Prince of Wales Hospital where her cardiologist, Dr Tony Freeman, practised. They admitted her immediately, called him and after the ubiquitous tests a decision was made to operate and install a pacemaker.

It was the end of the decade and the end of Margaret's career as a tour leader. Not that it stopped her travelling. Her motto is, 'Have globe, will travel.' For anyone like Margaret, who has travelled to most parts of the world, who has dined with kings and queens, stayed in grand castles and ritzy hotels and met a never-ending stream of famous people in all areas of society, there are always the inevitable questions about which city she liked best, which famous people most impressed her – on and on stretch the questions about the ranking of her experiences. Mostly, she avoids answering them. She does admit that if she were asked to close her eyes and just allow one scene to float into her consciousness it would probably be the Ringstrasse in Vienna – a wide avenue that encircles the old city. She always loved to hop on a tram and circle on it several times around the city. All the grand buildings like the opera house, Parliament, the university, the town hall and wonderful views of the Hofburg imperial palace can be seen from the tram.

Margaret loves trams, and she's also very fond of parks and gardens, seeking them out in whichever city she is visiting. She takes her greatest pleasure from such simple things. This is not an assumed humility, nor an attempt to be an 'everywoman', this is a genuine love of simple pleasures. That is not to say that she doesn't love a taste of the high life and indulgent luxury, but for her they are ephemeral treats. A simple picnic with sandwiches and a cup of coffee or a glass of wine in the park is still one of her favourite pastimes.

Her personal travel diaries, which she has kept from every trip she has ever taken, are crammed with the details of what she saw, where she stayed, what she ate, what she wore, the people she met along the way and the names of their children. Indeed, people who have become her friends constantly remark on her genuine, unending interest in their everyday lives and their children.

She has an amazing memory for faces and names, which has no doubt developed and been honed by decades of being a politician's wife. With Margaret, however, it is much more than duty. She is an endlessly curious person and is always interested in human beings, whatever their power, rank or status. While her husband may have an extraordinary memory for historical detail, Margaret has an extraordinary memory for faces and families.

People sense this quality when they meet her for the first time. She always looks whomever she is talking to directly in the eye, asks them about themselves and actually listens to the answers. While she is talking with someone, however short the time, she gives them her total attention. You will never see Margaret looking past someone to whom she is speaking to see who else is in the vicinity.

This respect of other people, regardless of their status, goes to the core of her character. It is thirty years since she was the wife of a politician and as such expected to smile and pay attention to members of her husband's electorate and, indeed, any person who approached her. She is never bored with meeting new people and this authenticity is sensed by everyone who has met her.

She never brings up famous names in order to impress anyone – it would never occur to her. She has no need to try and impress, and isn't very impressed with those who have that need.

Only if a name comes up in conversation will she say something like, 'Oh, Stephen Sondheim. He came here to Darling Point for lunch. I think I cooked spaghetti.'

What was he like?

'A charming man.'

What did you talk about?

'I can't remember, but he certainly wasn't a bore.'

It is always very hard to get her to talk about any of the well-known people she has met. For example, John Mortimer – London barrister and creator of Rumpole of the Bailey – liked her so much he was prepared to meet the members of her study tour in the London pub where Rumpole spent so much of his time.

'He's a funny, roly-poly man. Very much like Rumpole. He's terrific fun. I first met him at Kathy Lette's.'

Gore Vidal?

'He came to Canberra when Gough was Prime Minister. He made himself known and was invited to lunch at the Lodge. I found him very diverting. And then Gough ran into him in Venice and he asked us to have a drink with Joanne Woodward and Paul Newman that evening.'

So! What were they like?

'She was delicious. Very delicately handsome. Finely made. They're both very small. He'd be about Bob Hawke's size. Both of them had the most beautiful blue eyes. He, of course, was absolutely edible.'

And what did you do with them?

'We had drinks on their terrace. People were going past on the canal and calling out "Hello Paul." When it got too much he changed seats so he wasn't so prominently displayed. They took us over to Peggy Guggenheim's to say hello for her recent eightieth birthday. Now she was really ratty – a bit like Miss Haversham in *Great Expectations* – her birthday cake, which she insisted we eat a slice of, had been around for a while. It was nice, but a bit dusty.'

Unlike many people who have mixed with those at the top of their professions, Margaret has not rehearsed a catalogue of stories on a range of topics, or a series of sound bites on big names for every occasion. It's very hard to squeeze an anecdote out of her. She is more interested in the person she is talking to than in reciting a well-rehearsed story from her own life.

On 19 November 1999 Margaret turned eighty and celebrated with a big party in a lovely restaurant at Fox Studios in Sydney. It was very much her party – only her family and friends were invited, no politicians were in evidence. Her children were determined that it was to be her night. Tony, as the eldest child, sang her praises on their behalf, and Margaret replied with her usual self-deprecating humour. Gough, even though he sat on the front table, did not speak. Nor was he invited to do so. The spotlight for once shone solely on Margaret, who looked radiant. There's nothing she likes better than a good party, and it was a long time since she'd had a big, special celebration solely dedicated to her pleasure. Not, in fact, since her twenty-first birthday, which had been quite a while ago.

NEW CENTURY

New year 2000. New decade. New millennium.

At one minute past midnight Margaret and Gough were sitting on a balcony with their old friends Georgie and Snow Swift at the Swifts' apartment in Darling Point, together with twenty or so other friends, marvelling at the fireworks that were exploding all over Sydney Harbour.

Artist Margaret Olley and Gough had been part of a national celebration earlier in the day. While they were waiting for John Howard to arrive Gough, leaning on his stick, said ponderously to Olley, leaning on her frame, 'I never sleep with anybody unless they're over eighty.'

Olley sees a lot of the Whitlams at the various arts events they all support and she is always highly amused when Margaret, looking over Olley's shoulder, says, 'I'm just trying to see who the old bugger is boring now.'

There was not, alas, as they would have liked, a republic of Australia to be celebrated at the New Year's celebrations. John Howard was firmly ensconced in government, living in Kirribilli House, no doubt watching the same fireworks exploding over the Harbour Bridge.

But Margaret was very excited about the year 2000, not just because she had actually survived to see the new millennium, but also because her home town of Sydney was to host the Olympic Games.

Prior to the Olympics, however, in January she had the special treat of going to London as part of those invited by Prime Minister Howard to celebrate the centenary of Australia's Federation. All the former prime ministers and their wives, and the current state premiers and their wives, travelled at great expense to the government to London and spent five days there engaged in celebrations. Margaret and Gough had a very enjoyable time – the stand-outs for Margaret were the service in Westminster Abbey and the banquet in the Guildhall. They were also invited to dinner at Buckingham Palace, together with the former prime ministers and wives, and the current high commissioner and his wife.

There was no column in *Woman's Day* for Margaret to record what the Queen wore, or what they ate, and off what crockery, but she says Her Majesty was 'very jolly. She said that she often asked after us, and I think that's because she really liked the old chap. And he really liked her.'

Margaret also greatly admires many of the women whom she spent time with that week and whom she has met over the years; women who have – like her – previously played public roles in Australian political life.

> Dame Enid Lyons was a very talented and admirable woman. She was modest, but not suffocatingly so. She made a mark in her own right because she succeeded her own husband as a member of Parliament.
>
> I was rather intimidated by Dame Pattie Menzies when I was the wife of a young member. She seemed so terribly proper and correct, and I felt like a large plum dropping off a tree at the wrong moment. She didn't go out of her way to make anybody uncomfortable – I'm sure she tried to do the opposite.
>
> Lady Casey [wife of Richard Casey] did a splendid job as

the Governor-General's wife. She always communicated with me when times were difficult, and had a word of comfort and consideration to offer. She sometimes used to send me little verses, or drawings, and shared her love of the arts with me.

Of course, Malcolm [Fraser] often sounds like a member of the Labor Party these days. He keeps making the distinction between the Liberal Party that he led and the conservative party that Howard now leads. He is an old-style Liberal. I couldn't have put up with being in his company in the 1970s or '80s, but now I find him *almost* engaging.

I've always felt that Tamie was good company. She seemed to affect a very twee voice when she was young, but she doesn't now. She was a bit – as Menzies was – what I call 'eeny, meeny, miny, mo'. His vowels were not always open. The closed vowels were accentuated. He'd say, 'I laike this.'

But that's just my little fixation. Tamie does have a good sense of humour and I've had a few giggles with her. I think she was very pleased with me, and I with her, after the coup: the new prime minister's wife always has all the wives to morning tea and I was invited and I went. People would expect that I wouldn't have gone. She was so pleased and saw to it that we were pictured together. Also she was terribly pleased to have the letter I left, telling her about the physical peculiarities of the Lodge, and made it known, which was nice.

Betty Gorton was good fun.

I could have a giggle with Zara [Holt]. Hazel [Hawke] was the one I felt closest to – you could have a down-to-earth conversation with her, and a giggle. I didn't have much in common with Annita [Keating].

As for the present Prime Minister's wife, I have made a few remarks saying that I wondered what Janette does all day, and that I thought she was useless. I said it publicly in some interview. I really think she *is* useless in terms of how little she really gives to the community. She doesn't even go to the old people's homes that Howard visits. She's not there. The only thing she goes to is big public things. There's Howard shaking hands and kissing old ladies in retirement homes. If you've got a wife, your wife should be there, too.

I fear she's a steely woman. Never contributing anything else but a smile. Not a grin – a grin indicates some sense of humour.

When I was in New Guinea for the tenth anniversary of their independence, John Howard had just usurped Andrew Peacock's position. Again. In the course of the evening party I ran into Janette. I said, 'Congratulations on John's acquisition of office – or should I say, commiseration?'

She visibly bridled and said, 'You don't commiserate with somebody who's got what they always wanted.'

I thought, you silly person. No sense of humour whatever. And now that she is the wife of the Prime Minister, she is practically invisible. As I say, I think you have certain obligations to make the most of the position, to accept invitations, to support charitable causes, to let yourself be known to the people of Australia. I mean, people want to see you. What is she hiding? And when you do see them together in public, when they are delivering a wreath at a cemetery, they are holding hands. For God's sake, they've been married for over thirty years!

What on earth does she do with all her time? She doesn't play sport. None of her children are at home now. As for refusing to live at the Lodge because her youngest son had two years of school left – he could have been a boarder. It was insulting to the people of Canberra and Australia that they wouldn't live in the Lodge. That is where the Prime Minister lives. It's just correct behaviour to do so. Kirribilli is for the weekends and for official guests. It was improper of them to claim it for their permanent home. Imagine the president's wife refusing to live in the White House!

Margaret recalls with some annoyance an incident that left a bad impression on her. Some years ago Janette Howard had asked her to find something that had been given to the Whitlams that could be donated to the Lodge or Kirribilli House. Margaret had finally chosen a very handsome silver box from Mexico that had been inscribed to her. She cleaned it up and packaged it off, together with a personal letter to Janette. Several months later, having received no response, she rang Mrs Howard's secretary to ask whether the parcel had, in fact, arrived. The secretary had no knowledge of it but assured her she would ring her back, which she did, assuring her that Mrs Howard had received it and would be writing a letter of acknowledgement. Seven months passed and Margaret received no response from Mrs Howard. The letter finally arrived after ten months, addressed to Gough from the chairman of the Australiana Fund, of which Janette Howard is the patron. Margaret rarely indulges in personal criticism but failure to respond politely and correctly to a gift is, for her, inexcusable behaviour.

On their way back from London the Whitlams travelled to Greece at their own expense, where they met up with Gough's permanent driver, Michael, who had been with them for eight years. They had breakfast with him in the little village house where his mother had lived. Michael is devoted to them both and they treat him like one of the family. Dinner at a palace, or breakfast in a little village house – it makes no difference to them, they enjoy each experience for what it is.

The Olympic Games were everything that Margaret, as a former lobbyist, had promised the delegates they would be, and more. At the opening ceremony on 15 September 2000 she was bursting with excitement, like everyone else in the stadium, particularly when Cathy Freeman stood in the chill and the rain and lit the flame.

Margaret was in the stands most days for the swimming events and then for the track and field athletics. On the night of 25 September she nearly exploded with pride, together with millions of her fellow Australians, when Cathy stormed home to win the 400 metres.

Along with most other Australians, she was sentimental about how the Sydney Olympics made her feel. For a brief period all were united for the cause of peace and goodwill. In Sydney, everyday life in the city was transformed; people smiled at total strangers. Margaret couldn't help reminisce about the 1956 Olympics in Melbourne – how she and Gough had taken Tony and Nick along to watch the opening ceremony – and remind herself of all the major events that had occurred in their lives since then.

The year 2001 was marked for her by the implantation of a new pacemaker. She had been feeling particularly awful, so bad in fact, that she rang Catherine. The two of them had made an arrangement with Margaret's cardiologist, Tony Freeman, that if she felt unwell she was to be taken by car to Emergency at the Prince of

Wales Hospital and her doctor was to be called. When Catherine arrived with her mother that day, Freeman immediately prepared her for an operation.

The year also produced heartache of a different kind. Her son Nick was the subject of repeated media attacks and criticisms regarding his role as chairman of the National Roads and Motorists' Association (NRMA), which were followed by an Australian Securities and Investment Commission (ASIC) investigation.

It is always hard for any parent to be forced to withstand public criticism of their offspring. Both she and Gough knew that bearing the name Whitlam did produce strong reactions from some members of the public and the press, but they had taught their children to always fiercely defend their own reputations, and to take responsibility for their own actions.

Margaret is aware that her children are not perfect, but she couldn't help being shocked by an exchange she had with one woman, who said, 'Mrs Whitlam, I've always admired you, who which is more than I can say for your son.'

Margaret asked, 'Which son? I have three sons,' pretending she didn't know who the woman was talking about.

The woman replied, 'Nick – he's been a very bad boy.'

Margaret said, 'No, he's not, he's a good boy.'

'Well, I'm very angry with what he's doing to the NRMA.'

Margaret replied, 'As far as I'm concerned he's not a bad person at all.'

She told Nick about the exchange some time later and confessed to him that she didn't really understand all the issues regarding demutualisation or corporatisation. She told him she thought that it was probably better that she didn't, and he agreed, as he didn't want to worry her any more than was necessary.

I trusted him and had every confidence in his capacity to deal with it. I was shocked when I saw the foul things the media was saying, most of which were not true.

Nick is very outgoing. He was always a bit of a showoff and we used to pull him in. At the same time, he did have something to show off. He is charming, good-looking, intelligent and loves being in the thick of everything. I can understand some people thinking him arrogant in this manner. My private view is that the NRMA conflict was a tall-poppy thing stemming from envy and Nicholas's determination to have his way.

Gough and I discussed it, but we didn't attempt to interfere. We interest ourselves but we don't busy ourselves in the kids' activities.

They were both, however, greatly relieved when in 2004 the court dismissed ASIC's case against him and ordered that the organisation pay costs. Margaret told him to keep his mouth shut and not give the media any more headlines.

She knew from past experience how the press could take a simple thing and distort it. For example, they had criticised Nick for going for a swim in the middle of one of the hearings, implying that he was not taking it very seriously. Margaret knew why he would go for a swim: for exactly the same reason that she or Catherine would have done so. She had taught all her children to swim, particularly to relieve stress or tension. Swimming helps you relax, water is soothing. It made absolute sense to her that her son would have a swim at such a time.

Nick's wife, Judy, was aware that part of her husband's determination to be exonerated from the ASIC investigations was his concern that the accusations had disgraced the Whitlam name.

'I remember Gough saying when Nick was exonerated something like, "Now I can die happy." Margaret never interfered, but you always knew she was there. Like a rock. Nick had an example from 1975 and the way his parents coped then – you don't whinge, you get on with your life and never let your enemies beat you down.'

When Nick wrote a book, which Margaret read – skipping, she admits, the sections on the NRMA and focusing on his memories of his childhood – she felt that writing it had helped him 'sort things out'. Unfortunately, even though ASIC's case against him had been dismissed, the damage to his reputation had been thorough and Nick decided to leave Sydney. They moved to Scarborough on the south coast of New South Wales, where he bought a cottage for himself and Judy to live in, and a pub, which his daughter, Alice, and her husband, Chris now run. True to his mother's example he didn't sit around sobbing, but assessed the situation, made decisions and got on with the rest of his life.

As Margaret says, 'You can have regrets, but you don't harp on them. Just occasionally you wish you'd done something differently, but you can't change what's past. You just have to find practical solutions to your problems.'

In February 2002 Margaret's cane slipped on a wet floor in the mall in Bondi Junction. By the time she had let go of her cane she was halfway to the floor. She tried to break the fall with her elbow and it immediately swelled up painfully. Even though she was feeling faint she refused an ambulance and made her way to a coffee shop. By this time Catherine had become her mother's unofficial carer and Margaret realised that she needed to call her to confess that she didn't really feel up to driving herself home. Nevertheless, she hated having to ask for help, even from her daughter.

The twenty-second of April 2002 marked the sixtieth anniversary of the wedding of Margaret Elaine Dovey to Edward Gough Whitlam.

In a television interview to commemorate it Gough said, 'I've established all political records for matrimonial endurance. A couple of years ago we beat the Menzies' record, and now we have established sixty years.'

Margaret was more droll. When asked in a radio interview to what she attributed the success of her sixty-year marriage her reply was, 'Inertia.'

They celebrated with a special family dinner at Lucio's in Paddington, a favourite place for what Margaret called their 'inner family celebrations', and by spending three weeks in a villa in Tuscany with Anne and John Wellings and two other close friends, Hugh and Elfie Taylor, who had been on many tours with them.

Towards the end of the year Margaret drove her little old Honda to the Woollahra Golf Club in order to pay her subscription fees. Even though she hadn't played golf for several years, she liked the club and clung to the thought that one day she might pick up her clubs again. As she was preparing to leave the car park, her foot slipped from the brake to the accelerator and the Honda careered into the flower beds.

Even though it was a bit of a shock she took herself back into the clubhouse to tell them, 'I'm sorry, I've just cleaned up your daisy beds.'

No one seemed too perturbed, but the accident weighed on Margaret's mind. Her children had been telling her that it was time for her to give up driving but she had always resisted their entreaties because she knew that the car was the passport to her independence. Nevertheless, in December of that year she gave her sixteen-year-old car to her granddaughter, Alice, her heart full of regrets for the loss of her freedom to come and go as she pleased. Now she was dependent on others for transport. Not that it stopped her usual round of lunches, dinners, concerts, theatre and opera. It just took a little more organising, but her diary was always full and 2003 was another busy year, full of political, social and charitable functions.

'I want to get on with the rest of my life. I want to experience as much as I can of the life around me. Even though at this stage in my life my usefulness is declining, I like to make a contribution of some kind to the community,' she says.

In February 2004 all this nearly came to a stop. That same dizzy, weird feeling that Margaret dreads suddenly returned and she was taken by ambulance to the Prince of Wales Hospital.

They had been through the admissions procedures, Margaret was lying on the trolley-bed and her cardiologist, Tony Freeman, had just arrived when the room started to spin and Margaret experienced what she describes as 'an awful sense of nothingness'. As if through a haze she noticed that there seemed suddenly to be ten people in the room and Freeman was thumping on her chest, shouting, 'Cough, Margaret, cough!'

This time she had suffered a major heart failure. Freeman decided to remove her current pacemaker and insert a new bi-lateral cardioverta. While Margaret doesn't like to dwell on the incident she is prepared to admit it was 'very scary'.

Then, in August 2004, a bad bout of bronchitis and the excessive coughing it engendered caused the broken bones in her spine to press on a nerve. She was eventually hospitalised for the daily agonising back pain she was enduring.

When she was visited during this period she would point out what she called her latest Jeffrey Smart painting, which was the urban landscape to be seen from her window. Even in her hospital bed, constantly interrupted by nurses taking temperatures and blood pressure, she was smiling and warm and gracious, totally open and accepting of the indignities to which the failings of the human body subject us all. She laughed at the theatre-of-the-absurd play in which she had been cast: 'This medication is making me fart – I'm so sorry but I can't help it. Go out if it gets too much.'

Phone calls from Gough were numerous. She would say to him, 'Can you ring me back, darling, I've just got nurses here,' and then comment, 'The old boy is hopeless in hospitals so he rings me all the time to see how I am and tell me about invitations to events and dinners to put in my diary. Funny old thing. He knows I like to have things to look forward to.'

On 19 November, now out of hospital, she celebrated her eighty-fifth birthday at the Boathouse Restaurant in Glebe with her children and their partners.

'We all had a good time – very relaxed – and Gough managed to arrive in time for pudding. He loves those chocolate desserts where they give you five different styles on one plate.'

Margaret had a bloody mary, then oysters followed by grilled kingfish and a slice of cheesecake. Ever since the heart incident she had been trying to lose weight on the doctor's instructions and Catherine's supervision, but she was allowed dessert on her birthday.

She remembers, 'Tony stood up and said, "Margaret, this is not a speech, it's an appreciation." I looked at them all and thought how jolly they all are in their different ways. I like them all individually and they are all so totally different. They are all pretty disciplined about their fitness and their body shape. Unlike me. That's probably why I've turned into an elongated, misshapen potato.'

A year later Gough's sister, Freda, celebrated her eighty-fifth birthday. This time the family went to Lucio's for lunch. Gough arranged the seating, as he likes to do, and – like all close families – they loved an occasion when it was just them and they could enjoy each others' company away from the prying stares of strangers.

That night when they were settled down in front of the television Gough said to Margaret, 'It went really well today, didn't it?'

Margaret replied, 'It was a great success, my darling.'

And Gough remarked, 'Our kids have really all turned out well, haven't they?'

Margaret agreed and had to allow herself a quiet moment of self-congratulation for how she had brought them up – and practically on her own, a fact that her husband readily acknowledged.

Margaret says that Gough is a deeply emotional man who is easily moved by any reference to his family and his children. Even though the kids are always sending her up for being sentimental, it's their father who often wells up in public, no matter how he tries to hide it.

His mobility, due to a neurological problem, is now not as good as Margaret's and, frustrated with the indignities and limitations of old age, Gough has a tendency to fly into rages, at times for what Margaret considers the most insignificant or bizarre reasons.

'Sometimes we've just arrived somewhere and he suddenly launches into a fierce argument with somebody, contorting his face and making a total show of himself. I've apologised to people about it and they say, "Don't worry about it, he's been so marvellous in the past."'

When he turns on Margaret she either ignores him and goes into another room, or she quietly tells him that his behaviour is not acceptable, and he calms down.

'In the past if he'd spoken to me like that I'd have burst into tears and not spoken to him for days. But now I don't cry any more because I know it's his old age and his frustrations, and plenty of women my age have to deal with worse.'

In 2005 Gough's spirits seemed to revive, however, with the arrival of the thirtieth anniversary of his dismissal. He was asked to give numerous talks and speeches on the topic, and the events of thirty years ago came fully alive to him again.

Well aware of the dictum 'history is determined by those who write it', at the invitation of his publisher he revised his book *The Truth of the Matter*, writing a new introduction that included supportive evidence from honoured men who believed that Kerr had acted wrongly.

Still convinced that everything he had done before and on 11 November 1975 was right and proper – his only failing being to trust his Governor-General – he appeared on television, in print and on the front cover of magazines, reinforcing his position. The media's frenzy to discuss and analyse the events was still in evidence.

The Australian ran a countdown of daily events from 18 October to 11 November 1975, when the editorial focused on the fact that the way Whitlam was evicted from the Lodge made him a hero, and that the loser of 1975 was the ultimate winner. Gough relishes any opportunity to remind people of this fact and is of the firm belief that he achieved more in his three years of being Prime Minister than anyone else did with several terms.

Margaret, while understanding Gough's emotional need to revisit the dramatic events of 1975, no longer has any passion for the memories. She has no wish to be dragged back into the past, preferring instead to dwell in the present and look forward to the future.

In August 2005 the Whitlams celebrated the birth of Stephen's grandson and their first great-grandson, Oscar, and a month later that of their first great-granddaughter, Isabella – Nick's first grandchild. Then, on 7 February 2006, *The Sydney Morning Herald* announced that Gough and Margaret were welcoming their great-grandson on his first visit to Sydney. 'Stephen Whitlam, the grandfather, is delighted that the boy, Oscar Cyrus, is named after kings of Sweden and Persia. Gough is tickled, too.'

By now Margaret had been advised by her doctors that there were to be no more overseas trips, but she and Gough were constantly being sent invitations to visit towns and districts within Australia, so she certainly made up for it by travelling within her own country. Eventually Catherine had to start restricting her mother's activities to one event a day even if she was at home, otherwise Margaret would be out for lunch and dinner, or a performance, every day. Catherine also organised a series of 'helpers' for her, one of whom is a personal exercise physiotherapist who does her best to keep Margaret's legs supple and her muscles strong.

Their mother–daughter relationship has now reversed its roles and, even though Margaret relies on Catherine a great deal, she still likes to assert her right to 'do my own thing'. As the youngest, Catherine saw the least of her mother as a child – now she is her strength and support, seeing her almost daily.

Margaret has played many roles in her life, some centre-stage, some off-stage. Now, looking back, her children all agree on one thing: she has been and is a wonderful mother.

Tony thinks that her general confidence is based on the fact that 'she was the apple of her father's eye'. He calls her 'Margaret' and talks to her about his father and how she is coping with their physical deterioration. He and his wife, Pip, take her to the theatre on their subscription and are constantly amused by the fact that she is so uncritical and likes most productions that they see.

'Nevertheless, she has a degree of confidence in her opinions, which is unusual for a woman of her vintage and era.

'She's very gregarious. All my life people have been saying to me, "I met your parents and I really like your mother." She has given Gough a more level grounding in mainstream life. He came from such an ascetic family and he was always driven by doing good in his political life. And she took her role as PM's wife seriously – she was always there in the gallery when Parliament was sitting.'

Nick is the swimmer and as a schoolboy he was always winning competitions. He is – according to Tony – Margaret's favourite. In fact, there is a family joke about the word 'fave'. Stephen says, 'If I ring my parents and Father answers the phone and I say I want to speak to Mother, he'll call out, "Mum, it's the fave on the phone." Or, if we all arrive at their apartment and he sees you first he'll say, "Mum, the fave is here."'

Nick says, 'We were never latch-key kids. She was always there when we came home from school. She was admirable in the way she adjusted herself to her husband's career and facilitated a lovely childhood for all of us in circumstances that were so different from how she was brought up.'

He is very pleased that he had the opportunity to travel with his mother, alone. Neither of them had much money at that time, but they had the chance to enjoy each other's company. He also admires the way in which she used her position as Gough's wife – both while he was Prime Minister and afterwards – to promote worthy causes and to work for the community. She really made something of the role, he thinks.

Stephen is the most different to the other Whitlam offspring – he's not interested in sport, he doesn't drink, he doesn't entertain, he has been divorced and he is the least competitive of them. He loves to read at home or go to the latest films.

He was much more domestic than his elder brothers and would often help his mother with ironing, pea-shelling or picking vegetables from the garden. His brothers used to call him derogatory nicknames, and tell him that he wouldn't live to see thirteen because he had nearly died as a baby.

'Mother was very firm, but in the way that parents were. If we had been behaving badly she would say, "Wait until your father gets home," and he would administer the punishment. Usually a slipper on the bottom.'

Stephen describes Margaret as 'Father's secret weapon' because she can mix with all sorts of people. He sees her as very strong-willed. He agrees with his father when he says that all the women in the family are bossy – from Margaret's mother to Catherine – and he says that he's closest to Catherine, though he gets on with them all.

Catherine agrees with her brothers about her mother's strengths, adding that she thinks Margaret is too forgiving of people. Except, of course, anyone who attacks her children.

The same height as Margaret used to be – 6 foot 2 inches – Catherine says that, as women, being so tall means that both of them had to put up with a lot of unkind remarks, so they learnt the importance of being kind to people.

Catherine says that unlike Margaret, who is very even-tempered, unfortunately she and her brothers have all inherited their father's temper. No wonder Margaret intones, 'Let us speak of fruit and flowers.'

She has never seen her mother trying to exert any political influence over Gough, even though Margaret considers him, quite rightly in Catherine's opinion, to be extraordinarily naïve about people, and particularly susceptible to flattery. What is clear to Catherine is that her mother 'made it possible for Dad to achieve what he did, but in doing that she sacrificed a hell of a lot of herself. But, she doesn't see that she's made any sacrifices or that she is special for doing that.'

As far as the events of 1975 are concerned, she thinks Margaret was personally wounded for many years by Kerr's deceit.

'But basically she just got on with it. She still had a lot of living to do. She loves travelling, reading and meeting people. She also loves watching popular programs on television like *The Bill*. That drives Dad nutty. He can't believe that she will watch such "garbage", as he puts it.

'They sometimes get up each other's craw. They know each other's sore spots and Mum is naughty the way she does things that she knows will annoy Dad. I reprimand her about it, but I know it comes from years of living together.'

Daughter-in-law Judy Whitlam arrived in Sydney from London with Nick one week before Gough was dismissed. People she had known well in England suddenly turned their backs on her, but she felt immediately accepted into the Whitlam family.

'Margaret is totally non-judgemental. She just took it for granted that I was the person to make their son happy.'

Once they had children, however, Judy realised that even though Margaret would knit for her grandchildren and would fundraise for their schools, she would not baby-sit them.

'She put Gough first and he is quite demanding, and also shy, so he needs a supportive wife. I also think that she's spent so much time by herself bringing up four children that she didn't want to help bring up any more. She's definitely not a stay-at-home wife and you just have to learn to share her with so many other people.'

However, when Judy needs to talk out her problems, Margaret always takes the time to listen and offer advice. 'Even with the difficulties of having a handicapped child she always made me feel I could cope. And I did.'

Judy thinks that Margaret's assertiveness is a necessary balance to Gough's opinionated persona, and that Gough was attracted to her because, 'She was always her own person.' Nevertheless, she is touched by their vulnerability and their dependence on each other, which is firmly based on more than sixty years of very deep love for each other.

'Margaret always insists on doing things for Gough. She wants to be the one to look after him. He says, "I'll do it," and she'll say, "No, I'll do it," and neither of them is hugely mobile.'

She says she has never, ever heard Nick say one disparaging word about either of his parents. 'It's all a credit to Margaret because she is so ordinary as well as extraordinary. Her great talent is to make you feel more positive about yourself.'

Pip, Tony's wife, says she thinks of Margaret 'as a ship sailing through rough seas. Old age buffets her now, but she is forever stable and steering a straight course. The good ship Margaret sails on.'

Margaret is realistic and honest in her approach to the problems of ageing couples who have been together a long time. As Bette Davis once famously said, 'Old age ain't for sissies.' And Margaret is no sissy.

When I was writing this book, one Saturday I had an early morning call from Margaret.

'I'm in trouble. You know Gough's book that I lent you?'

'Yes.'

'Well, he wants it back. He has to work on a speech and he needs it and all his other copies are locked up in his office.'

'I'll drop it around in about an hour or so.'

'That would be simply marvellous. Are you sure I'm not putting you to any trouble?'

'Not at all. I have to get my glasses fixed.'

'Don't expect us to be dressed.'

'Don't worry about it.'

'I don't mean we'll be naked.'

'I'll avert my eyes.'

Much laughter.

Later in the morning I went around to their apartment and buzzed the door.

'Come up, my friend.' Margaret opened the door. 'I decided to get dressed.'

'Needn't have bothered.'

'Time for a coffee?'

'Of course.'

'Come and look at my old boy.'

There he was, asleep – an angelic head above the blanket.

'Doesn't he look sweet? Like a big baby.'

When I was about to leave, Margaret ushered me back to the bedroom.

'Come and say goodbye, he'll be awake now.'

And there he was, sitting up in bed, wearing blue pyjamas and looking handsome with his good complexion and smiley eyes.

''Bye, biographer.'

I told him I had been researching a bit from his book about Elizabeth Reid and Kerr's proposal.

'Ah, yes. "Why work for number two when you can marry number one?"'

'That's okay if you want to live with a man with a white bouffant hair-do.'

Gough roared with laughter. And Margaret said, leading me to the door, 'Silly old thing, isn't he?'

Weeks later, when I was ready to interview Gough, I asked Margaret, 'Shall I conduct it in his office or at home?'

She said immediately, 'I think his office would be better. There he can sit at his desk and be lord of all he surveys. At home I keep moving him around.'

Gough mostly resists talking personally about his life and his relationship with Margaret, but he is effusive in his praise for her as an excellent mother and an excellent member's wife – not only because she gave so much back to the electorate but because, he says, she always got along with people on both sides of the House.

> She is very talented at getting along with people, that's why she was so good at leading those study tours. While she was wife of the Prime Minister she wrote those columns like Eleanor Roosevelt. Margaret was never a political player, nor ideological like Eleanor, but her accounts of visits with the Windsors were very good. She did speak out about legalising marijuana before I did, and she has, of course, always believed in freedom of choice and equality of pay for women.

His only criticism of his wife is what he calls her bossiness, which he blames on generic inheritance. 'Her mother was bossy and she has inherited that characteristic, as has our daughter. But her mother was also very committed to doing good works in the community and Margaret did that very well and naturally. Margaret is addicted to conversation, which has been a great asset.'

And what of the rumours that have circulated about their marriage over the years?

The Liberals have, of course, always put around hurtful rumours about our marriage – there are some vicious bastards and bitches out there – but, apart from her bouts of illness, we have always slept in the same bed.

It's the longest prime ministerial marriage in Australian history and we've been compatible in that we've had broadly similar cultural interests for over six decades. I've never thought our marriage might break up. Most of it has been lived in the limelight and it's been pretty good. Whenever we've talked about our marriage we tell each other that neither of us could have done better. I think that we're both happy that we married and have stayed married.

I'm kept pretty busy in my office and I try to accept invitations to functions put on by political, educational and ethnic groups with which I've had a long association. And then, of course, there are our various subscriptions to opera and ballet. Margaret goes to more of those than I do because she's more mobile now. I have to go in the blasted wheelchair. If we're not going out we watch a bit of television, or I read. I don't usually get home until six o'clock because she watches all those silly *Pick-A-Box*-style programs. We share a great interest in ABC and SBS programs, but I could do without *The Bill* and the various Italian and German versions of it. You know, there's even an Austrian one with dogs.

As with all older people, who are reminded on an almost daily basis of their mortality, as more and more of their friends are 'gathered', Gough, having helped plan his own funeral with the help of a self-selected committee, likes to leave nothing to chance.

'If she goes before me I've made arrangements for her to have a send-off in St Andrew's, which is afflicted by the Jensenite heresy, but will be big enough as she is very popular and well-regarded in her own right. What is really amazing is that she has no enemies.'

Asked whether he'd speak on such an occasion and whether he could imagine his life without her, Gough's eyes brim with tears and words literally choke in his throat.

'I'd find it very difficult to speak at her funeral . . . It would be very difficult without her . . . I mustn't get maudlin, but let's just say . . . I've grown accustomed to her face . . .'

The 1956 song by Lerner and Lowe was made famous in the musical *My Fair Lady* and the next line is, 'She almost makes the day begin.'

Margaret rarely sleeps in unless her health dictates she stay in bed. She gets up early to collect the morning papers for Gough and, apart from various trips to her many doctors, the home calls of her personal exercise trainer and her hydrotherapy sessions, her social calendar would rival that of a woman twenty years her junior.

Her role model on ageing and how to ignore it is her old friend Claire Nichols, whom Margaret first met in Bayreuth. At 103 years of age, Claire lives alone, does her own shopping – with the help of a community car to get her to and from the Edgecliff centre – and has at least two dinner parties a week, for which she cooks. The only assistance she needs is with carrying plates to and from the dining-room table. She is cheerful, reads

The Sydney Morning Herald every day and usually completes the crossword. She is interested in what's happening in the world, has a large circle of friends and family, and still goes to the ballet and the opera.

Georgie Swift is Margaret's longest-standing friend and, having met over sixty years ago at university they still go to films and lunches together on a regular basis. After a recent outing when they had been to the cinema, Georgie wanted to hail a taxi but Margaret insisted that they take a bus to David Jones in Bondi Junction for some oysters for lunch. Georgie remembers it well:

> We got on the bus, paid our fare and I was laughing at it all, but Margaret loves catching public transport. The driver eventually stopped the bus at the end of the section at Bondi Junction and everyone got off. We looked out of the window and David Jones was at the end of the street. Neither of us is up to walking too far, so we asked, 'Is this really the last stop?'
>
> The bus driver said, 'Don't worry, I'll get you there, Mrs Whitlam.'
>
> And he drove the bus right up to the entrance to David Jones, just for us. He'd clearly have done anything for her. She's always had this presence. It's something to do with her height but it's also something about her. She's always had it.

Meg Renshaw became friends with Margaret in 1966 after Meg married Jack Renshaw, a former premier of the New South Wales Labor government. Meg was new to politics and had no idea that at political functions the men disappear, leaving the women to fend for themselves. The first night she met Margaret they were both stranded without their husbands at the top table and a little bloke came up to Margaret and asked her to dance.

'It was absolutely hilarious. He had his head tucked between Margaret's boobs and his hand on her bottom. Every time I'd pass her on the dance floor, we'd both laugh our heads off. It was our sense of humour that made us such good friends.'

Often when they went out to lunch they would book under the names of Mrs Lamb and Mrs Shaw, just so they could be themselves and not the wives of well-known politicians. They felt like naughty schoolgirls on a lark. Once, they took out a lottery ticket in those names and won over $100. After the dismissal and the 1975 defeat Margaret would play golf with Meg at the public course in Northbridge near Meg's home. Meg also travelled on Margaret and Gough's first study trip to China and had a great time with them both.

'They don't always agree. They'll really sound off against each other. Margaret was never backward in coming forward to say what she thought. The dynamic between them only made them more human and interesting.'

Meg always admired her as a wife because she would never go out without ensuring that Gough's lunch or dinner was ready for him. 'There's a very deep love and respect between the two of them.'

Now, whenever Margaret and Meg go to a charity event together, people flock to Margaret. Often when they have been out at lunch, Meg says they will both 'admire a good sort. We'll have a look but neither of us would be game to follow it up. Margaret has never had any affairs outside her marriage. She loves Gough dearly.'

What of the media, who have a tendency to build up their tall poppies, only to rejoice in cutting them down?

Piers Akerman, the political columnist, says he has the greatest respect for the wife of any politician because it is the worst job in the world, and he reiterates that Margaret has consistently taken on the role with great dignity.

Laurie Oakes, the revered political print and television journalist, says in all his years of reporting and analysing politics and people in the public spotlight, 'Never have I heard or could I make a criticism of her.' He agrees with Adams' assessment of her as quite simply, 'A class act.'

Dame Leonie Kramer sees Margaret as a good example of how to behave in today's world; of the importance of courtesy and of not making enemies or gossiping. There are no boundaries to cross in order to make contact with her. Dame Leonie doesn't believe that Margaret has any enemies and, as the wife of a politician who has been in the public eye for over fifty years and has been outspoken on many issues, that is quite amazing.

Is Margaret a candidate for sainthood? Or canonisation? Certainly not. She's far too human for that. And she loathes being described or labelled 'a national treasure', 'a living legend' or a 'public icon', as she has never seen herself in such a light.

Did Gough make Margaret who she is today? Given her background, her private schooling and her university education, she could quite easily have married another lawyer, who would ultimately become a judge, or even a chief justice, and have lived her life in a beautiful house around the corner from her parents in Vaucluse. She could have devoted herself to her children, her various charities, her dinner parties and her love of the arts.

But when she met the young Gough Whitlam she realised they were a pair. Like the music of Wagner, which she came to adore, she too wanted a life that was dramatic, romantic and exuberant in its scope. Standing next to him she felt right. Neither of them, although they liked to flirt with the idea, were bohemians. Essentially conformist, they formed a synchronistic union that enabled them to balance each other.

She wanted to fly but did not have the confidence to do it on her own. He was a meteor, destined for great things. She hooked onto his meteoric path, kept him sane and made him human. His head was full of Greek and Roman heroes and she constantly reminded him that he was, after all, just a man. And she learnt to match him step for step, both of them striding fast and standing tall through the world of Australian politics.

Gough's sister is convinced that he never would have become Prime Minister without Margaret. He was handsome, brooding, shy, lived in his head, had flashes of brilliance, but was an innocent in the ways of the world. Determined to make a better world for those less well off than himself, he convinced her that politics was the best path to follow and she took his hand.

He crashed up against people who didn't share his vision, many of whom were on his own side. The other side, his sworn political enemies, never forgave both of them for joining the other team. When Gough became Prime Minister and Margaret the mistress of the Lodge, it was as if they had stolen the Ashes from their rightful owners. The opposition were determined to cut him down, one way or another.

After Kerr's ambush, Gough and Margaret were both shocked. Stunned. But they had faith that the Australian people would maintain the rage, hold the faith. Economics defeated ideology. Fear defeated faith. Inflation and interest rates defeated rage. Margaret, with her strength, her stability and her unconditional love, refused to let her husband wallow in defeat.

Margaret never gives up. There are no rewards for trying and failing, other than the knowledge that you tried, and what's more you survived. She refused to allow them to sink into depression, or despair, or self-pity. There was a world out there and every day was to be lived to the full. A firm believer that it takes no more energy to be optimistic than to be depressed, she chooses blind optimism every time.

Margaret neither berates nor blames Gough for anything that has happened. She created a full life far from her home and her friends, first in Cronulla on the coast, then in Cabramatta on the plains. She brought up four children almost on her own. His world was her world and she did her best to make that work.

Their three years in the Lodge changed the culture of the nation forever. It was three years that shook Australia, and they walked tall on the international stage. When it was all over and they were given minor roles, they did not turn their back on them. In their fifties and sixties they invented a new life. Together they faced the world, unashamed of what they had tried to achieve for their country.

For Gough, security is a home-cooked meal and someone who makes his domestic life smooth and comfortable. He doesn't mind Margaret doing other things, as long as his life isn't disrupted. At home with his books, his newspapers, his music, his wife and visits from his children, he is content. He never wanted the trappings of wealth and thought the pursuit of money and power for its own sake to be crass. He didn't want to own the world, simply to change it for what he considered the better for everyone. Margaret knew this and understood his single-minded pursuit of his goals. Although she was more worldly than her husband, even she believed that most people, certainly those in positions of power, wanted to do good for others, if given a chance.

Gough's political idealism and Margaret's social-worker training were the basis for them both to fulfil their belief that those with privileges had a responsibility, even a duty, to help those less fortunate. Not in any *noblesse oblige* manner, but rather by facilitating the means to help people help themselves, through education and government services. Theirs has been a true partnership, both publicly and privately.

What Margaret has to teach us is how to hang in there for the long haul, how to really love someone for better or worse, how to deal with life's misadventures, disappointments and failures, and not become obsessed, bitter or cynical.

She has learnt to look forward to each day and make the most of life's ordinary pleasures; to keep loving one person for over sixty years, forsaking all others; to maintain a genuine interest in the lives of others when you are constantly meeting new people; and to sustain a sense of humour, no matter how many broken bones and illnesses you are forced to endure.

Margaret Whitlam is no saint. She is not even a heroine in the strict sense of the word. Hers has been, on one level, an ordinary life lived as a daughter, a wife, a homemaker and a mother. On another level the fact that her husband was prime minister of this country in one of its most tumultuous and exciting decades has catapulted her into an extraordinary life. She has faced the ordinary and the extraordinary with equanimity and embraced them with curiosity.

A large part of her life has been and is still lived in the public eye and yet she remains greatly admired and even loved. No one seems to have a harsh word to say about her.

Politics is the toughest, roughest game in town. It is hard enough for a politician to end a career still respected, admired or even loved. So how does the wife of a prime minister, standing always beside him, not exactly silently, manage to capture the public's attention to the extent that she creates her own persona, her own reputation, her own following?

There is no other wife of an Australian politician or a prime minister in the twentieth or twenty-first centuries who has not only survived, but blossomed and become beloved like Margaret Whitlam.

No one is lukewarm about her husband: Gough Whitlam is either adored or reviled. And yet Margaret has prevailed and bloomed as her own person, on her own terms. That she has done so with energy, with dignity, with humility and humour is the story of her life.

Picture her now, sitting on her balcony overlooking the harbour that she has grown up with and loved, her eyes closed, soaking up the afternoon sun. Rachmaninoff's *Piano Concerto No. 2* is playing in the background. She has already organised her husband's dinner for the evening as she is going to a new play at the Sydney Theatre Company with her son Tony and her daughter-in-law, Pip. Stephen is taping the evening's episode of *The Bill* for her. Nick has rung her to say he is taking his father to lunch tomorrow. Catherine has spent the morning driving her to her various medicos for check-ups, the results of which are good.

Luxuriating in the warmth of the winter sun with the romantic waves of Rachmaninoff washing over her, she's relishing the prospect of an evening at the theatre.

Let's leave her there, enjoying it all, shall we?

ACKNOWLEDGEMENTS

It is not possible to name and thank all the people who have helped and encouraged me in the writing of this book; nevertheless, some names should be mentioned. My heartfelt thanks go to the following.

First and foremost, thanks to Margaret Whitlam, because she finally stopped refusing my requests to tell her story. If she had not had the courage and given me the time to talk to me in detail about her life, my task would have been a great deal harder. She also gave me access to all her personal diaries, letters, papers, clippings, photos and memorabilia.

So, too, the family of Whitlams: Gough, Freda, Tony and Pip, Nick and Judy, Stephen and especially Catherine Dovey, who generously took us out on our research expeditions.

Margaret's friends – Georgie Swift, Claire Nichols, Kate Maclaren, Kathy Lette, Meg Renshaw, Jeanette Leahy, John and Anne Wellings, John Menadue, Richard Butler, Richard Glover, Barbara Stuart, Lady Marjorie Pagan and Margaret Olley

– provided many wonderful memories and anecdotes from the past and the present.

So, too, did James Strong, Bill and Dallas Hayden, Barry Jones, John Faulkner, Susan Ryan, Elizabeth Reid, Dame Leonie Kramer and Tamie Fraser.

Journalists Laurie Oakes, Alan Ramsey, Phillip Adams, Alex Mitchell and Piers Akerman shared their opinions with me about Margaret's importance to Australian life and history.

I am indebted to the following authors for allowing me to incorporate their research and insights, particularly from the following books:

Laurie Oakes – *Whitlam PM: a biography*
Gough Whitlam – *The Truth of the Matter*
Nick Whitlam – *Still Standing*
Stephan Whitlam – *Scenes from a Life*
John Menadue – *Things You Learn Along the Way*
Diane Langmore – *Prime Ministers' Wives*
Paul Kelly – *November 1975*

I also wish to thank Fenella Souter for her article entitled 'Year of Women and Wonders' in the 'Good Weekend' magazine of July 2005. Ian Duncan and the Whitlam Institute and Penny and Aaron from Gough Whitlam's office were generous in their help with research.

My personal support team – Richard, Nicholas and James Beasley, Trish Hobson, Maggie Tabberer, Susie Carleton, Noel Staunton, Tony Richards, Bern Barry, David and Ingaborg Caplice, Helen Norman and Cate Fowler – provided me with delicious food, fine wine, good conversation and most importantly the best laughs. Vicki Busteed gave me honest and sustaining feedback on the first draft.

My literary agent and friend, Deborah Callaghan, encouraged me to ask Margaret just one more time and never let me feel alone through out the entire journey.

My accountant and guardian angel, John Masselous, gave his time generously to keep me on the straight and narrow.

Gillian Harvie transcribed and typed all my material with her usual calm and genius, and my computer expert, Ravi, never let me feel helpless.

Nikki and the concierge staff at the Elan saved me in many emergencies.

Random House Australia's managing director Margie Seale, my publisher Jeanne Ryckmans, senior editor Catherine Hill, marketing and publicity manager Briony Cameron, senior publicist Peta Levett and designer Gayna Murphy all gave their energy, their enthusiasm and their best talents to the book's fruition.

Above all, my thanks go to Mary Beasley, who never stops believing in me and who has lived though every word in this book.

INDEX